Iliad
Book 1

Homer

with notes and vocabulary by
P. A. Draper

Ann Arbor
THE UNIVERSITY OF MICHIGAN PRESS

*A CIP catalog record for this book is available from
the British Library.*

Library of Congress Cataloging-in-Publication Data

Homer.
    Iliad. Book 1 / Homer ; with notes and vocabulary by P. A. Draper.
      p.   cm.
    Includes bibliographical references.
    Homer's text in Greek with introduction, annotations, and criticism in English.
    ISBN 0-472-09792-X (acid-free paper) — ISBN 0-472-06792-3 (pbk. : acid-free paper)
    1. Greek language—Readers. 2. Achilles (Greek mythology)—Poetry. 3. Trojan
War—Poetry. I. Draper, P. A. (Pamela Ann), 1952– II. Title.

    PA4020 .P1   2002
    883'.01—dc21

                                      2002018718

The Greek text of book 1 of the *Iliad* is reprinted
by permission of Oxford University Press from
volume I of Homer, *Iliad (Books I–XII),* edited by
D. B. Monro and T. W. Allen, Oxford Classical
Texts, 3rd edition (Oxford, 1920): 1–21.

Contents

Preface

This annotated edition of the first book of Homer's *Iliad* is intended to make it possible for students who have completed elementary Greek to read, enjoy, and appreciate Homer. Vocabulary and grammar notes are included liberally, conveniently placed so as to be visible at the same time as the text. To help ease the transition to a world very different from our modern one, explanations are provided of the people, deities, objects, and customs mentioned. For those new to Homer, figuring out the language itself may leave little time or energy to appreciate the artistry of the poetry, so there are also notes on scansion, literary interpretation, and Homer's skill in manipulating the language. My goal has been to give readers the idea that there is more to Homer than learning the vocabulary for a sacrifice scene, recognizing an unaugmented aorist or a short-vowel subjunctive, and remembering that the article is often used as a pronoun.

I owe a tremendous debt to the many commentaries, books, and articles that I mined extensively for explanations and interpretations of the first book of the *Iliad*. Credit is given in Appendix 2 rather than in the notes themselves in order to keep the contents of the notes focused on the text.

The Greek text is essentially that of the Oxford Classical Text. In a few places I have altered a word or a punctuation mark where such a change seemed to provide a better reading. Since the purpose of this book is primarily to help first readers of Homer grapple with vocabulary, grammar, meter, and style, not to delve into issues of textual criticism, I have not provided explanations of such changes or any apparatus criticus. Simon Pulleyn's *Iliad Book One* (Oxford: Oxford University Press, 2000) has an excellent introduction to textual criticism and extensive explanations of specific words and passages; anyone wanting to learn more about this aspect of Homeric criticism should definitely consult it.

I am very grateful to all the people who helped in so many ways as I worked on this book, especially Susan Shelmerdine and her Greek students at the University of North Carolina-Greensboro; Peggy Tyler; everyone in the Resource Sharing Office of the Clemson University Libraries for getting countless interlibrary loan requests for me; the anonymous reviewers, whose suggestions led to significant improvements; and Ellen Bauerle, Colin Day, Collin Ganio,

Claudia Leo, Jennifer Wisinski, Christina Milton, and Jill Butler Wilson at the University of Michigan Press. Special thanks are due to my fellow Clemson University faculty members Elizabeth Carney, Elizabeth Dale, and Sarah Mc-Cleskey, who agreed to read this text in our weekly Greek reading sessions and provided me with many valuable suggestions; and to my patient husband, Richard Cowan. Finally, I offer my deepest gratitude to Cathy Callaway and Robert Seelinger, *amicis optimis,* without whose encouragement, support, editorial comments, and advice I would never have completed this book.

Introduction

Who Was Homer?

It's like the question of the authorship of the *Iliad*. . . . The author of that poem is either Homer or, if not Homer, somebody else of the same name.

—Aldous Huxley, *Those Barren Leaves,* Part 5, chapter 4

The only thing we can say with complete certainty about Homer is that there is nothing we can say with complete certainty about Homer. We do not know who he was (or if he even existed at all), where he lived, what he looked like, or how he composed his poetry. Scholars have been arguing for centuries (the famous "Homeric Question") about the author of the *Iliad* and the *Odyssey*. The following are some of the theories that have been proposed.

- Homer did not exist at all. The poetry ascribed to him is just a collection of early poems.
- Homer composed/wrote both works (to account for differences in the two works, many have suggested that he wrote the *Iliad* as a young man and the *Odyssey* when he was older).
- Homer wrote the *Iliad,* and someone else (some have suggested a woman) wrote the *Odyssey.*
- Homer was not the author of the *Iliad* and the *Odyssey* but merely an editor who compiled traditional stories into longer works.
- Homer compiled the *Iliad* from traditional tales but created the *Odyssey* himself.

The ancient Greeks, who considered Homer the greatest of poets, and for whom the *Iliad* and the *Odyssey* were not only magnificent poetry but a source of moral, religious, political, and historical instruction, did have certain ideas about him, but they actually knew very little. They thought the author of the *Iliad* and the *Odyssey* was a blind itinerant poet who lived some time after the Trojan War (which they dated to around 1200 B.C.) but well before the age of Pericles. Smyrna, a city in Ionia (*Ionia* was the ancient Greek name for the central area of the west coast of modern Turkey), was believed to be his birthplace (although several other cities also claimed that honor). Chios, an island off the coast of Ionia, was thought to be his home (though again, other places also claimed him).

Modern scholars cannot do much better. We now think the author (or authors) of the *Iliad* and the *Odyssey* lived sometime around 750–700 B.C., somewhere in Ionia. Possibly he was born in Smyrna and lived on Chios. He probably traveled a good deal in Asia Minor, which would explain his use of words from many dialects and his familiarity with the regions of Asia Minor and the eastern Mediterranean. Linguistic analysis suggests that the *Iliad* was written a decade or two earlier than the *Odyssey*.

There is very convincing evidence that Homer worked within a long tradition of oral poetry. His works show some knowledge of conditions and objects that existed several centuries before the eighth century B.C., and as far as we know, this knowledge could not have been passed down in written form, because writing was apparently unknown in Greece from about 1100 to 770 B.C. Therefore, it must have been passed down orally. Also, Homer's poetry shows similarities to oral poetry from other cultures, particularly in its use of repetitive or formulaic word combinations and typical characters and episodes.

Beyond that, we can only make guesses. To appreciate the *Iliad* and the *Odyssey* as works of great literature, it is not essential to know precisely who the author was. It is important to realize that he was a poet who worked within an oral tradition, since this explains some of the characteristics of his poetry that seem strange to us now. Acknowledging, then, that the identity of the person (or persons) responsible for the *Iliad* is a mystery, I will, for the sake of convenience, call that person Homer.

How Was the *Iliad* Composed?

For generations before Homer, traveling poets or bards provided entertainment by reciting traditional stories composed in verse, specifically in dactylic hexameter, about heroic figures. Accompanying their performances with a lyre, they performed at various gatherings, probably during or after meals in the homes of aristocrats or at festivals or games. The subjects of these epic poems were gods and heroes and their adventures—for example, the war of the gods and the Titans, episodes from the Trojan War, the story of the Argonauts, the labors of Heracles, or the war against Thebes.

Since the art of writing was not known in the two to three centuries before Homer, these poets would have had no written texts of the stories to memorize.

This means they were not just reciting lines they had learned from a script. We believe that they composed as they sang or chanted, creating, in effect, a new poem each time they performed.

Ancient Greek poetic meters were patterns of long and short syllables (see the fuller explanation of dactylic hexameter and the determination of syllable length later in this introduction). Over time, word combinations that fit the requirements of the meter were passed orally from poet to poet and became part of a standard poetic vocabulary. These phrases, lines, and even whole scenes are referred to as formulas and were the building blocks used by these oral poets.

For example, a poet wanting to say "he went in silence" at the beginning of a line in the metrical pattern – ⌣ ⌣ – could use the phrase βῆ δ' ἀκέων (as does Homer at *Il.* 1.34). A poet needing a reference to Achilles at the end of a line, in the nominative case, and filling the pattern ⌣ ⌣ – – ⌣ ⌣ – –, could use the standard descriptive phrase πόδας ὠκὺς Ἀχιλλεύς ("swift-footed Achilles"; see *Il.* 1.58). If a poet needed a reference to the goddess Dawn in the same position and the same case, the poet could use ῥοδοδάκτυλος Ἠώς ("rosy-fingered Dawn"; see *Il.* 1.477).

To describe actions that happened frequently, the poets developed not only phrases but entire lines (for example, Ἦτοι ὅ γ' ὣς εἰπὼν κατ' ἄρ' ἕζετο· τοῖσι δ' ἀνέστη ["so, having spoken, he sat down, and he [another man] stood up before them"] (*Il.* 1.68, 101). Typical scenes (serving a meal, making a sacrifice, launching a ship) also had standard vocabulary.

We should not assume, however, that because Homer employed traditional formulas, his work was not creative or original. In fact, a considerable number of lines in Homer's works are *not* formulaic. Estimates of the nonformulaic portion of the *Iliad* and the *Odyssey* range from one-third to as high as two-thirds. Though Homer's use of formulas is often ornamental and unrelated to the immediate context, he can also utilize them creatively, choosing a specific formulaic word or phrase to create a desired effect.

The *Iliad* and the *Odyssey* are our only complete examples of early Greek epic poetry. Summaries and fragments of other poems that survive suggest that Homer's works differ from them in significant ways. First, Homer's works are considerably longer than any others. Second, rather than telling the complete story of an event, such as the Trojan War, Homer focuses on episodes within longer stories. The *Iliad* covers only a short period during the tenth year of the Trojan War, concentrating on Achilles' anger and its consequences. Within this framework, Homer describes events that represent the whole story (the duel between Paris and Menelaus reminds us of the beginning of the war, and the death of Hector looks forward to the fall of Troy), but his focus is considerably narrower.

How Homer fit into the tradition of oral poetry is not entirely clear. He may have been a traveling bard himself, or he may simply have used the elements of the oral tradition to create his own works. If the belief that he lived around 750–700 B.C. is correct, then he lived at the time writing was reintroduced in Greece. We do not know whether he wrote down his works himself, dictated them to someone else, or orally composed poetry that was written down later over a long period of time.

Though not the first to propose that the works of Homer came out of an oral tradition (Josephus made the suggestion in the first century A.D.), the German scholar Friedrich Wolf set in motion in his *Prolegomena ad Homerum* (1795) the modern debate on how the *Iliad* and the *Odyssey* came into being. Wolf believed that Homer composed without writing anything down and that others added to his work as it was transmitted orally over several hundred years. When it was eventually written down, it was the work not only of Homer but also of many other poets.

In the 1930s, the work of the American scholar Milman Parry on the formulaic phrases, lines, and episodes in Homeric poetry offered proof that Homer's work came out of an extensive oral tradition. Parry showed that the system of formulas was quite complex but also very economical. There was very little duplication; unique formulaic phrases existed for a large number of different metrical requirements. Parry theorized that such a sophisticated system must have been developed by many poets over a long period of time.

Most scholars today see Homer at the end of a long tradition of oral poetry. He used what many others had developed over time, but he used it creatively and he also added his own material. How much of his poetry was his own invention and how much was taken from traditional material is impossible to tell, although we suspect that considerable portions of it reflect his own creativity. It is important to understand the tradition in which he was working; otherwise, the repetitions in his poetry strike a modern reader as strange. But even if he borrowed material, he was the one who selected and organized it into a meaningful whole. As W. B. Stanford wrote,

> when the name of a single person is attached to two superb poems, he is likely to have been a genius of outstanding originality, though, like any master-architect he would freely use materials that had been cut and shaped by others before him.[1]

---

1. W. B. Stanford, "Homer," in *Ancient Writers: Greece and Rome*, vol. 1, ed. T. James Luce (New York: Scribner's, 1982), 5.

What Historical Period Does the *Iliad* Represent? Is the *Iliad* "True"?

Another long-debated question is the "truth" of the events related in the *Iliad.* Homer clearly describes a time in the past, but how far in the past? Was there really a Trojan War? Did Achilles and Agamemnon and Helen and Odysseus and the others really exist?

The Greeks after Homer, with few exceptions or reservations, believed that when Homer described the Trojan War, he was describing an actual historical event—the most important event in their early history. They dated this war to around 1200 B.C. But having no written records from that time, and lacking knowledge gained from modern archaeology, they had no way of confirming Homer's accuracy.

Beginning with the work of Heinrich Schliemann, who excavated Troy, Mycenae, and Tiryns in the 1870s and 1880s, and continuing to the present day, archaeology has given us much more information about the period around 1200 B.C., a time in the late Bronze Age (the period in which bronze was the principal material used to make tools and weapons). Greece did not then exist as a unified country in the modern sense. Homer did not speak of "Greeks," calling them instead by several names, Argives ('Αργεῖοι), Danaans (Δαναοί), and, most frequently, Achaeans ('Αχαιοί).

The Greek-speaking peoples who lived in the area that is now Greece had a society organized around great palaces at such places as Mycenae, Tiryns, Pylos, and Thebes. (Since Mycenae was one of the largest centers of this culture, we refer to the civilization as Mycenaean.) The Mycenaeans had a sophisticated culture. They built enormous palaces and tombs. Palace bureaucrats kept detailed records in a syllabic script now called Linear B. Frescoes decorated the palace walls, and artisans did beautiful work in gold and bronze and ivory. Their pottery has been found throughout the Mediterranean, which shows that they traveled and traded extensively.

The city of Troy, located at modern Hisarlik in northern Turkey, was actually built and destroyed and rebuilt in the same place many times, with the original city dating to around 2800 B.C. About 1220 B.C., the seventh Troy was destroyed by fire. We do not know whether a force of Mycenaeans besieged, captured, and burned it down; there is no conclusive archaeological evidence on this point. It is possible that this destruction of Troy (or perhaps an earlier one) provided the inspiration for the later stories of the Trojan War, but this is merely a guess. Recent excavations of the sixth Troy (1700–1250 B.C.) have revealed it to be larger than previously thought and surrounded by outer fortifications, making it another candidate for the city Homer described as "broad" (*Il.* 13.433; 24.256, 494, 774; *Od.* 1.62; 4.99; 5.307; 11.499; 12.189).

For some reason, around 1100 B.C., Mycenaean civilization itself collapsed. It was long believed that invaders from the north (the Dorians, a less civilized Greek people) brought about the destruction of the great palaces. However, archaeological evidence has not supported this theory, and it is now thought that a combination of factors (perhaps including internal conflicts among the Mycenaeans, the influx of the Dorians, non-Dorian invaders, earthquakes, famine, and climate changes) led to the downfall of the palace-centered society. Whatever the reason, the level of culture fell drastically, and the period from 1100 to 950 B.C. is referred to as the Dark Age. Violence, isolation, population decline, and poverty marked this period; many Greeks migrated to the Aegean islands or to the coast of Asia Minor. Ionia was settled by Greeks at this time. The art of writing seems to have been lost. One important technological advance did occur during this time: the Greeks entered the Iron Age and began to make tools and weapons from iron.

By the ninth century, Greece was emerging from the Dark Age into what we now call the Geometric period (because of the geometric style of pottery decoration used at this time). The Greek alphabet that we are familiar with was then developed, adapted from the Phoenician alphabet. It was a period of expanding horizons, with exploration and colonization beyond Greece itself. Monarchies declined, and the polis, or city-state, emerged as the political unit. We think that it was during this period, around 750–700 B.C., that the *Iliad* and the *Odyssey,* the earliest works of Greek literature we possess, were composed.

It seems impossible to believe that Homer and the oral poets who preceded him invented every detail of the world they described. It is much more plausible to think it was based on some real society. But was it that of the Mycenaeans, the Dark Age, or the "Greeks" of his own time? The answer actually seems to be "all of the above," though it appears that the late Dark Age (the late ninth and early eighth centuries B.C.) was probably the time period chiefly depicted in Homeric poetry.

Homer knew the locations of the main centers of Mycenaean civilization and that the Mycenaeans had had great palaces. But he mentions no details of palace life—the elaborate bureaucracies, the writing they used, their dress, their frescoes.

Homeric heroes carry bronze weapons, which the Mycenaeans did have. But Homer also mentions iron tools, which were known only during the Dark Age and later. He describes Mycenaean large shields, boar's-tusk helmets, and bronze greaves, but also smaller shields and breastplates, which seem to be characteristic of Dark Age armor. Homer knows about chariots, which the

Mycenaeans used in battle, but not about how they were used (his chariots are nothing more than transportation to carry the Homeric hero to the fighting).

When Homeric heroes die, they are cremated, which reflects the customs of Dark Age Greece, not Mycenaean times, when the dead were buried (although excavations at Troy have produced evidence of Bronze Age cremations there). Homer mentions many things that did not exist in the time period he was supposedly describing—freestanding temples, the wealth at the temple of Apollo in Delphi, the use of the hoplite phalanx in battle, and Phoenician ships sailing the Aegean—but which did exist later.

The Homeric world is not just a reflection of the realities of many different time periods; it is also a product of poetic invention. In addition to trying to identify historical elements in Homer's works, we should also remember that part of what he describes is purely a fictional and exaggerated glorious past, when wars went on for ten years, enormous expeditions were mounted, and men were far stronger than they are in the present time.

Some memories of past times were correctly preserved through the centuries; others were not. But Homer was not trying to write accurate history; he was telling stories of a glorious heroic past for the entertainment and enjoyment of an audience. As he used words, details, and episodes that had been passed down for generations and added material from his own observations, it is not surprising that the Homeric world contains details of life from many periods and from his own imagination.

How Were the Homeric Poems
Passed Down over the Centuries?

Sometime after the composition of the *Iliad* and the *Odyssey,* professional reciters known as rhapsodes traveled throughout the Greek world, reciting Homer's poetry. One group of rhapsodes in Chios called themselves the Homeridae (meaning "sons of Homer") and claimed to be actual descendants of the poet. An evening's performance undoubtedly consisted not of the entire *Iliad* or *Odyssey* (each would have been far too long) but of episodes from them. As various rhapsodes performed over time, some changes and additions undoubtedly crept into the text.

By 650 B.C., the *Iliad* and the *Odyssey* were evidently well known, both in Ionia and on mainland Greece. We know this because other poets seem to quote from them and because artists were depicting scenes from the works.

Between 650 and 550 B.C., perhaps even earlier, the poems were probably written down. The story is told that Pisistratus, the tyrant of Athens, tried to establish an authentic text in the second half of the sixth century. There is some evidence that during the sixth century, a law was passed in Athens requiring that only Homer's works be performed at the Panathenaic festival, but there is no real proof that Pisistratus or anyone else tried to compile a standard text. Perhaps it was simply at this time that a complete written text first came to Athens.

The text we have now is based in large part on the work of three great Alexandrian scholars: Zenodotus, Aristophanes of Byzantium, and especially Aristarchus. Working during the third and second centuries B.C., these men, who each served as librarian at the Museum of Alexandria, created a standard text of the Homeric poems. They studied many manuscripts of the poems, removed lines that they thought had been added to the original poem, and made critical notes on the works. It was probably also during this time that each poem was divided into twenty-four books.

From the second century B.C. until the second or third century A.D., the Homeric poems were preserved on papyrus rolls. Many rolls were required for the complete texts of the *Iliad* and the *Odyssey*. The invention of the paged book (codex) in the late first or early second century A.D. and the use of parchment (prepared animal skins) for pages changed the way in which long works could be recorded. The earliest Homeric text on parchment comes from the third century A.D. Parchment books had larger pages than papyrus rolls, allowing more room for illustrations and notes in the margins. (Homeric scholars from the time of the great Alexandrians on had been making textual notes in the margins and sometimes between the lines of manuscripts. Many of these notes or scholia can be seen in existing manuscripts.)

Byzantine scholars played an important role in the preservation, transmission, and study of the Homeric texts. From A.D. 500 to 1300, such men as Photius, John Tzetzes, and Eustathius collected and critiqued Homeric manuscripts and scholia. Many Byzantine manuscripts and commentaries made their way to the West, especially to Italy.

The earliest complete extant manuscript of either Homeric poem is the Venetus A manuscript, a tenth-century A.D. manuscript of the *Iliad* that came to the library of St. Mark in Venice in the fifteenth century and was rediscovered there in the eighteenth century. This manuscript is especially important because, in addition to the text, it transmits considerable information about Aristarchus's critical work.

In the fourteenth century, many Greek texts and scholars came to Italy, where most of our extant manuscripts were copied. Then the invention of printing introduced a new method of preserving and transmitting the Homeric texts. The first printed edition of the *Iliad* was published in Florence in 1488.

The text we have today is based mainly on medieval manuscripts (none earlier than the tenth century), on scholia and commentaries, and on fragments of papyri containing lines from the *Iliad* that go back to the third century B.C.

The Story of the *Iliad*

The *Iliad* takes its name from Ἴλιος, another name for the city of Troy, and is therefore "a story of Troy." To place the first book of the *Iliad* in context, it is necessary to know what happened before and after this segment of the story, as an ancient audience would have. The *Odyssey* recounts Odysseus's journey home from the Trojan War, and several shorter poems composed during the seventh and sixth centuries B.C. took the story of the Trojan War beyond both the *Iliad* and the *Odyssey.* The poems in this epic cycle told of events before, during, and after the war and included the fall of Troy and the return of other Greek leaders.

Background

From sources outside the *Iliad,* we learn that Zeus, the king of the gods, was attracted to the sea nymph Thetis. When he learned that her son was destined to be more powerful than his father, he decided to marry her to the human Peleus, a Greek king. (Peleus and Thetis became the parents of Achilles, the pivotal figure in the *Iliad.*) All the gods were invited to the wedding except Eris, the goddess of strife. Angry at being snubbed, she arrived at the festivities anyway, bringing a golden apple that she announced was for the fairest of the goddesses. As she planned, this set in motion a bitter dispute among Hera, Athena, and Aphrodite over who should have the apple. When the three goddesses appealed to Zeus to decide, he (the husband of Hera and the father of Aphrodite and Athena) wisely refused and said that a mortal, Paris, should make the decision.

So the three goddesses appeared before Paris, a prince of Troy, and asked him to select the fairest. Each offered him a bribe. Hera promised him power; Athena, victory in war; and Aphrodite, the most beautiful woman in the world as his wife. The golden apple went to Aphrodite.

Unfortunately, Helen, the most beautiful woman in the world, was already married to Menelaus, the king of Sparta. Aphrodite helped Paris abduct Helen (stories vary as to whether she went willingly or not) and bring her back to Troy. Menelaus, furious at the loss of his wife, appealed to his brother, Agamemnon, the king of Mycenae, for help in getting her back, and Agamemnon organized a great expedition of Greeks to do just that. Among the many heroes who joined the endeavor were Achilles, Odysseus, Nestor, and Diomedes.

As the Greek expedition was poised to sail from Aulis, the goddess Artemis sent unfavorable winds that prevented them from sailing. Calchas, a Greek seer, said that Agamemnon's daughter, Iphigenia, must be sacrificed to appease the goddess. Agamemnon summoned his daughter from Mycenae and sacrificed her.

The Greeks then sailed to Troy, where a long war began. The king of the Trojans, Priam, had many sons, one of whom, Hector, led the defense of the city. For nine years, Greeks and Trojans fought on the plain in front of the heavily fortified city, but neither side was able to gain the advantage. At this point, the *Iliad* begins.

The *Iliad*

The *Iliad* covers only a short period (about seven weeks) in the tenth year of the Trojan War. As it opens, we learn that Chryses, a priest of Apollo, came to the Greek camp to ransom his daughter, Chryseis, whom the Greeks had captured. However, she had been given to Agamemnon as a prize, and he refused to give her up. In answer to Chryses' prayer that he punish the Greeks, Apollo sent a plague on the Greek army. Achilles, the greatest of the Greek warriors, called an assembly to determine why Apollo was angry with them and what could be done about it. Calchas, the seer, revealed that the cause of Apollo's anger was Agamemnon's refusal to return Chryseis to her father. Agamemnon was forced to return the woman for the good of the army, but he threatened to take Achilles' prize woman, Briseis, to replace her. Angry words were exchanged, with Achilles vowing that if he were treated with such dishonor, he would withdraw himself and his troops from the fighting. Undeterred, Agamemnon took Briseis. Achilles then refused to fight and also asked his mother, Thetis, to persuade Zeus to allow the Trojans to defeat the Greeks in battle, so they would suffer for Agamemnon's treatment of him. Zeus granted her request.

When the Trojans pushed the Greeks back to their fortified camp, Agamemnon sent a delegation to Achilles, offering to return Briseis and give him many gifts if he would return to battle. But Achilles, still angry, refused to return. When the fighting continued, the Trojans drove the Greeks back all the way to their ships, which were drawn up on the shore.

Grieving at the misfortunes of the Greeks, Patroclus, Achilles' best friend, asked if he could wear Achilles' armor into battle, hoping to fool the Trojans into thinking that Achilles had returned. Achilles agreed to this, warning Patroclus only to drive the Trojans away from the Greek ships and not to pursue them back to the city. Patroclus, however, carried away by his success, chased the Trojans back to the walls of Troy. There Hector killed him and took Achilles' armor.

When Achilles heard that Patroclus had died, he was devastated with grief and swore to avenge his death. After getting new armor, which his mother arranged for the god Hephaestus to make for him, he returned to battle and killed Hector. Priam, Hector's father, then went secretly to the Greek camp to ransom his son's body. Achilles, remembering his own aged father, accepted the ransom and returned the body to Priam. The *Iliad* ends with the funeral of Hector.

After the *Iliad*

We must turn to sources outside the *Iliad* to complete the story. Achilles, aware all along that if he fought at Troy he would die, was killed by Paris, with Apollo's help. The Greeks finally took Troy through a trick. Having constructed a giant wooden horse, the Greeks left it before the walls of Troy and sailed to a nearby island, making the Trojans think they had given up and returned home. The Trojans brought the horse into the city and celebrated the end of the war. During the night, Greek soldiers hidden inside the horse crept out and opened the gates of the city to the Greek army. Troy was destroyed, Priam was killed, and Helen was returned to Menelaus. The Greeks then set sail for home. Agamemnon reached Mycenae only to be murdered by his wife and her lover. Menelaus and Helen wandered for some years before getting back to Sparta. It took Odysseus ten years to reach his home, the island of Ithaca, and reclaim his throne.

Homeric Greek

Homeric Greek is an artificial language. No one ever actually spoke it. It is a composite of words from many different dialects and time periods developed over centuries as the language of epic poets. While it consists mainly of the Ionic Greek dialect from the west coast of Asia Minor, it has traces of Aeolic, the Greek spoken farther north on the coast of Asia Minor. It has words from Arcadia and Cyprus that appear to be survivals of Mycenaean Greek (carried to Arcadia and Cyprus when Mycenaeans from the Peloponnese moved there). It also contains words that seem to have been simply invented by poets.

The reason for the combination of so many different forms was meter. The poets needed words to fit complex metrical patterns. If a form from another dialect fit the meter when an Ionic form did not, they used the other form. If an augmented verb would not fit the meter but an unaugmented one would, they did not use an augment. This language of the epics was created not single-handedly by Homer or any one poet but by many poets over long periods of time. Eventually, some of the words or expressions were so old that even the poets using them were not sure of their meaning.

When reading Homeric Greek, expect to see forms that do not look like standard Attic forms. Verb augments may or may not be present. Vowels that are contracted in Attic appear uncontracted. Words that have single consonants in Attic may have doubled consonants, and other spellings will be slightly different. The following variations are very common in Homeric Greek.

1. Verb augments are not always present (for example, λίσσετο for ἐλίσσετο in *Il.* 1.15).

2. These variations in declensional endings occur frequently.

First Declension	Attic	Homeric
gen. sing. (masc)	-ου	-ᾱ, -εω
gen. plur.	-ῶν	-άων, -έων
dat. plur.	-αις	-ῃσι(ν), -ῃς

Second Declension		
gen. sing.	-ου	-οιο
dat. plur.	-οις	-οισι(ν)

Third Declension		
dat. plur.	-σι(ν)	-εσσι(ν)

3. The following personal pronoun variations occur.

ἐγώ (I)	Attic	Homeric
gen. sing.	ἐμοῦ or μου	ἐμεῖο, ἐμεῦ, μευ, ἐμέθεν
nom. plur.	ἡμεῖς	ἄμμες
dat. plur.	ἡμῖν	ἄμμι(ν)
acc. plur.	ἡμᾶς	ἄμμε

σύ (you)		
gen. sing.	σοῦ or σου	σεῖο, σέο, σεῦ, σέθεν
dat. sing.	σοί or σοι	τοι
nom. plur.	ὑμεῖς	ὔμμες
dat. plur.	ὑμῖν	ὔμμι(ν)
acc. plur.	ὑμᾶς	ὔμμε

him, her, it	Attic	Homeric
gen. sing.	αὐτοῦ,-ῆς,-οῦ	εἷο, ἕο, εὗ, ἕθεν
dat. sing.	αὐτῷ,-ῇ,-ῷ	ἑοῖ, οἷ
acc. sing.	αὐτόν,-ήν,-ό	ἑέ, ἕ, μιν
gen. plur.	αὐτῶν	σφείων, σφέων
dat. plur.	αὐτοῖς,-αῖς,-οῖς	σφίσι(ν), σφι(ν)
acc. plur.	αὐτούς,-άς,-ά	σφέας, σφε

4. Infinitives can end in -έμεναι or -έμεν, as well as -ειν.

5. The article (ὁ, ἡ, τό) is more frequently used as a personal, demonstrative, or relative pronoun than as an article. It can be translated as "he," "she," "it," "this," "that," "who," or "which," in addition to "the."

6. Aorist participles can indicate the same time as the main verb and are often translated as though they were present participles.

See appendix 2 for more information on Homeric forms and grammar.

Dactylic Hexameter

Meter is the rhythmical pattern of poetry. Unlike English poetry, whose meters involve patterns of stressed and unstressed syllables, Greek meters are patterns of long and short syllables. The meter of Homeric poetry, *dactylic hexameter,* has the following characteristics.

- Each line is divided into six sections (ἕξ = "six," hence "*hex*ameter") called *feet.*

- The patterns of long and short syllables that can occur within the feet are called *dactyls* and *spondees.*

  dactyl—a pattern of one long, then two short syllables: — ˘ ˘. (It gets its name from δάκτυλος (finger). Look at your index finger; notice how it has one long and two short sections).

  spondee—a pattern of two long syllables: — —.

- Each of the first five feet can be either a dactyl or a spondee. About 95 percent of the time, the fifth foot is a dactyl. A line with a spondee in the fifth foot is called a *spondaic line.*

- The sixth foot is always a spondee.

- The first syllable of each foot receives the *ictus* (stress or emphasis in pronunciation).

A syllable is short if:

- it has a single short vowel (ᾰ, ε, ῐ, ο, ῠ) followed by another vowel or a single consonant.

But it can be scanned as a long syllable if:

- it is the first or last syllable of a word and receives the ictus. See the last syllable of πόλιν in *Iliad* 1.19.

$$— —\ |\ —\quad ⌣⌣\ |—⌣\quad ⌣\ |—\ —\ |\ —\quad ⌣\quad ⌣\ |—\quad —$$

ἐκπέρσαι Πριάμοιο πόλ<u>ιν</u>, εὖ δ᾽ οἴκαδ᾽ ἱκέσθαι·

(If it is the final syllable of a word, it will often be followed by a *caesura,* or pause in the verse, as in this example.)

- the short vowel is the last letter of a word and the next word begins with a liquid (λ, μ, ν, ρ), a digamma (ϝ), or a sigma (σ). See the last syllable of ἐπί in *Iliad* 1.233.

$$—\quad —|—\quad ⌣\quad ⌣|—\quad ⌣\quad ⌣|—\quad ⌣\quad ⌣\ |\ —\quad ⌣\quad ⌣|—\quad —$$

ἀλλ᾽ ἔκ τοι ἐρέω καὶ <u>ἐπὶ μέγ</u>αν ὅρκον ὀμοῦμαι·

A syllable is long if any of the following are true.

- it has a long vowel (ᾱ, η, ῑ, ῡ, ω). (Hint: any vowel with a circumflex accent is long.)

- it has a diphthong (two vowels pronounced together, e.g., αι, ει, οι, υι, αυ, ευ, ηυ, ου).

- it has a short vowel followed by two or more consonants. (Note: This is very common.) The consonants do not have to be in the same word as the vowel. The letters ρ (at the beginning of a word), ζ, ξ, and ψ are considered double consonants. See the last syllable of ἀνά and the next to the last syllable of ὀλέκοντο in *Iliad* 1.10.

$$— \; ⌣ \; ⌣ \; | — \quad ⌣ \; ⌣ \; | — \; ⌣ \; ⌣ \; | — \; ⌣ \; ⌣ \; | — \; ⌣ \; ⌣ \; | — \; —$$

νοῦσον ἀνὰ στρατὸν ὦρσε κακήν, ὀλέκοντο δὲ λαοί,

- it is the first or last syllable in the line. Even if these syllables have short vowels, they are scanned as long syllables. See the last syllable of Ἀπόλλωνα in *Iliad* 1.21.

$$—⌣ \; ⌣ \; | — \quad ⌣⌣ \; | —⌣ \quad ⌣ \; | —⌣ \; ⌣ \; | \quad — —| — \quad —$$

ἁζόμενοι Διὸς υἱὸν ἑκηβόλον Ἀπόλλωνα.

But it can be scanned as a short syllable if:

- the long vowel or diphthong comes at the end of a word and the next word begins with a vowel. (Note: This is very common.) See the last syllable of ἑκηβόλου in *Iliad* 1.14.

$$— \quad ⌣ \; ⌣ \; | — \; — | \; — \quad ⌣ \; ⌣ \; | — ⌣ \; ⌣ \; | — \; — | — \quad —$$

στέμματ᾽ ἔχων ἐν χερσὶν ἑκηβόλου Ἀπόλλωνος

- the long vowel or diphthong is followed by another vowel within the same word. Note the first syllable of υἱός, in *Iliad* 1.489.

$$—⌣ \; ⌣ \; | — \; — | — ⌣ \; ⌣ \; | \quad ⌣ \; ⌣ \; | — ⌣ \quad ⌣ \; | — \quad —$$

διογενὴς Πηλῆος υἱός, πόδας ὠκὺς Ἀχιλλεύς·

- it does not receive the ictus. In *Iliad* 1.43, the α in Ἀπόλλων is long, but the syllable is scanned short because it does not receive the ictus.

$$— \; ⌣ \; ⌣ \; | \; — \; ⌣ \; ⌣ \; | — \; — | \; \quad — \; ⌣⌣ \; | \; — \; ⌣ \; ⌣ | — \quad —$$

Ὣς ἔφατ᾽ εὐχόμενος, τοῦ δ᾽ ἔκλυε Φοῖβος Ἀπόλλων,

Diaeresis, or When Is a Diphthong Not a Diphthong?

When a double dot (¨), indicating a *diaeresis* (separation), appears over an ι or υ, it means that letter does not form a diphthong with the preceding vowel and the two vowels are pronounced as separate syllables. This occurs, for example, in *Iliad* 1.3.

— | — ˘ ˘ | —

ψυχὰς Ἄϊδι

Digamma

The digamma (Ϝ), pronounced like the English *w,* was a consonant used in early Greek but no longer in use in Homeric Greek. Sometimes, but not always, a digamma that was once in a word still affects the determination of long and short syllables. For example, in *Iliad* 1.33, the first syllable of ἔδεισεν is scanned long because ἔδεισεν was originally spelled ἔδϜεισεν, putting two consonants after the short ε.

— ˘ ˘ | — — | — ˘ ˘ | — ˘ ˘ | — ˘ ˘ | — —

Ὣς ἔφατ, <u>ἔδ</u>εισεν δ᾿ ὁ γέρων καὶ ἐπείθετο μύθῳ·

Synizesis

Sometimes two vowels or a vowel and a diphthong that are side by side (either in the same word or in separate words) and that would normally be pronounced as two syllables are run together, scanned, and pronounced as one long syllable. See -εοι in θεοί in *Iliad* 1.18.

— — | — — | — ˘ ˘ | — ˘˘| — ˘ ˘ | — —

ὑμῖν μὲν θ<u>εοὶ</u> δοῖεν Ὀλύμπια δώματ᾿ ἔχοντες

Elision

Elision occurs when a short final vowel (and sometimes a final diphthong) is dropped before a word beginning with a vowel. An apostrophe takes the place of the missing vowel or diphthong. For example, in *Iliad* 1.2, μυρί᾿ equals μυρία and ἄλγε᾿ equals ἄλγεα.

οὐλομένην, ἣ <u>μυρί᾿</u> Ἀχαιοῖς <u>ἄλγε᾿</u> ἔθηκε,

Caesura

A pause in a verse that falls within a foot is called a *caesura*. (One that falls at the end of a foot is called a *diaeresis*.) Almost all Homeric verses have a caesura in either the third or the fourth foot. In *Iliad* 1.13, the caesura is marked with ‖.

— ‿ ‿ | — ‿ ‿ | — ‿ ‖ ‿ | — ‿ ‿ | — ‿ ‿ | — —
λυσόμενός τε θύγατρα ‖ φέρων τ᾽ ἀπερείσι᾽ ἄποινα,

Characters in Book 1 of the *Iliad*

Ἀγαμέμνων, -ονος, ὁ	Agamemnon	king of Mycenae; chief commander of the Greek forces at Troy; brother of Menelaus (who is the king of Sparta and the husband of Helen); also called Ἀτρεΐδης, "son of Atreus"
Ἀθήνη or Ἀθηναίη, -ης, ἡ	Athena	goddess of the arts and war; daughter of Zeus; supporter of the Greeks
Ἀπόλλων, -ωνος, ὁ	Apollo	son of Zeus and Leto; god of archery, music, and prophecy; supporter of the Trojans
Ἀχιλ(λ)εύς, -ῆος, ὁ	Achilles	greatest Greek hero; son of the sea goddess Thetis and the mortal Peleus; also called Πηλεΐδης or Πηληϊάδης or Πηλεΐων, "son of Peleus"
Βρισηΐς, -ΐδος, ἡ	Briseis	woman given to Achilles as his γέρας (war prize)
Εὐρυβάτης, -αο, ὁ	Eurybates	one of Agamemnon's heralds
Ζεύς, Διός, ὁ	Zeus	king of the gods; husband of Hera; also called Κρονίδης or Κρονίων, "son of Cronus"
Ἥρη, -ης, ἡ	Hera	wife of Zeus; friend of the Greeks; enemy of the Trojans
Ἥφαιστος, -ου, ὁ	Hephaestus	lame son of Zeus and Hera;

		god of fire and all arts that use fire, especially metalworking
Θέτις, -ιδος, ἡ	Thetis	sea goddess; mother of Achilles; wife of Peleus; daughter of Nereus
Κάλχας, -αντος, ὁ	Calchas	Greek seer
Νέστωρ, -ορος, ὁ	Nestor	king of Pylos; oldest of the Greek leaders
Ὀδυσ(σ)εύς, -ῆος, ὁ	Odysseus	king of Ithaca; Greek leader renowned for his craftiness
Πάτροκλος, -ου, ὁ	Patroclus	Achilles' closest friend; also called Μενοιτιάδης, "son of Menoetius"
Ταλθύβιος, -ου, ὁ	Talthybius	one of Agamemnon's heralds
Χρυσηΐς, -ΐδος, ἡ	Chryseis	woman given to Agamemnon as his γέρας (war prize); daughter of Chryses
Χρύσης, -αο, ὁ	Chryses	priest of Apollo; father of Chryseis

Further Reading

The following list, a very brief and highly selective introduction to the thousands of books and articles written about Homer and the *Iliad,* includes basic introductions to Homer, classics of Homeric scholarship, historical studies, articles that investigate very specific topics or suggest interesting interpretations, modern fiction, and relevant web sites on ancient Greece, Homer, and Troy. This section is intended merely to suggest the vast resources that are available for further exploration of the world of Homer.

General Works

Beye, Charles Rowan. *The Iliad, the Odyssey, and the Epic Tradition.* New York: Anchor, 1966. An excellent introduction to Homer and his poetry; extremely informative and readable.

Bowra, C. M. *Homer.* New York: Scribner's, 1972. An overview of Homeric poetry; includes a chapter on the shape and character of the *Iliad* and another on the "obstacles and difficulties" faced by a modern audience as they read Homer.

Camps, W. A. *An Introduction to Homer.* Oxford: Oxford University Press, 1980. A brief overview of the essential character of Homeric poetry.

Edwards, Mark W. *Homer: Poet of the Iliad.* Baltimore: Johns Hopkins University Press, 1987. A discussion of all aspects of Homeric poetry, as well as a detailed analysis of each book of the *Iliad.*

Griffin, Jasper. *Homer on Life and Death.* Oxford: Clarendon, 1980. Essays on the Homeric poems stressing unifying themes, such as heroism, life, and death; chapter 2, "Characterization," includes considerable discussion of Achilles and Agamemnon.

Kirk, G. S. *The Iliad: A Commentary.* Vol. 1, *Books 1–4.* Cambridge: Cambridge University Press, 1985. A detailed commentary on the language, style, poetics, structure, background, and interpretation of specific words, lines, and passages in the first four books of the *Iliad.*

Latacz, Joachim. *Homer: His Art and His World.* Trans. James P. Holoka. Ann Arbor: University of Michigan Press, 1996. Discussion of how Homeric poetry must have differed from other Greek epic poetry and how an ancient audience, familiar with the stories, would have appreciated Homer's art in a different way from a modern audience; includes a lengthy section on book 1 of the *Iliad.*

Lord, Albert Bates. *Epic Singers and Oral Tradition.* Ithaca, N.Y.: Cornell University Press, 1991. A collection of articles providing an overview of oral traditional epic.

McAuslan, Ian, and Peter Walcot. *Homer.* Greece and Rome Studies, vol. 4. Oxford: Oxford University Press, 1998. A collection of articles on a variety of Homeric topics, including Homer as a poet of the Dark Ages, the search for the "real" Homer, and a critical appreciation of the first fifty-two lines of the *Iliad.*

Morris, Ian, and Barry Powell. *A New Companion to Homer.* Leiden: Brill, 1997. Essays on all aspects of Homeric poetry, including language and meter, Homer as literature, and the world of Homer.

Nardo, Don, ed. *Readings on Homer.* San Diego: Greenhaven, 1998. Excerpts of essays on Homeric style, imagery, and cultural values, as well as themes and characters in the *Iliad.*

Owen, E. T. *The Story of the Iliad.* Toronto: Clarke, Irwin, 1946. Reprint, Bristol: Bristol Classical; Wauconda, Ill.: Bolchazy-Carducci, 1989. A book-by-book analysis of what makes the *Iliad* a "well-told story."

Parry, Milman. *The Making of Homeric Verse: The Collected Papers of Milman Parry.* Ed. Adam Parry. Oxford: Clarendon, 1971. The works of the man who conclusively demonstrated the formulaic nature of Homeric poetry; the introduction has an excellent overview of the "Homeric Question" and of Parry's significance.

Rutherford, Richard. *Homer.* Greece and Rome New Surveys in the Classics, no. 26. Oxford: Oxford University Press, 1996. An excellent introduction to Homeric epic; see especially chapter 2 for discussion of structure, characterization, and themes in the *Iliad.*

Seymour, Thomas Day. *Life in the Homeric Age.* 1907. Reprint, New York: Biblo and Tannen, 1963. Not an attempt to identify historical elements in Homer, but an organization of information on all aspects of life as presented in the Homeric poems themselves.

Silk, Michael. *Homer: The Iliad.* Landmarks of World Literature Series. Cambridge: Cambridge University Press, 1987. Reprint, 1993. An introduction to Homer, the composition of the *Iliad,* its themes and characters, and its influence on later literature; section 8 of chapter 1 contains an interesting comparison of oral composition and jazz.

Stanford, W. B. "Homer." In *Ancient Writers: Greece and Rome,* vol. 1, ed. T. James Luce, 1–41. New York: Scribner's, 1982. An essay providing an excellent general overview of the *Iliad* and the *Odyssey,* as well as an appreciation of Homer's artistry.

Taplin, Oliver. "Homer." In *The Oxford History of the Classical World,* ed. John Boardman, Jasper Griffin, and Oswyn Murray, 50–77. Oxford: Oxford University Press, 1986. A good introduction to Homer and his poetry.

Works on Specific Issues

Bernheim, Frederick, and Ann Adams Zener. "The Sminthian Apollo and the Epidemic among the Achaeans at Troy." *Transactions of the American Philological Association* 108 (1978): 11–14. Suggests an identification of the disease sent by Apollo to the Greeks in book 1 of the *Iliad.*

Bowra, C. M. *Tradition and Design in the Iliad.* Oxford: Clarendon, 1930. See especially chapters 1 and 9 on the character of Achilles and chapter 12 on when and where Homer lived.

Casson, Lionel. *The Ancient Mariners: Seafarers and Sea Fighters of the Mediterranean in Ancient Times.* 2d ed. Princeton: Princeton University Press, 1991. A history of ships and their uses in the ancient Mediterranean world.

Donlan, Walter. "Homer's Agamemnon." *Classical World* 65, no. 4 (December 1971): 109–15. A sympathetic analysis of the development of Agamemnon's character through the *Iliad.* See Taplin's 1990 article for a very different view.

Landels, John G. *Music in Ancient Greece and Rome.* London: Routledge, 1999. An introduction to the music of the ancient Greeks and Romans; includes discussion of musical instruments, the performance of epic poetry, and meter.

Luce, J. V. *Celebrating Homer's Landscapes: Troy and Ithaca Revisited.* New Haven and London: Yale University Press, 1998. A detailed survey of Homeric geography, illustrated with photographs of the modern terrain; argues that Homer's topographic descriptions are quite accurate.

Rabel, Robert J. "Chryses and the Opening of the *Iliad.*" *American Journal of Philology* 109 (1988): 473–81. Suggests that the Chryses story provides the model for Achilles' actions, although Achilles carries the anger—which he mistakenly thought motivated the old priest—too far.

Redfield, James M. "The Wrath of Achilles as Tragic Error." In *Essays on the Iliad: Selected Modern Criticism,* ed. John Wright, 85–92. Bloomington: Indiana University Press, 1978. Discusses the errors that lead to tragedy in book 1 of the *Iliad.*

Scott, John A. "Dogs in Homer." *Classical Weekly* 41 (1947–48): 226–28. Argues against the notion that a different attitude toward dogs in the *Iliad* and the *Odyssey* suggests that the two works are by different authors.

Segal, Charles. "Nestor and the Honor of Achilles (*Iliad* 1.247–84)." *Studi Micenei ed Egeo-Anatolici* 13 (1971): 90–105. Argues that Achilles is entirely justified in his actions in book 1 of the *Iliad.*

Shay, Jonathan. "Achilles: Paragon, Flawed Character, or Tragic Soldier Figure?" *Clas-

sical Bulletin 71, no. 2 (1995): 117–24. Looks at previous interpretations of Achilles' character (as glorious hero or psychologically and/or morally deformed man) and suggests that Achilles should be seen as a real soldier whose tragic mistakes can be blamed on the intense stress of nine years of war.

Taplin, Oliver. "Agamemnon's Role in the *Iliad*." In *Characterization and Individuality in Greek Literature,* ed. Christopher Pelling, 60–82. Oxford: Clarendon, 1990. Presents a very negative view of Agamemnon. See Donlan's 1971 article for an opposing view.

Warry, John. "Homeric and Mycenaean Warfare." In *Warfare in the Classical World,* 10–23. London: Salamander, 1980. Reprint, Norman: University of Oklahoma Press, 1995. A beautifully illustrated account of warfare in the Homeric poems, with discussion of both the literary and the archaeological evidence.

Whittaker, A. J. "Homer Sings the Blues." *Greece and Rome* 41, no. 1 (April 1994): 19–22. Highlights the main characteristics of Homeric oral composition by comparing it to the work of blues singers.

Youman, A. Eliot. "Climactic Themes in the *Iliad*." *Classical Journal* 61, no. 5 (February 1966): 222–28. A concise discussion of several recurring themes in the *Iliad.*

History

Dickinson, Oliver. *The Aegean Bronze Age.* Cambridge: Cambridge University Press, 1994. A general introduction to Bronze Age Minoan, Cycladic, and Helladic cultures of the southern Aegean.

Finley, M. I. *The World of Odysseus.* Rev. ed. New York: Viking, 1978. A standard work on the historicity of Homer's poetry; argues that the world Homer describes was that of the early Dark Age and that there is no historical or archaeological proof for a Trojan War.

Fitton, J. Lesley. *The Discovery of the Greek Bronze Age.* Cambridge: Harvard University Press, 1996. Describes the history of the excavation of Troy and sites in Crete and Greece that provide the only real evidence we have for life in the Bronze Age.

Hurwit, Jeffrey M. *The Art and Culture of Early Greece, 1100–480 B.C.* Ithaca, N.Y.: Cornell University Press, 1985. Places Archaic Greek art and architecture in "its literary, historical, and intellectual contexts"; presents arguments for the theory that two different people wrote the *Iliad* and the *Odyssey* and for the idea that "Homer" used writing in the composition of the epics.

Lemonick, Michael D. "Troy's Lost Treasure." *Time,* April 22, 1996, 78–80. A news report on the golden artifacts discovered by Schliemann at Troy, smuggled out of Turkey, and donated to Germany; the golden vessels and jewelry, believed to be lost during World War II, were actually taken to Russia, and they were put on exhibit in Moscow in 1996. See also Plagens's *Newsweek* article.

Luce, J. V. *Homer and the Heroic Age.* New York: Harper and Row, 1975. A very readable, well-illustrated look at what archaeology has revealed about the historicity and interpretation of the Homeric poems.

Martin, Thomas R. *Ancient Greece: From Prehistoric to Hellenistic Times.* New Haven: Yale University Press, 1996. An overview of Greek history. An on-line version is available on the *Perseus Digital Library* web site, ⟨http://www.perseus.tufts.edu⟩.

Ottaway, James H., Jr. "New Assault on Troy." *Archaeology* 44, no. 5 (September/October 1991): 54–59. A discussion of Homer, Troy, and Manfred Korfmann's excavations at Hisarlik. For the latest information on these excavations, see the *Project Troia* web site ⟨http://classics.uc.edu/troy/index.html⟩.

Plagens, Peter. "The Golden Hoard." *Newsweek,* April 8, 1996, 72–73. Another news report about the 1996 Moscow exhibit of the treasures of Troy. See also Lemonick's *Time* article.

Pomeroy, Sarah B., Stanley M. Burstein, Walter Donlan, and Jennifer Tolbert Roberts. *Ancient Greece: A Political, Social, and Cultural History.* New York: Oxford University Press, 1999. Chapters 1 and 2 provide an excellent introduction to Bronze Age and Dark Age Greece, with especially good discussions of Homer and Homeric society.

Taylour, William. *The Mycenaeans.* Rev. ed. London: Thames and Hudson, 1983. Survey of what we know about the Mycenaean Greeks.

Wood, Michael. *In Search of the Trojan War.* New York: Facts on File, 1985; updated ed. Berkeley: University of California Press, 1998. A popular account of the archaeological discoveries of Schliemann, Dorpfeld, Evans, Blegen, and others; examines the evidence for the existence of a Trojan War.

Fiction

Bradley, Marion Zimmer. *The Firebrand.* New York: Simon and Schuster, 1987. A novel about the Trojan War and centered on Cassandra, the daughter of King Priam of Troy; although the main events and characters from the *Iliad* are here, the story is told from a modern feminist perspective, with several changes to the story. See Mary Lefkowitz's review of this book in *New York Times Book Review,* November 29, 1987, 27.

Euripides. *Iphigenia at Aulis.* A play depicting the sacrifice of Agamemnon's daughter Iphigenia so the Greek fleet could sail from Aulis to Troy.

Franklin, Sarah B. *Daughter of Troy.* New York: Avon, 1998. A novel about the Trojan War and narrated by Briseis, centering on her passionate love affair with Achilles.

McCullough, Colleen. *The Song of Troy.* London: Orion, 1998. This novel, narrated in turn by all the major characters of the Trojan War, is a fascinating speculation on what real events might stand behind the stories in Homer and other ancient authors. Especially interesting is McCullough's presentation of the "quarrel" between Achilles and Agamemnon.

Powell, Richard. *Whom the Gods Would Destroy.* New York: Scribner's, 1970. A novel whose central character, an unacknowledged son of King Priam of Troy, lives through the Trojan War and meets most of the leading characters on both the Greek and the Trojan sides.

Renault, Mary. *The Praise Singer.* New York: Pantheon, 1978. A novel about the sixth-century poet Simonides that highlights the transition from oral to written poetry. It includes an account of Pisistratus's supposed efforts to establish the text of Homer.

Vaughan, Agnes Carr. *Within the Walls.* New York: Macmillan, 1935. Set within the city of Troy during the Trojan War, this novel follows the life of Andromache, the wife of Hector, from her marriage to the fall of the city.

Wallin, Florence. *According to Helen.* Alexander, N.C.: Pine Tree, 1997. Narrated by Helen, this novel tells of her life from the time before her marriage to Menelaus until after the end of the Trojan War.

Web Sites

The Perseus Digital Library (home of the Perseus Classics Collection—texts in original languages and translation, modern reference works and secondary sources, digital images and maps), ⟨http://www.perseus.tufts.edu⟩.

Project Troia (the web site of the archaeological excavation at Troy run by the University of Tübingen and the University of Cincinnati), ⟨http://classics.uc.edu/troy/index.html⟩.

The National Archaeological Museum of Athens, ⟨http://www.culture.gr/2/21/214/21405m/e21405m1.html⟩.

The Library of Congress Greek and Latin Classics Internet Resources, ⟨http://lcweb.loc.gov/global/classics/claslink.html⟩.

Iliad
Book 1

Homer announces his subject: the anger of Achilles and its terrible consequences.

Μῆνιν ἄειδε, θεά, Πηληϊάδεω ᾿Αχιλῆος	1
οὐλομένην, ἣ μυρί᾿ ᾿Αχαιοῖς ἄλγε᾿ ἔθηκε,	2
πολλὰς δ᾿ ἰφθίμους ψυχὰς ῎Αϊδι προΐαψεν	3
ἡρώων, αὐτοὺς δὲ ἑλώρια τεῦχε κύνεσσιν	4
οἰωνοῖσί τε πᾶσι, Διὸς δ᾿ ἐτελείετο βουλή,	5
ἐξ οὗ δὴ τὰ πρῶτα διαστήτην ἐρίσαντε	6

1   **μῆνις, -ιος, ἡ**—anger, wrath.

    ἀείδω—sing about (poetry of this type was sung to the accompaniment of a lyre); **ἄειδε**—present active imperative.

    θεά—vocative sing. (The goddess referred to is the Muse who inspires the poet. The Muses are the goddesses of literature, music, and dance. In Homer, they do not have individual names and areas of responsibility, as they do later. In addition to acknowledging the Muse as his source of inspiration, calling on her may serve as a divine guarantee for the quality of the story as well as a signal for the audience to be quiet since the performance is beginning.)

    Πηληϊάδης, -εω, ὁ—son of Peleus (i.e., Achilles, the son of the mortal Peleus and the sea nymph Thetis). (The suffix -δης adds the meaning "son of" to the name to which it is attached, in this case Πηλεύς. See ᾿Ατρεΐδης in line 7. Such names are called *patronymics*, literally, "names from the father.")

    ᾿Αχιλεύς, -ῆος, ὁ—Achilles (also spelled with two λ's; see line 7).

2   **οὐλόμενος, -η, -ον**—destructive, ruinous. (The position of οὐλομένην at the beginning of the line and the end of its clause emphasizes the terrible destructive quality of this anger.)

    ἥ—which (a relative pronoun, referring to the μῆνιν . . . οὐλομένην and introducing a relative clause with three verbs: ἔθηκε [line 2], προΐαψεν [line 3], and τεῦχε [line 4]).

    μυρίος, -η, -ον—countless; μυρί᾿ = μυρία (an example of elision).

    ᾿Αχαιοί, -ῶν, οἱ—Achaeans (one of the names Homer uses for the Greeks).

    ἄλγος, -εος, τό—pain, hardship, trouble, suffering; ἄλγε᾿ = ἄλγεα.

    τίθημι, θήσω, ἔθηκα—put, cause, make.

3   **δ᾿** = δέ.

    ἴφθιμος, -ον—strong, mighty, stalwart.

    ᾿Αΐδης, -αο, ὁ—Hades, god of the underworld, where the spirits of all the dead went; ῎Αϊδι—dative (although a first-declension noun, it also has genitive and dative third-declension forms). Mention of spirits being sent to the underworld is not meant to be a comforting thought for those facing death. In the Homeric view, there was no survival as an individual in the afterlife. Rather it was a gloomy existence as a flitting ghostly spirit or shade that could neither think nor speak. Reference to the fate of the dead here at the very beginning of the poem sets the stage for events to come by reminding us of the "facts of life," so to speak. As one scholar wrote, "The heroes of the *Iliad* have no afterlife to look forward to. By risking their lives they risk all that they have or could ever hope to have." The only way a Homeric hero can achieve any sort of immortality is to perform heroically while alive, doing glorious deeds that will be remembered and celebrated by future generations.

προϊάπτω, προϊάψω, προῖαψα—send, hurl.

4   ἥρως, ἥρωος, ὁ—warrior, hero; ἡρώων—understand with ψυχάς in line 3.

αὐτούς—"them," "the men themselves" (their bodies as opposed to their ψυχάς).

ἐλώρια, τά—prey.

τεύχω, τεύξω, ἔτευξα—make, cause to be or become; τεῦχε = ἔτευχε (an unaugmented imperfect).

κύων, κυνός, ὁ—dog; κύνεσσιν—dat. plur.

5   οἰωνός, -οῦ, ὁ—bird of prey; οἰωνοῖσι—dat. plur.

τε—and.

Dogs and birds never actually eat the bodies of heroes in the *Iliad,* although such a fate is often threatened. The soul of a person who did not receive proper funeral rites could not enter the underworld, hence the fear of such a fate. This early mention of corpses and what happens to them foreshadows important themes in the later books of the *Iliad,* where a key issue is the fate of the bodies of Patroclus and Hector.

Ζεύς, Διός, ὁ—Zeus, ruler of the gods.

τελείω, τελέσσω, ἐτέλεσσα—accomplish, bring to completion.

βουλή, -ῆς, ἡ—plan, purpose, "the will."

Διὸς δ᾽ ἐτελείετο βουλή—"and the will of Zeus was being accomplished." (The will of Zeus will be made clear by the end of this book, when Zeus agrees to let the Trojans defeat the Greeks, at least temporarily, to punish Agamemnon for dishonoring Achilles.)

6   ἐξ οὗ δή—beginning, from the day when.

τὰ πρῶτα—first.

διίστημι, διαστήσω, διέστην—stand apart, separate; διαστήτην = διεστήτην—aorist active, 3rd pers. dual.

ἐρίζω, ἐρίσω, ἤρισα—quarrel; ἐρίσαντε—aorist active participle, nom. dual masc.

Scanning Notes

1   The α in θεά is long.

-δεω in Πηληϊάδεω is scanned as one long syllable. This is an example of synizesis (two vowels run together and pronounced as one long syllable).

2   The υ in μυρί᾽ is long.

3   The second ι in ἰφθίμους and the υ and the α in ψυχάς are long.

Ἀτρεΐδης τε ἄναξ ἀνδρῶν καὶ δῖος Ἀχιλλεύς.   7

Apollo is angered by the disrespect shown to his priest Chryses, who came to the Greeks to ransom his daughter.

Τίς τ᾽ ἄρ σφωε θεῶν ἔριδι ξυνέηκε μάχεσθαι;   8
Λητοῦς καὶ Διὸς υἱός· ὁ γὰρ βασιλῆϊ χολωθεὶς   9
νοῦσον ἀνὰ στρατὸν ὦρσε κακήν, ὀλέκοντο δὲ λαοί,   10
οὕνεκα τὸν Χρύσην ἠτίμασεν ἀρητῆρα   11
Ἀτρεΐδης· ὁ γὰρ ἦλθε θοὰς ἐπὶ νῆας Ἀχαιῶν   12
λυσόμενός τε θύγατρα φέρων τ᾽ ἀπερείσι᾽ ἄποινα,   13

---

7   Ἀτρεΐδης, -αο, ὁ—son of Atreus; refers to Agamemnon, the commander in chief of the Greek forces, or to Menelaus, Agamemnon's brother and the husband of Helen. Here, Ἀτρεΐδης = Agamemnon.
   ἄναξ, ἄνακτος, ὁ—lord, king.
   δῖος, -α, -ον—godlike, glorious, noble, excellent.
      The first word of the *Iliad*, μῆνιν, introduces one of its main themes—Achilles' anger—and the first seven lines reveal some of what is to come. After Achilles and Agamemnon quarrel, Achilles, angry at his treatment by Agamemnon, withdraws from the fighting. His withdrawal has terrible consequences for the Greeks, as lines 2–5 predict. These introductory lines do not tell of the terrible consequences for Achilles—the death of his best friend Patroclus—nor do they reveal that after Patroclus's death, his anger is redirected against the Trojans and especially against Hector. Finally, they say nothing of how his anger will finally end, in a gesture of compassion for an enemy.
      The story of the Trojan War was familiar to the ancient Greek audience. These first seven lines may demonstrate the originality of Homer's approach to the story. He focuses on the anger, an inner condition and its effects, rather than on a hero and his deeds, and he gives a negative connotation to that anger (Achilles' anger is not directed at the enemy, leading to glorious deeds, but hurts his own comrades). Such an approach may have been Homer's way of catching the attention of an audience used to hearing more standard heroic songs.
8   τίς—with θεῶν, a partitive genitive indicating the whole.
   τ᾽ = τε.
   ἄρ, ἄρα, ῥα—then, in fact.
   σφωε—acc. dual of εἷο: "these two," "the two of them," "them both."
   ἔρις, -ιδος, ἡ—quarrel, strife; ἔριδι—dative of manner: "in strife."
   ξυνίημι, ξυνήσω, ξυνέηκα—bring together.
   μάχομαι, μαχήσομαι, ἐμαχεσ(σ)άμην—fight, battle.
9   Λητώ, -οῦς, ἡ—Leto, mother (by Zeus) of Apollo and Artemis; Λητοῦς καὶ Διὸς υἱός = Apollo.

ὁ—"he," "that one" (refers to Apollo). (It is common in Homeric Greek for the article to be used as a personal, demonstrative, or relative pronoun.)

βασιλῆϊ=βασιλεῖ—"at the king" (i.e., at Agamemnon).

χολόω, χολώσω, ἐχόλωσα, κεχόλωμαι, ἐχολώθην—anger, enrage; χολωθείς—aorist passive participle, nom. sing. masc.: "enraged, angered." (The person at whom one is angry will be in the dative.)

10   νοῦσος, -ου, ἡ—sickness, plague, disease.

ἀνά—upon, up through, throughout (+ acc.).

στρατός, -οῦ, ὁ—army, camp.

ὄρνυμι, ὄρσω, ὦρσα—stir up, start, let loose.

ὀλέκω—destroy; *middle*—perish, die; ὀλέκοντο = ὠλέκοντο—imperfect middle.

λαός, -οῦ, ὁ—(in sing. and plur.) the people, the army, the troops.

11   οὕνεκα—because.

τόν—"that man" (an article used as a demonstrative pronoun).

Χρύσης, -αο, ὁ—Chryses, a priest of Apollo at Chryse, a town near Troy. When the Greeks captured Chryse, they took his daughter, Chryseis, prisoner, and she was allotted to Agamemnon as his prize.

ἀτιμάζω, (aor.) ἠτίμασα—dishonor, treat with disrespect, insult.

ἀρητήρ, -ῆρος, ὁ—priest.

12   Ἀτρεΐδης = Agamemnon.

ἔρχομαι, ἐλεύσομαι, ἦλθον—come, go.

θοός, -ή, -όν—swift.

νηῦς, νηός, ἡ—ship. (Coming "to the ships of the Achaeans" is equivalent to coming to the Greek camp. The ships have been drawn up out of the water onto the land, and huts have been built beside them.)

13   λύω, λύσω, ἔλυσα—loosen, free, set free; *middle*—ransom; λυσόμενος—future participle of purpose.

θυγάτηρ, -τρός, ἡ—daughter.

ἀπερείσιος, -ον—boundless, immeasurable, unlimited; ἀπερείσι᾽ = ἀπερείσια. (What is this called when a short final vowel is dropped before a word beginning with a vowel?)

ἄποινα, -ων, τά—ransom.

Scanning Notes

10   The α in λαοί is long.

11   The υ in Χρύσην, the ι in ἠτίμασεν, and the first α in ἀρητῆρα are long.
      Line 11 is a spondaic line, i.e., a line with a spondee in the fifth foot. Only about 5 percent of all Homeric lines follow this pattern. The two spondees at the end of the line add emphasis to the final word.

12   The α in θοάς is long.

13   The υ in λυσόμενος is long.

στέμματ᾽ ἔχων ἐν χερσὶν ἑκηβόλου Ἀπόλλωνος   14
χρυσέῳ ἀνὰ σκήπτρῳ, καὶ λίσσετο πάντας Ἀχαιούς,   15
Ἀτρεΐδα δὲ μάλιστα δύω, κοσμήτορε λαῶν·   16

Chryses wishes the Greeks success in the war and asks that they accept the ransom he has brought for his daughter.

"Ἀτρεΐδαι τε καὶ ἄλλοι ἐϋκνήμιδες Ἀχαιοί,   17
ὑμῖν μὲν θεοὶ δοῖεν Ὀλύμπια δώματ᾽ ἔχοντες   18
ἐκπέρσαι Πριάμοιο πόλιν, εὖ δ᾽ οἴκαδ᾽ ἱκέσθαι·   19
παῖδα δ᾽ ἐμοὶ λῦσαί τε φίλην, τὰ τ᾽ ἄποινα δέχεσθαι,   20
ἁζόμενοι Διὸς υἱὸν ἑκηβόλον Ἀπόλλωνα."   21

---

14 **στέμμα, -ατος, τό**—band of fabric, ribbon; στέμματ᾽ = στέμματα. (These are sacred bands of wool that Chryses has wrapped around his staff [ἀνὰ σκήπτρῳ, line 15]; they may indicate either his status as a priest or the fact that he is approaching the Greeks as a suppliant.)

χείρ, χειρός, ἡ—hand; χερσίν—dat. plur.

ἑκηβόλος, -ον—far-shooting, sharp-shooting.

Ἀπόλλων, -ωνος, ὁ—Apollo, god of archery, music, and prophecy. (He is one of the gods who sides with the Trojans in the Trojan War.)

15 **χρύσεος, -η, -ον**—made of gold, golden, decorated with gold.

ἀνά—on, upon (+ dat.).

σκῆπτρον, -ου, τό—staff (in this case, a staff indicating priestly authority). (The details Homer mentions in his description of Chryses [the στέμματα and the σκῆπτρον indicating he is a priest of Apollo] are significant. They show he is someone who should be listened to and appeased, as he has a god behind him.)

λίσσομαι, (aor.) **ἐλισάμην**—beg, beseech; λίσσετο = ἐλίσσετο.

16 **Ἀτρεΐδα**—acc. dual.

μάλιστα—especially.

κοσμήτωρ, -ορος, ὁ—commander; κοσμήτορε—acc. dual.

17 **ἐϋκνήμις, -ιδος**—well-greaved. (Greaves, thin plates of bronze covering the lower leg as shin guards, were part of the Homeric warrior's armor. It is likely that knowledge of greaves is one of the things that was handed down from Mycenaean times through the oral poetic tradition.)

18 **μέν**—indeed, to be sure.

δίδωμι, (δι)δώσω, ἔδωκα—give; δοῖεν—aorist active optative, 3rd pers. plur.: "may they grant." (The optative without κε[ν] or ἄν is common in wishes referring to a future possibility.)

Ὀλύμπιος, -η, -ον—Olympian, on Mt. Olympus (the mountain in northern Greece where the gods lived).

δῶμα, -ατος, τό—home, house; δώματ᾽ = δώματα.

ἔχοντες—modifies θεοί.

19 ἐκπέρθω, ἐκπέρσω, ἐξέπερσα or ἐξέπραθον—sack, utterly destroy;
    ἐκπέρσαι—aorist active infinitive.

Πρίαμος, -ου, ὁ—Priam, king of Troy; Πριάμοιο—gen. sing.

εὖ—"successfully."

οἴκαδ᾽ = οἴκαδε—home(ward), home.

ἱκνέομαι, ἵξομαι, ἱκόμην—arrive at, reach. (The ancient audience, knowing the misfortunes ahead for the Greek heroes after Troy's fall [Odysseus and Menelaus wandered for years before reaching home, the lesser Ajax died in a shipwreck, and Agamemnon was murdered when he arrived home], would have appreciated the irony of Chryses' wish for a successful return home. His words may even have inspired pity for Agamemnon.)

20 παῖς, παιδός, ὁ, ἡ—child, son, daughter.

λῦσαι—an infinitive is often used as an imperative in Homer.

δέχομαι, δέξομαι, ἐδεξάμην—accept, receive; δέχεσθαι—infinitive used as an imperative.

21 ἅζομαι—respect, stand in awe of; ἁζόμενοι—agrees with an understood ὑμεῖς. Chryses ends his speech by offering the Greeks an excellent reason to grant his request—they would be honoring Apollo by doing so. Or is it actually a subtle threat, as he urges the Greeks to respect (ἁζόμενοι—implication: "do not dishonor") Apollo the far-shooting god (ἑκηβόλον—implication: "he can hurt you if you do not")?

Scanning Notes

14 The α in Ἀπόλλωνος is long.

15 The υ in χρυσέῳ is long.

    The -εῳ in χρυσέῳ is scanned as one syllable. Although synizesis (two vowels run together and pronounced as one long syllable) occurs here, this syllable is scanned short because the next word begins with a vowel.

16 The second α in Ἀτρεΐδα and the α in λαῶν are long.

17 The ι in ἐϋκνήμιδες is long.

18 θεοί is scanned and pronounced as one long syllable (synizesis).

19 The last syllable of πόλιν is scanned long. A short final syllable that receives the ictus can be scanned long. It is common to find, as here, a sense pause, or caesura, occurring after such a lengthened syllable.

21 The first α in Ἀπόλλωνα is long.

    How does the scansion of this verse help emphasize the last word? What is a line of this type called?

*All the other Greeks want to accept Chryses' offer, but Agamemnon refuses
and sends him away with threats.*

Ἔνθ᾽ ἄλλοι μὲν πάντες ἐπευφήμησαν Ἀχαιοὶ   22
αἰδεῖσθαί θ᾽ ἱερῆα καὶ ἀγλαὰ δέχθαι ἄποινα·   23
ἀλλ᾽ οὐκ Ἀτρεΐδῃ Ἀγαμέμνονι ἥνδανε θυμῷ,   24
ἀλλὰ κακῶς ἀφίει, κρατερὸν δ᾽ ἐπὶ μῦθον ἔτελλε·   25
"μή σε, γέρον, κοίλῃσιν ἐγὼ παρὰ νηυσὶ κιχείω   26
ἢ νῦν δηθύνοντ᾽ ἢ ὕστερον αὖτις ἰόντα,   27
μή νύ τοι οὐ χραίσμῃ σκῆπτρον καὶ στέμμα θεοῖο·   28
τὴν δ᾽ ἐγὼ οὐ λύσω· πρίν μιν καὶ γῆρας ἔπεισιν   29
ἡμετέρῳ ἐνὶ οἴκῳ, ἐν Ἄργεϊ, τηλόθι πάτρης,   30

---

22 ἔνθ᾽ = ἔνθα—then.

  ἐπευφημέω, ἐπευφημήσω, ἐπευφήμησα—approve, shout assent, speak favor-
     ably, agree.

23 αἰδέομαι, αἰδέσομαι, ᾐδεσάμην—respect, have regard for.

  θ᾽ = τε.

  ἱερεύς, -ῆος, ὁ—priest.

  ἀγλαός, -ή, -όν—splendid, shining.

  δέχθαι = δέξασθαι—aorist infinitive of δέχομαι. (Forms lacking thematic vow-
     els [the connecting vowels between the verb stem and the ending] are more fre-
     quent in Homer than in later Greek.)

24 ἀλλ᾽ = ἀλλά.

  Ἀγαμέμνων, -ονος, ὁ—Agamemnon, the king of Mycenae and leader of the
     Greeks; brother of Menelaus. Often referred to as Ἀτρεΐδης, the son of Atreus.

  ἀνδάνω—be acceptable, please; ἥνδανε—imperfect.

  θυμός, -οῦ, ὁ—heart, soul, mind; θυμῷ—"in his mind" or "in his heart" (dative of
     place, indicating the place where an action, or in this case, a feeling, occurs).

25 κακῶς—harshly, wickedly, "humiliatingly."

  ἀφίημι, ἀφήσω, ἀφῆκα—send away, dismiss, drive off; ἀφίει—imperfect.

  κρατερός, -ή, -όν—harsh, stern, powerful.

  μῦθος, -ου, ὁ—word, command, speech, "threat."

  ἐπιτέλλω—lay (a command) on, impose, inflict. (ἐπὶ . . . ἔτελλε is a compound
     verb whose parts are separated. In Homer's time, some prepositions and verbs
     were used to convey an idea that in later times would be expressed by a com-
     pound verb formed from their union. This occurred because most prepositions
     were originally adverbs, and Homer often used them in this way to modify a
     verb's meaning. In later Greek, the two parts evolved into a compound verb. The
     technical name for the separation is *tmesis* [from τέμνω, "cut"]. This is not
     really a very accurate name, since the preposition has not been "cut" from the
     verb. Rather, in Homeric Greek, the two have not yet joined together.)

κρατερὸν δ' ἐπὶ μῦθον ἔτελλε—"he commanded harshly," "he threatened."

26 γέρων, -οντος, ὁ—old man; γέρον—vocative.

κοῖλος, -η, -ον—hollow (refers to the fact that the ships were almost completely without decks).

νηυσί—dat. plur. of νηῦς (ship).

κιχάνω, κιχήσομαι—come upon, find, overtake; κιχείω is a present subjunctive.

μή . . . κιχείω is a negative hortatory subjunctive used to express a warning or threat: "let me not find you."

27 ἢ . . . ἤ—either . . . or.

δηθύνω—linger, delay, tarry; δηθύνοντ᾽ = δηθύνοντα (present active participle, acc. sing. masc.).

ὕστερον—later, afterward.

αὖτις—again, back again.

ἰόντα—present active participle of εἶμι, acc. sing. masc.

δηθύνοντ᾽ and ἰόντα—both modify σε (line 26).

28 μή—lest.

νυ—indeed.

τοι = σοί.

χραισμέω, χραισμήσω, ἔχραισμον—help, avail, benefit (+ dat.); χραίσμη is an aorist subjunctive, 3rd pers. sing. Both σκῆπτρον and στέμμα are subjects of χραίσμη, although it is a singular verb. Grammatically it agrees with the nearer noun, σκῆπτρον.

29 πρίν—sooner, before that.

μιν—him, her, it (acc. sing.).

γῆρας, -αος, τό—old age; καὶ γῆρας—"old age itself."

ἔπειμι, ἐπείσομαι—come upon; ἔπεισιν—present tense used for future tense.

30 ἡμέτερος, -η, -ον—our.

Ἄργος, -εος, τό—Argos, the area in the Peloponnese ruled by Agamemnon.

τηλόθι—far from (+ gen.).

πάτρη, -ης, ἡ—native land.

In this line, Homer effectively uses three adverbial phrases that, with rising intensity, stress Chryseis's future distant location and emphasize the separation from her father.

Scanning Notes

24 The υ in θυμῷ is long.

27 The υ in δηθύνοντ᾽ is long.

29 The υ in λύσω is long.

ἱστὸν ἐποιχομένην καὶ ἐμὸν λέχος ἀντιόωσαν·　　31
ἀλλ' ἴθι, μή μ' ἐρέθιζε, σαώτερος ὥς κε νέηαι."　　32

Chryses goes to the shore of the sea and prays to Apollo, asking the god to
make the Greeks pay for the pain they have caused him.

Ὣς ἔφατ', ἔδεισεν δ' ὁ γέρων καὶ ἐπείθετο μύθῳ·　　33
βῆ δ' ἀκέων παρὰ θῖνα πολυφλοίσβοιο θαλάσσης·　　34
πολλὰ δ' ἔπειτ' ἀπάνευθε κιὼν ἠρᾶθ' ὁ γεραιὸς　　35
Ἀπόλλωνι ἄνακτι, τὸν ἠΰκομος τέκε Λητώ·　　36

31　**ἱστός, -οῦ, ὁ**—loom.
　　ἐποίχομαι, ἐποιχήσομαι—work at, apply oneself to, ply.
　　λέχος, -εος, τό—bed.
　　ἀντιάω, ἀντιάσω, ἠντίασα—share.
　　ἐποιχομένην and **ἀντιόωσαν**—present participles, acc. sing. fem.; both modify
　　　　μιν (line 29).
32　**ἴθι**—imperative of εἶμι.
　　μ' = με.
　　ἐρεθίζω, ἐρεθίσω, ἠρέθισα—provoke, irritate, anger; **ἐρέθιζε**—imperative.
　　σαώτερος—"more safely."
　　ὥς κε—so that, in order that.
　　νέομαι—go, return; **νέηαι**—present subjunctive, 2nd pers. sing.: "you may re-
　　　　turn." (νέηαι = νέῃ, the contracted Attic form. It was originally νέησαι, but the
　　　　σ is often lost between two vowels.)
　　ὥς κε νέηαι—purpose clause.
　　Homer lets Agamemnon unpleasantly characterize himself with his own words.
　　He shows no respect for either an old man or a representative of a god; the senti-
　　ments of the rest of the army mean nothing to him; he is extremely discourteous to
　　one who has been courtesy itself to him; and he does not consider at all what Apollo
　　might do to the army if his priest is insulted. The irony of his threat (μή μ' ἐρέθιζε—
　　"don't make me angry") will soon become apparent as we see the truly threatening
　　effects of Apollo's and then Achilles' anger. This incident at the beginning of the
　　Iliad, Agamemnon's refusal to accept the ransom offered by Chryses for his daugh-
　　ter, foreshadows other occasions when ransoms are accepted or rejected. Warriors
　　defeated in battle or captured offer ransoms for their lives, as Dolon does in book
　　10. And just as the *Iliad* begins with a ransom offer, so too does it end, with the ran-
　　soming of Hector's body.
33　**ὥς**—so, thus, in this way.
　　φημί, φήσω, ἔφησα—speak; ἔφατ' = ἔφατο—imperfect middle (with active
　　　　meaning).
　　δείδω, δείσομαι, ἔδεισα—fear, be afraid.

πείθω, πείσω, ἔπεισα or ἔπιθον or πέπιθον—persuade; *middle*—obey (+ dat.).

34   βαίνω, βήσω, ἔβησα or ἔβην—come, go, walk; βῆ = ἔβη—aorist, 3rd pers. sing.

ἀκέων, -ουσα, -ον—in silence, silent.

θίς, θινός, ἡ—beach, shore.

πολύφλοισβος, -ον—loud roaring, ever roaring, πολυφλοίσβοιο—gen. sing. fem.

θάλασσα, -ης, ἡ—sea (= Attic θάλαττα).

With just a few key words and phrases, Homer sketches a picture of a pitiful old man walking frightened and alone by the roaring sea. Notice the contrast between ἀκέων and πολυφλοίσβοιο. Chryses is not, however, nearly as powerless as this description might suggest.

On the lighter side, a poem that makes an English adjective out of the word πολύφλοισβος comments on some characteristics of Homeric grammar.

> Poluphloisboisterous Homer of old
>   Threw all his augments into the sea,
> Although he had often been courteously told
>   That perfect imperfects begin with an *e:*
> But the Poet replied with a dignified air,
>   "What the Digamma does any one care?"
>
> (A. Godley, *Verses to Order* [1892])

35   πολλά—"earnestly," "fervently" (neuter plural adjective used as an adverb; πολλά is from πολλός, -ή, -όν, a variant form of πολύς, πολλή, πολύ).

ἔπειτ᾽ = ἔπειτα—then.

ἀπάνευθε—(adv.) far away, away.

κίω—come, go.

ἀράομαι, ἀρήσομαι, ἠρησάμην—pray; ἠρᾶθ᾽ = ἠρᾶτο.

γεραιός, -ή, -όν—old; ὁ γεραιός—"the old man."

36   τόν—an article used as a relative pronoun (= ὅν).

ἠΰκομος, -ον—having beautiful hair, beautiful-haired.

τίκτω, τέξω, ἔτεκον—give birth to, bear; τέκε = ἔτεκε.

Scanning Notes

33   The first syllable of ἔδεισεν is scanned long because ἔδεισεν was originally spelled ἔδϝεισεν, putting two consonants after the short ε.

The υ in μύθῳ is long.

36   *Iliad*, Book 1

"κλῦθί μευ, ἀργυρότοξ᾽, ὃς Χρύσην ἀμφιβέβηκας   37
Κίλλαν τε ζαθέην Τενέδοιό τε ἶφι ἀνάσσεις,   38
Σμινθεῦ, εἴ ποτέ τοι χαρίεντ᾽ ἐπὶ νηὸν ἔρεψα,   39
ἢ εἰ δή ποτέ τοι κατὰ πίονα μηρί᾽ ἔκηα   40
ταύρων ἠδ᾽ αἰγῶν, τόδε μοι κρήηνον ἐέλδωρ·   41
τείσειαν Δαναοὶ ἐμὰ δάκρυα σοῖσι βέλεσσιν."   42

Apollo hears Chryses' prayer. He hurries down from Mt. Olympus and rains arrows of plague on the Greeks.

῞Ως ἔφατ᾽ εὐχόμενος, τοῦ δ᾽ ἔκλυε Φοῖβος Ἀπόλλων,   43
βῆ δὲ κατ᾽ Οὐλύμποιο καρήνων χωόμενος κῆρ,   44

---

37   **κλύω,** (aor.) **ἔκλυον**—hear (+ gen.); **κλῦθι**—aorist active imperative, 2nd pers. sing.

μευ—gen. sing. of ἐγώ.

ἀργυρότοξος, -ον—equipped with a silver (ἄργυρος) bow (τόξον), (god) of the silver bow; ἀργυρότοξ᾽ = ἀργυρότοξε.

ὅς—[you] who.

Χρύση, -ης, ἡ—Chryse, a town near Troy (Chryses' home).

ἀμφιβαίνω, ἀμφιβήσω, ἀμφέβησα, ἀμφιβέβηκα—protect; ἀμφιβέβηκας—perfect; translate as present. (In Homer, a perfect tense often indicates something true in the present time and should be translated with an English present tense.)

38   **Κίλλα, -ης, ἡ**—Cilla, a town near Troy; Κίλλαν and Χρύσην (line 37) are both objects of ἀμφιβέβηκας.

ζάθεος, -η, -ον—very sacred, holy.

Τένεδος, -ου, ἡ—Tenedos, a small island near Troy; Τενέδοιο—gen. sing.

ἶφι—with might, with power, by force.

ἀνάσσω—be lord or master of, rule over (+ gen.).

39   **Σμινθεύς, -ῆος, ὁ**—Smintheus (a name given to Apollo); Σμινθεῦ—vocative. Smintheus may mean "Mouse God," referring to Apollo as a destroyer of the field mice who could devastate crops, or it may refer to mice as carriers of plague and therefore indicate Apollo's power to bring plague. Or it may refer to a city near Troy called Sminthe and merely mean "Apollo of Sminthe."

χαρίεις, -εσσα, -εν—pleasing, lovely, fine; χαρίεντ᾽ = χαρίεντα.

νηός, -οῦ, ὁ—temple.

ἐπερέφω, ἐπερέψω—roof over, build; ἐπὶ . . . ἔρεψα—tmesis; aorist.

40   **ἤ**—or.

δή—indeed.

κατακαίω, κατακαύσω, κατέκηα—burn; κατὰ . . . ἔκηα—tmesis.

πίων, πίειρα, πῖον—fat.

μηρίον, -ου, τό—thigh piece, thighbone; μηρί᾽ = μηρία.

41 ταῦρος, -ου, ὁ—bull.

ἠδ᾽= ἠδέ—and.

αἴξ, αἰγός, ὁ, ἡ—goat.

εἰ δή ποτέ τοι κατὰ πίονα μηρί᾽ ἔκηα / ταύρων ἠδ᾽ αἰγῶν (lines 40–41)—
Chryses refers to sacrifices he has made to Apollo. When an animal was
sacrificed, the bones and fat were burned for the gods, who were thought to enjoy the smell conveyed to them in the smoke. The people participating in the
sacrifice then roasted and ate the meat.

κραίνω—accomplish, perform, bring to pass, fulfill; κρήηνον—aorist active imperative, 2nd pers. sing.

ἐέλδωρ, τό (indeclinable)—desire, wish.

42 τίνω, τείσω, ἔτεισα—pay, atone for; τείσειαν—aorist active optative: "may
they pay for."

Δαναοί, -ῶν, οἱ—Danaans (another name Homer uses for the Greeks; it may
come from the name of Danaus, a mythical king of Argos).

δάκρυ, -υος, τό—tear.

σός, σή, σόν—your.

βέλος, -εος, τό—arrow, missile; σοῖσι βέλεσσιν—dative of means: "by means
of your arrows," "through your arrows."

43 εὔχομαι, εὔξομαι, ηὐξάμην—pray.

τοῦ—him (an article used as a personal pronoun).

τοῦ δ᾽ ἔκλυε—Saying that a god "heard" a prayer is a common Homeric way of
indicating that the prayer was granted.

Φοῖβος, -ου, ὁ—Phoebus (a name given to Apollo, possibly meaning "bright" or
"shining").

44 κατ᾽= κατά.

Οὔλυμπος, -ου, ὁ—Mt. Olympus, the home of the gods.

κάρηνον, -ου, τό—peak, summit.

χώομαι, χώσομαι, ἐχωσάμην—be angry.

κῆρ, κῆρος, τό—heart; κῆρ—accusative of respect: "in his heart."

Scanning Notes

37 The υ in Χρύσην is long.

40 The ι in πίονα is long.

43 The α in Ἀπόλλων is long, but the first syllable is scanned short. A long vowel that
does not receive the ictus can be scanned short.

τόξ᾿ ὤμοισιν ἔχων ἀμφηρεφέα τε φαρέτρην·   45
ἔκλαγξαν δ᾿ ἄρ᾿ ὀϊστοὶ ἐπ᾿ ὤμων χωομένοιο,   46
αὐτοῦ κινηθέντος· ὁ δ᾿ ἤϊε νυκτὶ ἐοικώς.   47
ἕζετ᾿ ἔπειτ᾿ ἀπάνευθε νεῶν, μετὰ δ᾿ ἰὸν ἕηκε·   48
δεινὴ δὲ κλαγγὴ γένετ᾿ ἀργυρέοιο βιοῖο·   49
οὐρῆας μὲν πρῶτον ἐπῴχετο καὶ κύνας ἀργούς,   50
αὐτὰρ ἔπειτ᾿ αὐτοῖσι βέλος ἐχεπευκὲς ἐφιεὶς   51

---

45 **τόξον, -ου, τό**—bow; τόξ᾿ = τόξα—plural used for singular.
   ὦμος, -ου, ὁ—shoulder; ὤμοισιν—dative of place: "on his shoulders."
   ἀμφηρεφής, -ές—closed, covered at both ends, closely covered; ἀμφηρεφέα—
   acc. sing. fem.
   φαρέτρη, -ης, ἡ—quiver. (Homer focuses attention on the quiver that contains the
   plague arrows with the repetition of the φ sound in ἀμφηρεφέα.)
46 **κλάζω, κλάγξω, ἔκλαγξα**—rattle, clang.
   ἄρ᾿ = ἄρα.
   ὀϊστός, -οῦ, ὁ—arrow.
   ἐπ᾿ = ἐπί.
   χωομένοιο—"of the angry god," "the angry god's."
47 **κινέω, κινήσω, ἐκίνησα,** (aor. pass.) **ἐκινήθην**—move; *passive*—go, move
   oneself; κινηθέντος—aorist passive participle, gen. sing. masc.
   αὐτοῦ κινηθέντος—genitive absolute: "as he moved."
   ἤϊε—imperfect of εἶμι, 3rd pers. sing.
   νύξ, νυκτός, ἡ—night.
   ἔοικα—(perfect; translate as present) be like, resemble (+ dat.); ἐοικώς—perfect
   active participle, nom. sing. masc.
   νυκτὶ ἐοικώς—"like the night." (This simile may refer to the swiftness of night-
   fall or to the night as a time of darkness or terror. One critic said, "its effective
   imprecision conveys speed, suddenness, silence, and doom.")
48 **ἕζομαι, ἕσσομαι, εἷσα**—sit down, take a seat; ἕζετ᾿ = ἕζετο (an unaugmented
   imperfect).
   ἀπάνευθε—(prep.) far from, apart from (+ gen.).
   νεῶν—gen. plur. of νηῦς.
   ἰός, -οῦ, ὁ—arrow.
   μεθίημι, μεθήσω, μεθέηκα—let fly, send, "shoot"; μετὰ . . . ἕηκε—tmesis.
49 **δεινός, -ή, -όν**—terrible, awful, fearful.
   κλαγγή, -ῆς, ἡ—scream, shriek, noise.
   γίγνομαι, γενήσομαι, ἐγενόμην—arise, be, become; γένετ᾿ = ἐγένετο.
   ἀργύρεος, -η, -ον—silver, made of silver; ἀργυρέοιο—gen. sing. masc.
   βιός, -οῦ, ὁ—bow; ἀργυρέοιο βιοῖο—genitive of source: "from the silver bow."

Fig. 1. Apollo running with bow and arrow. Painting by the Brygos Painter on an Attic red-figure kylix, ca. 480–470 B.C. (Courtesy of the Museum of Fine Arts, Boston. James Fund and by Special Contribution, 1910. Reproduced with permission. © 2000 Museum of Fine Arts, Boston. All Rights Reserved.)

50 οὐρεύς, -ῆος, ὁ—mule.
    πρῶτον—first.
    ἐποίχομαι—go against, attack; ἐπῴχετο—imperfect.
    ἀργός, -ή, -όν—swift.
51 αὐτάρ—but, however.
    αὐτοῖσι—"at the men themselves."
    ἐχεπευκής, -ές—sharp.
    ἐφίημι, ἐφήσω—let go at, shoot; ἐφιείς—present active participle, nom. sing. masc.

Scanning Notes
45 The last syllable of ἀμφηρεφέα is scanned long. A short final syllable that receives the ictus can be scanned long.
47 The ι in κινηθέντος is long.
48 The ι in ἰόν is long.
51 Why is the last syllable of βέλος scanned long?

βάλλ᾿· αἰεὶ δὲ πυραὶ νεκύων καίοντο θαμειαί.   52

On the tenth day of the plague, Achilles calls a meeting of the troops.

Ἐννῆμαρ μὲν ἀνὰ στρατὸν ᾤχετο κῆλα θεοῖο,   53
τῇ δεκάτῃ δ᾿ ἀγορήνδε καλέσσατο λαὸν Ἀχιλλεύς·   54
τῷ γὰρ ἐπὶ φρεσὶ θῆκε θεὰ λευκώλενος Ἥρη·   55
κήδετο γὰρ Δαναῶν, ὅτι ῥα θνήσκοντας ὁρᾶτο.   56
οἱ δ᾿ ἐπεὶ οὖν ἤγερθεν ὁμηγερέες τ᾿ ἐγένοντο,   57
τοῖσι δ᾿ ἀνιστάμενος μετέφη πόδας ὠκὺς Ἀχιλλεύς·   58

---

52 **βάλλω**, (aor.) **ἔβαλον**—throw, shoot; βάλλ᾿ = ἔβαλλε—imperfect: "he shot and shot," "he kept shooting."
    αἰεί—always.
    πυρή, -ῆς, ἡ—funeral pyre.
    νέκυς, νέκυος, ὁ—corpse, dead body.
    καίω, καύσω, ἔκηα—burn; καίοντο = ἐκαίοντο.
    θαμέες, θαμειαί, θαμέα—numerous, frequent.
    Line 52 is particularly effective for several reasons. βάλλ᾿, emphasized by its position (at the beginning of the line and the end of a sentence) and by the brief pause following it, vividly imitates the sound of an arrow shot with the broken-off λλ sound. The repetition of the -αι sound in the rest of the line strengthens the force of αἰεί, especially the -ειαι at the end, which mirrors the sounds of αἰεί.
    Based on the fact that the mules and dogs died before the men, some scholars have theorized that the disease Homer is describing here was equine encephalomyelitis, which can be transferred from animals to men by mosquitoes. Another suggestion is that the disease was the result of many people living together with no knowledge of hygiene, that "the latrines or lack of them" were likely to have been responsible for the outbreak of disease.

53 **ἐννῆμαρ**—for nine days.
    μέν—marks the contrast with the δέ clause that follows.
    οἴχομαι—come, go; ᾤχετο—imperfect.
    κῆλον, -ου, τό—arrow.

54 **δέκατος, -η, -ον**—tenth; τῇ δεκάτῃ [ἡμέρῃ]—dative of time when: "on the tenth day."
    ἀγορή, -ῆς, ἡ—assembly; ἀγορήνδε—"to an assembly." (The suffix -δε adds the idea of "toward" or "to.")
    καλέω, (aor.) **ἐκάλεσ(σ)α**—call; *middle*—summon; καλέσσατο = ἐκαλέσσατο.

55 **φρήν, φρενός, ἡ**—mind, thoughts, heart (often used in plur.); φρεσί—dat. plur. (φρήν literally means "midriff" or "diaphragm." The Greeks thought of the midriff or chest area as the seat of thought and emotion.)
    θῆκε = ἔθηκε.

τῷ ... ἐπὶ φρεσὶ θῆκε—"put [it] into his mind" (literally, "put [it] upon the mind for him"). τῷ is a dative of interest, a construction frequently used where English would use a possessive.

λευκώλενος, -ον—white-armed. (Fair arms may have been considered a sign of feminine beauty, or a woman may have been called white-armed because basic female attire, the πέπλος, was sleeveless, hence her arms appeared pale in contrast to the colored garment. Another possibility is that white arms were a sign of upper-class status, indicating a woman who did not have to work outdoors. At any rate, it was conventional to portray women with white skin and men with reddish-brown skin on vase paintings of the eighth and seventh centuries.)

Ἥρη, -ης, ἡ—Hera, wife of Zeus and queen of the gods. She is a friend of the Greeks and an enemy of the Trojans.

56 κήδω, κηδήσω, ἐκήδησα—trouble, distress; *middle and passive*—be concerned about, care for (+ gen.); κήδετο = ἐκήδετο.

ὅτι—because.

θνήσκω, θανέομαι, ἔθανον—die, be killed; θνήσκοντας—present active participle, acc. plur. masc.; modifies an understood αὐτούς (= τοὺς Δαναούς).

ὁράω, ὄψομαι, εἶδον or ἴδον—see; ὁρᾶτο—imperfect middle; translate as active: "she kept seeing," "she was seeing."

57 ἐπεί—when.

ἀγείρω, (aor.) ἤγειρα, (aor. pass.) ἠγέρθην—gather, assemble; ἤγερθεν = ἠγέρθησαν—aorist passive, 3rd pers. plur.

ὁμηγερής, -ές—gathered, assembled together.

58 τοῖσι—dative of place: "before them."

ἀνίστημι—stand up, get up, rise, make to stand up; ἀνιστάμενος—present middle participle, nom. sing. masc.: "standing up."

μετάφημι, μεταφήσω, μετέφησα—address, speak to; μετέφη—imperfect active, 3rd pers. sing.

πούς, ποδός, ὁ—foot; πόδας—accusative of respect.

ὠκύς, -εῖα, -ύ—swift, fast, quick; πόδας ὠκὺς Ἀχιλλεύς—"swift-footed Achilles" (literally, "swift with respect to his feet").

Scanning Notes

54 The α in λαόν is long.
55 The α in θεά is long.

Achilles asks that they consult a prophet or a priest to learn why Apollo is angry.

" Ἀτρεΐδη, νῦν ἄμμε παλιμπλαγχθέντας ὀΐω   59
ἂψ ἀπονοστήσειν, εἴ κεν θάνατόν γε φύγοιμεν,   60
εἰ δὴ ὁμοῦ πόλεμός τε δαμᾷ καὶ λοιμὸς Ἀχαιούς·   61
ἀλλ' ἄγε δή τινα μάντιν ἐρείομεν ἢ ἱερῆα,   62
ἢ καὶ ὀνειροπόλον, καὶ γάρ τ' ὄναρ ἐκ Διός ἐστιν,   63
ὅς κ' εἴποι ὅ τι τόσσον ἐχώσατο Φοῖβος Ἀπόλλων,   64
εἴτ' ἄρ' ὅ γ' εὐχωλῆς ἐπιμέμφεται εἴθ' ἑκατόμβης,   65
αἴ κέν πως ἀρνῶν κνίσης αἰγῶν τε τελείων   66

---

59 **Ἀτρεΐδη**—vocative sing.
   ἄμμε = ἡμᾶς.
   παλιμπλάζομαι—be driven back; παλιμπλαγχθέντας—aorist passive participle, acc. plur. masc.
   ὀΐω, οἰήσομαι, ὠϊσάμην—think.
60 **ἄψ**—back, backward, back again.
   ἀπονοστέω, ἀπονοστήσω, ἀπενόστησα—return home, return; ἀπονοστήσειν— What kind of infinitive is this?
   ἄμμε παλιμπλαγχθέντας ὀΐω / ἂψ ἀπονοστήσειν (lines 59–60)—"I think that we, having been driven back, will return home."
   φύγοιμεν—aorist active optative of φεύγω; potential optative.
   εἴ κεν θάνατόν γε φύγοιμεν—"if, indeed, we even escape death at all" or "supposing that we should escape death."
61 **εἰ δή**—since, if as seems likely.
   ὁμοῦ—together, at the same time.
   τε . . . καί—both . . . and.
   δαμάζω, δαμάω, ἐδάμασα—subdue, overcome, tame; δαμᾷ—future, 3rd pers. sing. (Both πόλεμος and λοιμός are subjects of δαμᾷ, although it is a singular verb.)
   λοιμός, -οῦ, ὁ—plague.
62 **ἄγε**—come! (This imperative of ἄγω is used as an interjection).
   μάντις, -ιος, ὁ—seer, prophet.
   ἐρέω—ask; ἐρείομεν—present subjunctive: "let us ask" (hortatory subjunctive); ἐρείομεν = ἐρέωμεν. In Homer, long thematic vowels (the -η or -ω before the verb ending) of the subjunctive are often shortened (to -ε or -ο), especially in plural or dual forms. The endings -εται, -ομεν, and -ετε are the most frequent forms of the short-vowel subjunctive.
63 **ὀνειροπόλος, -ου, ὁ**—dream interpreter. (Dreams were believed to reveal the will of the gods.)

τ'—τε is not translated here; it marks this clause as a common or proverbial statement.

ὄναρ, τό (indeclinable)—dream.

καὶ γάρ τ' ὄναρ ἐκ Διός ἐστιν—"for a dream is also from Zeus" [as are other signs or omens].

64 κ' = κε.

εἶπον (aor.)—tell, say, speak, name; εἴποι—aorist optative, 3rd pers. sing.; potential optative.

ὅς κ' εἴποι—"who might tell [us]."

ὅ τι—why.

τόσσον—so, so very.

'Απόλλων—Achilles assumes Apollo is responsible for the disease afflicting the army because Apollo was the god associated with plague or sudden death among men.

65 εἴτ'... εἴθ'—whether ... or (= εἴ τε ... εἴ τε).

γ' = γε.

εὐχωλή, -ῆς, ἡ—vow

ἐπιμέμφομαι—blame, find fault with (+ gen.).

ἑκατόμβη, -ης, ἡ—hecatomb, sacrificial offering of a large number of animals. (Literally, the word means a sacrifice of one hundred (ἑκατόν) oxen (βοῦς), but it came to be used more generally for fewer than one hundred animals and not necessarily oxen.)

εἴτ' ἄρ' ὅ γ' εὐχωλῆς ἐπιμέμφεται εἴθ' ἑκατόμβης—"whether he is blaming [us] for an [unfulfilled] vow or an [unoffered] hecatomb."

66 αἴ κεν—in the hope that, on the chance that (+ subjunctive).

πως—in some way, somehow, perhaps; αἴ κέν πως—"to see if somehow," "in the hope that perhaps."

ἀρήν, ἀρνός, ὁ, ἡ—lamb.

κνίση, -ης, ἡ—odor of roast meat, steam or smell of burnt offerings (the part of the sacrifice the gods enjoyed).

τέλειος, -η, -ον—perfect, without spot or blemish. (An imperfect victim might offend the god.)

Scanning Notes

59 The ι in ὀΐω is long.

66 The ι in κνίσης is long.

βούλεται ἀντιάσας ἡμῖν ἀπὸ λοιγὸν ἀμῦναι."   67

Calchas, a gifted seer, rises to address the assembly.

Ἤτοι ὅ γ᾿ ὣς εἰπὼν κατ᾿ ἄρ᾿ ἕζετο· τοῖσι δ᾿ ἀνέστη   68
Κάλχας Θεστορίδης, οἰωνοπόλων ὄχ᾿ ἄριστος,   69
ὃς ᾔδη τά τ᾿ ἐόντα τά τ᾿ ἐσσόμενα πρό τ᾿ ἐόντα,   70
καὶ νήεσσ᾿ ἡγήσατ᾿ Ἀχαιῶν Ἴλιον εἴσω   71
ἣν διὰ μαντοσύνην, τήν οἱ πόρε Φοῖβος Ἀπόλλων·   72
ὅ σφιν ἐϋφρονέων ἀγορήσατο καὶ μετέειπεν·   73

---

67 **βούλομαι, βουλήσομαι**—wish, want; βούλεται = βούληται—present subjunctive: "he may wish" (another example of the short-vowel subjunctive).
ἀντιάω, ἀντιάσω, ἠντίασα—accept, partake of (+ gen.); ἀντιάσας—aorist active participle, nom. sing. masc.
ἡμῖν—"from us" (dative of advantage; literally, "for us").
λοιγός, -οῦ, ὁ—destruction, ruin, death.
ἀπαμύνω, (aor.) **ἀπήμυνα**—ward off (+ acc.) from (+ dat.); ἀπὸ . . . ἀμῦναι—aorist active infinitive (tmesis).
In lines 65–67, Achilles suggests that perhaps Apollo is angry because he blames (ἐπιμέμφεται) the Greeks for not fulfilling a vow (εὐχωλῆς) or not performing a sacrifice (ἑκατόμβης). If they make a sacrifice to him, after partaking of (ἀντιάσας) the odor (κνίσης) of the (roasted) lambs (ἀρνῶν) and goats (αἰγῶν), he may want (βούλεται) to ward off (ἀπὸ . . . ἀμῦναι) destruction (λοιγόν) from them (ἡμῖν). Does Achilles really have no idea why Apollo is angry, or is he just being extremely diplomatic in not mentioning Agamemnon's behavior to Chryses?

68 **ἤτοι**—in truth, to be sure; when followed by a δέ clause, may simply stress the contrast.
εἰπών—aorist active participle, nom. sing. masc.
καθέζομαι—sit down, take a seat; κατ᾿ . . . ἕζετο—tmesis.

69 **Κάλχας, -αντος, ὁ**—Calchas, a Greek seer.
Θεστορίδης, -αο, ὁ—son of Thestor.
οἰωνοπόλος, -ου, ὁ—seer (literally, "interpreter of birds"); Calchas was a man who could reveal the will of the gods. One way in which this might be done was by observing the flight of birds.
ὄχ᾿ = ὄχα—by far.

70 **οἶδα** (perfect; translate as present)—know; ᾔδη—pluperfect, 3rd pers. sing.: "knew."
ἐόντα—present active participle of εἰμί, acc. plur. neut; τά τ᾿ ἐόντα—"what is now" (literally, "the things being").
ἐσσόμενα—future active participle of εἰμί, acc. plur. neut.; τά τ᾿ ἐσσόμενα—"what will be" (literally, "the things going to be").

πρό—(adv.) before; πρό τ᾿ ἐόντα—"what was" (literally, "the things being before").

71   νήεσσ᾿ = νήεσσι—dat. plur. of νηῦς.

ἡγέομαι, ἡγήσομαι, ἡγησάμην—lead (+ dat.); ἡγήσατ᾿ = ἡγήσατο.

Ἴλιος, -ου, ἡ—Ilium (another name for Troy, derived from the name of Ilus, its founder).

εἴσω—to (+ acc.); Ἴλιον εἴσω—The preposition follows its object here.

72   ὅς, ἥ, ὅν—his own, her own, its own.

διά—by means of (+ acc.).

μαντοσύνη, -ης, ἡ—gift of prophecy.

τήν—the article used as a relative pronoun (= ἥν), refers to μαντοσύνην.

οἱ—to him; dat. sing. of εἷο.

πόρον (aor.)—give, bestow, grant.

73   σφιν—dat. plur. of εἷο.

ἐϋφρονέων, -ουσα, -ον—prudently, sensibly; well-meaning, with good intent.

ἀγοράομαι, (aor.) ἠγορησάμην—address (an assembly), talk; ἀγορήσατο = ἠγορήσατο.

μετέειπον (aor.)—speak.

ἀγορήσατο καὶ μετέειπεν—"he addressed them and said."

Scanning Notes

67   The third α in ἀντιάσας is long.

71   The first ι in Ἴλιον is long.

72   The α in Ἀπόλλων is long, but the first syllable is scanned short. A long vowel that does not receive the ictus can be scanned short.

Calchas reveals that he knows the cause of Apollo's anger, but he is afraid to name the person responsible until Achilles guarantees his safety.

"ὦ Ἀχιλεῦ, κέλεαί με, Διῒ φίλε, μυθήσασθαι   74
μῆνιν Ἀπόλλωνος ἑκατηβελέταο ἄνακτος·   75
τοιγὰρ ἐγὼν ἐρέω· σὺ δὲ σύνθεο καί μοι ὄμοσσον   76
ἦ μέν μοι πρόφρων ἔπεσιν καὶ χερσὶν ἀρήξειν·   77
ἦ γὰρ ὀΐομαι ἄνδρα χολωσέμεν, ὃς μέγα πάντων   78
Ἀργείων κρατέει καί οἱ πείθονται Ἀχαιοί·   79
κρείσσων γὰρ βασιλεὺς ὅτε χώσεται ἀνδρὶ χέρηι·   80
εἴ περ γάρ τε χόλον γε καὶ αὐτῆμαρ καταπέψῃ,   81
ἀλλά τε καὶ μετόπισθεν ἔχει κότον, ὄφρα τελέσσῃ,   82
ἐν στήθεσσιν ἑοῖσι· σὺ δὲ φράσαι εἴ με σαώσεις."   83

---

74 Ἀχιλεῦ—vocative.

κέλομαι, κελήσομαι—order, urge, request; κέλεαι—present, 2nd pers. sing. (The form was originally κέλεσαι, but the σ was lost between the two vowels; the Attic form would be κέλει.)

Διῒ—dat. of Ζεύς.

φίλε—vocative.

μυθέομαι, μυθήσομαι, ἐμυθησάμην—speak of, explain; μυθήσασθαι—What kind of infinitive is this?

75 μῆνιν—Homer began book 1 with this same word. Whose μῆνις is referred to in line 1 and whose here?

ἑκατηβελέτης, -αο—(adj.) far-shooting; ἑκατηβελέταο—gen. sing. masc.

76 τοιγάρ—therefore, accordingly.

ἐγών = ἐγώ.

εἴρω, ἐρέω—speak.

συντίθημι, συνθήσω, συνέθηκα—take heed, hear; σύνθεο—aorist imperative.

ὄμνυμι, ὀμοῦμαι, ὤμοσσα—swear, take oath; ὄμοσσον—aorist imperative.

77 ἦ—surely, truly.

πρόφρων—"zealously," "earnestly."

ἔπος, -εος, τό—word; ἔπεσιν—dative of means.

χερσίν—dat. plur. of χείρ; dative of means.

ἀρήγω, ἀρήξω, ἤρηξα—help, support (+ dat.).

78 ὀΐομαι—think, suspect.

χολωσέμεν = χολώσειν.

ἦ γὰρ ὀΐομαι ἄνδρα χολωσέμεν—"for, indeed, I think [that I] will anger a man" (an example of indirect statement or discourse after the verb ὀΐομαι—in this case an accusative/infinitive construction without the accusative (με), omitted here because the subject of χολωσέμεν is the same as the subject of ὀΐομαι).

μέγα—with power or might (literally, "exceedingly, greatly").

79 Ἀργεῖοι, -ων, οἱ—Argives (another name Homer uses for the Greeks in general; literally it would be those from Argos).

κρατέω—have power, rule over (+ gen.).

οἱ (dat. sing. of εἷο) = αὐτῷ.

80 κρείσσων, -ον—stronger, of superior strength, more powerful, better.

κρείσσων [ἐστίν] βασιλεύς.

ὅτε—when, whenever.

χώσεται = χώσηται, a short-vowel subjunctive in a present general condition, an expression of a general truth with a primary indicative verb (present, future, perfect, or future perfect) in the apodosis and a subjunctive verb in the temporal or conditional clause (the protasis). In Homer, there will often be no ἄν or κε(ν).

ἀνδρί—The person at whom the anger is directed will be in the dative.

χέρης, -ες—low, humble, poor, inferior.

81 περ—even, although, very, at least.

εἴ περ γάρ—"for even if."

χόλος, -ου, ὁ—anger, wrath, rage.

αὐτῆμαρ—on the same day.

καταπέσσω, (aor.) κατέπεψα—digest, repress, "swallow"; καταπέψῃ—aorist active subjunctive, 3rd pers. sing.; a subjunctive verb in the protasis of a present general condition.

82 ἀλλά—"nevertheless."

μετόπισθεν—afterward, behind.

κότος, -ου, ὁ—grudge, resentment, rancor, wrath.

ὄφρα—until (+ subjunctive).

τελέσσῃ—aorist active subjunctive of τελείω, 3rd pers. sing.

83 στῆθος, -εος, τό—chest, breast; "heart," i.e., the seat of emotion and feeling. (Only plural forms of στῆθος are used in Homer; translate as singular.)

ἑός, ἑή, ἑόν—his, her, its, his own, her own, its own.

φράζω, φράσω, ἔφρασα—point out, show; *middle*—consider; φράσαι—aorist middle imperative.

εἰ—"whether."

σαόω, σαώσω, ἐσάωσα—protect, rescue, preserve, save.

Scanning Notes

74 The second ι in Διΐ and the υ in μυθήσασθαι are long.

75 The last syllable of Ἀπόλλωνος is scanned long because ἑκατηβελέταο was originally spelled Ϝεκατηβελέταο, putting two consonants after the short o. The second α in ἑκατηβελέταο is long.

78 The first ι in ὀΐομαι is long.

Achilles promises Calchas protection.

Τὸν δ᾽ ἀπαμειβόμενος προσέφη πόδας ὠκὺς Ἀχιλλεύς·   84
"θαρσήσας μάλα εἰπὲ θεοπρόπιον ὅ τι οἶσθα·   85
οὐ μὰ γὰρ Ἀπόλλωνα Διῒ φίλον, ᾧ τε σύ, Κάλχαν,   86
εὐχόμενος Δαναοῖσι θεοπροπίας ἀναφαίνεις,   87
οὔ τις ἐμεῦ ζῶντος καὶ ἐπὶ χθονὶ δερκομένοιο   88
σοὶ κοίλης παρὰ νηυσὶ βαρείας χεῖρας ἐποίσει   89
συμπάντων Δαναῶν, οὐδ᾽ ἢν Ἀγαμέμνονα εἴπῃς,   90
ὃς νῦν πολλὸν ἄριστος Ἀχαιῶν εὔχεται εἶναι."   91

Calchas reveals that Apollo is angry because Agamemnon refused to allow
Chryses to ransom his daughter.

Καὶ τότε δὴ θάρσησε καὶ ηὔδα μάντις ἀμύμων·   92
"οὔτ᾽ ἄρ᾽ ὅ γ᾽ εὐχωλῆς ἐπιμέμφεται οὔθ᾽ ἑκατόμβης,   93

---

84   **ἀπαμείβομαι**—answer.

πρόσφημι, προσφήσω, προσέφησα—speak to, address; **προσέφη**—imperfect.

πόδας ὠκὺς Ἀχιλλεύς—This is not the first time Achilles has been called "swift-footed." The use of epithets (words or phrases that characterize a person or a thing) is a common feature of Homeric poetry. We have already seen several: line 75—the far-shooting lord Apollo (Ἀπόλλωνος ἑκατηβελέταο ἄνακτος); line 17—the well-greaved Achaeans (ἐϋκνήμιδες Ἀχαιοί); line 7—Agamemnon [son of Atreus], lord of men (Ἀτρεΐδης τε ἄναξ ἀνδρῶν). While the repeated use of these epithets may seem strange to us (especially in an instance like this, when the situation does not call for speed on Achilles' part), such standard phrases were building blocks used by oral poets. Whether Homer composed orally himself or simply used language and phrases from the oral tradition in the creation of his poetry, his works were undoubtedly intended for performance before live audiences. For such a performance, the use of epithets may have had a very practical purpose, similar to techniques used by radio broadcasters to catch the listener's ear. If the person who was reciting the speeches of many different characters marked the changes in speakers with only the name of the new speaker ("and Zeus answered" or "then Achilles said"), a listener might miss the name of the speaker. But if a descriptive phrase accompanied the name ("and Zeus, the cloud-gatherer, said"), someone who missed "Zeus" might still catch "cloud-gatherer" and know who was talking.

85   **θαρσέω,** (aor.) **ἐθάρσησα**—take courage, be bold; **θαρσήσας**—aorist active participle, nom. sing. masc.: "taking courage." In Homer, an aorist participle often indicates something happening at the same time as the main verb.

μάλα—by all means, certainly.

εἰπέ—aorist imperative of εἶπον.

θεοπρόπιον, -ου, τό—prophecy, oracle.

ὅ τι—whatever.

οἶσθα—2nd pers. sing. of οἶδα.

86 οὐ—translate with τις in line 88, where it is repeated for emphasis: "no, by Apollo,
     . . . not anyone . . ."

μά—by (+ acc.); used in an oath followed by the accusative of the god or object
     invoked.

μὰ γὰρ Ἀπόλλωνα Διΐ φίλον [ὄμνυμι].

Κάλχαν—vocative sing.

87 εὐχόμενος—translate with ᾧ in the preceding line: "by Apollo, . . . to whom you
     pray, Calchas, when you reveal" (literally, "praying to whom, Calchas, you re-
     veal").

θεοπροπίη, -ης, ἡ—oracle, prophecy.

ἀναφαίνω—reveal, show.

88 ἐμεῦ—gen. sing. of ἐγώ.

ζώω—live; ζῶντος—present active participle, gen. sing. masc.

χθών, χθονός, ἡ—earth, land.

δέρκομαι—see, look; δερκομένοιο—present participle, gen. sing. masc.

ἐμεῦ ζῶντος καὶ ἐπὶ χθονὶ δερκομένοιο—genitive absolute: "while I'm alive
     and breathing" or "while I'm living and seeing the light of day" (literally, "with
     me living and having the power of sight").

89 νηυσί—dat. plur. of νηῦς.

βαρύς, -εῖα, -ύ—heavy, "violent."

ἐπιφέρω, ἐποίσω, ἐπήνεικα—lay upon.

βαρείας χεῖρας ἐποίσει—"will lay violent hands upon."

90 σύμπας, σύμπασα, σύμπαν—all; συμπάντων Δαναῶν—with οὔ τις (line 88).

ἤν—if.

91 πολλόν—by far, much.

εὔχομαι—boast, claim.

92 τότε—then.

θάρσησε = ἐθάρσησε.

αὐδάω—speak; ηὔδα = ηὔδαε—imperfect.

ἀμύμων, -ον—excellent, blameless.

93 οὔτε—and not, nor; οὔτε . . . οὔτε—neither . . . nor.

ὁ—he (i.e., Apollo).

εὐχωλή, -ῆς, ἡ—vow.

ἐπιμέμφομαι—blame, find fault with (+ gen.).

Compare this line with line 65. How are they different?

Scanning Notes

86 The first α in Ἀπόλλωνα and the second ι in Διΐ are long.

87 The α in θεοπροπίας is long.

89 The second α in βαρείας is long.

92 The α in ηὔδα and the υ in ἀμύμων are long.

ἀλλ᾽ ἕνεκ᾽ ἀρητῆρος, ὃν ἠτίμησ᾽ Ἀγαμέμνων   94
οὐδ᾽ ἀπέλυσε θύγατρα καὶ οὐκ ἀπεδέξατ᾽ ἄποινα,   95
τοὔνεκ᾽ ἄρ᾽ ἄλγε᾽ ἔδωκεν ἑκηβόλος ἠδ᾽ ἔτι δώσει·   96
οὐδ᾽ ὅ γε πρὶν Δαναοῖσιν ἀεικέα λοιγὸν ἀπώσει,   97
πρίν γ᾽ ἀπὸ πατρὶ φίλῳ δόμεναι ἑλικώπιδα κούρην   98
ἀπριάτην ἀνάποινον, ἄγειν θ᾽ ἱερὴν ἑκατόμβην   99
ἐς Χρύσην· τότε κέν μιν ἱλασσάμενοι πεπίθοιμεν."   100

Agamemnon is furious with Calchas.

Ἦτοι ὅ γ᾽ ὣς εἰπὼν κατ᾽ ἄρ᾽ ἕζετο· τοῖσι δ᾽ ἀνέστη   101
ἥρως Ἀτρεΐδης εὐρὺ κρείων Ἀγαμέμνων   102
ἀχνύμενος· μένεος δὲ μέγα φρένες ἀμφὶ μέλαιναι   103
πίμπλαντ᾽, ὄσσε δέ οἱ πυρὶ λαμπετόωντι ἐΐκτην·   104
Κάλχαντα πρώτιστα κάκ᾽ ὀσσόμενος προσέειπε·   105
"μάντι κακῶν, οὐ πώ ποτέ μοι τὸ κρήγυον εἶπας·   106
αἰεί τοι τὰ κάκ᾽ ἐστὶ φίλα φρεσὶ μαντεύεσθαι,   107

94 ἕνεκ᾽ = ἕνεκα—because of, on account of (+ gen.).
    ἀτιμάω, ἀτιμήσω, ἠτίμησα—dishonor, treat with disrespect, insult; ἠτίμησ᾽ = ἠτίμησε.
95 ἀπολύω, ἀπολύσω, ἀπέλυσα—release.
96 τοὔνεκ᾽ = τοὔνεκα—for this reason, therefore, because of this (τοὔνεκα = τοῦ ἕνεκα).
    ἔτι—still.
97 πρίν—before, until (+ infinitive).
    ἀεικής, -ές—grievous, ruinous.
    ἀπωθέω, ἀπώσω, ἀπέωσα—push away, push back, drive off.
    πρίν ... πρίν (lines 97–98)—not necessary to translate the first πρίν: "And he will not remove [push back] the grievous destruction from the Danaans until . . ."
98 ἀποδίδωμι, ἀποδώσω, ἀπέδωκα—give up, restore, give back; ἀπὸ ... δόμεναι tmesis; ἀπὸ ... δόμεναι = ἀπὸ ... δοῦναι—aorist active infinitive; understand "we" as the subject: "until [we] give back . . ."
    ἑλικῶπις, -ιδος—(fem. adj.) quick-eyed, flashing-eyed; possibly "black-eyed" or "dark-eyed."
    κούρη, -ης, ἡ—young woman, girl.
99 ἀπριάτην—(adv.) without a price.
    ἀνάποινον—(adv.) without a ransom.
    ἀπριάτην ἀνάποινον—an example of *asyndeton*, a figure of speech in which an expected conjunction (καί) is omitted, adding a feeling of urgency or emphasis.
    ἱερός, -ή, -όν—sacred, holy.

100 Χρύση, -ης, ἡ—Chryse, a town near Troy (Chryses' home).

ἱλάσκομαι, ἱλάσσομαι, ἱλασσάμην—appease, propitiate.

πεπίθοιμεν—aorist active optative of πείθω: "Then, having appeased him, we may persuade [him to stop the plague]."

101 Compare this line with line 68. Who is the subject of each verb in the two lines?

102 εὐρύ—(adv.) widely.

κρείων, -ουσα, -ον—ruling.

103 ἄχνυμαι—be distressed, grieve.

μένος, -εος, τό—fury, rage.

ἀμφί—(adv.) on both sides.

μέλας, μέλαινα, μέλαν—dark, black.

104 πίμπλημι, πλήσω, ἔπλησα—fill (what something is filled with will be in the genitive); πίμπλαντ᾽ = ἐπίμπλαντο—imperfect passive.

μένεος δὲ μέγα φρένες ἀμφὶ μέλαιναι / πίμπλαντ᾽ (lines 103–4)—"His mind, dark on both sides [i.e., completely darkened by emotion], was greatly filled with anger."

ὄσσε—eyes (nom. dual neut.).

οἱ—dative of interest; ὄσσε δέ οἱ—"and his eyes."

πῦρ, πυρός, τό—fire, flame.

λαμπετάω—shine, gleam, blaze, flash; λαμπετόωντι—present active participle, dat. sing. neut.

ἐΐκτην—pluperfect of ἔοικα (translate as imperfect), 3rd pers. dual.

105 κάκ᾽= κακά—neuter accusative adjective used as an adverb.

ὄσσομαι—look, glare.

κάκ᾽ ὀσσόμενος—"with a look boding ill" (literally, "glaring evil things").

προσέειπον (aor.)—address, speak to.

106 μάντι—vocative.

πω—yet, ever.

κρήγυος, -ον—good, useful, helpful; τὸ κρήγυον—"good" or "a good thing."

εἶπας—aorist active, 2nd pers. sing.

107 τοι—dative of interest with φρεσί.

τὰ κάκ᾽= τὰ κακά—"evil" or "evil things"; τὰ κάκ᾽ ἐστί—neuter plural subject with a singular verb.

φρεσί—dat. pl. of φρήν.

μαντεύομαι, μαντεύσομαι, ἐμαντευσάμην—predict, prophesy.

Scanning Notes

94 The α in ἀρητῆρος and the ι in ἠτίμησ᾽ are long.

100 The υ in Χρύσην is long.

ἐσθλὸν δ᾽ οὔτε τί πω εἶπας ἔπος οὔτ᾽ ἐτέλεσσας·   108

Agamemnon says he refused to ransom Chryseis because he wants to take her home with him. For the sake of the army, however, he will give her up, but he demands another prize to replace her.

καὶ νῦν ἐν Δαναοῖσι θεοπροπέων ἀγορεύεις   109
ὡς δὴ τοῦδ᾽ ἕνεκά σφιν ἑκηβόλος ἄλγεα τεύχει,   110
οὔνεκ᾽ ἐγὼ κούρης Χρυσηΐδος ἀγλά᾽ ἄποινα   111
οὐκ ἔθελον δέξασθαι, ἐπεὶ πολὺ βούλομαι αὐτὴν   112
οἴκοι ἔχειν· καὶ γάρ ῥα Κλυταιμνήστρης προβέβουλα   113
κουριδίης ἀλόχου, ἐπεὶ οὔ ἑθέν ἐστι χερείων,   114
οὐ δέμας οὐδὲ φυήν, οὔτ᾽ ἂρ φρένας οὔτέ τι ἔργα.   115
ἀλλὰ καὶ ὣς ἐθέλω δόμεναι πάλιν, εἰ τό γ᾽ ἄμεινον·   116
βούλομ᾽ ἐγὼ λαὸν σόον ἔμμεναι ἢ ἀπολέσθαι·   117

---

108   **ἐσθλός, -ή, -όν**—good.
     "Not ever did you speak any good word nor bring to pass any good [deed]."
     Agamemnon may be referring to what happened as the Greeks were on their way
     to Troy. When the Greek fleet was becalmed at Aulis, Calchas said they would not
     get favorable winds until Agamemnon's daughter, Iphigenia, was sacrificed to
     Artemis. Agamemnon was forced to summon his daughter to Aulis and sacrifice
     her.
109   **ἐν Δαναοῖσι**—"among the Greeks."
     θεοπροπέω—prophesy, predict; **θεοπροπέων**—present active participle.
     ἀγορεύω—speak, say, declare.
110   **ὡς**—that.
     τοῦδ᾽= τοῦδε; **τοῦδ᾽ ἕνεκα**—refers ahead to the next line.
     σφιν—dat. plur. of εἷο: "for them."
111   **Χρυσηΐς, -ΐδος, ἡ**—Chryseis, the daughter of Chryses. (Here we learn her name
     for the first time. Her name, a patronymic, literally means "daughter of Chry-
     ses." The suffix -ίς, -ίδος performs the same function for a feminine name that
     -δης does for a masculine name like Πηληϊάδης or Ἀτρεΐδης.)
     κούρης Χρυσηΐδος—"for the young woman Chryseis."
112   **ἐθέλω, ἐθελήσω, ἠθέλησα**—wish, want; ἔθελον = ἤθελον.
     ἐπεί—since.
     πολύ—much, by far.
     βούλομαι, βουλήσομαι—prefer, want.
     αὐτήν—"[the girl] herself."
113   **οἴκοι**—at home.
     καί—even.
     γάρ ῥα—"for in fact."

Κλυταιμνήστρη, -ης, ἡ—Clytemnestra, wife of Agamemnon.

προβέβουλα (perfect; translate as present)—prefer to, prefer before (+ gen.).

Κλυταιμνήστρης προβέβουλα—"I prefer [her] to Clytemnestra." (As the ancient Greek audience well knew, Clytemnestra would murder Agamemnon when he came home after the war was over.)

114 κουρίδιος, -η, -ον—wedded, legally married.

ἄλοχος, -ου, ἡ—wife.

κουριδίης ἀλόχου—in apposition to Κλυταιμνήστρης in line 113.

ἔθεν—genitive of comparison.

χερείων, -ον—worse, inferior, less worthy.

115 δέμας, -αος, τό—build, body, stature.

φυή, -ῆς, ἡ—form, physique, appearance, figure.

φρένας—"wit," "intelligence."

οὔτέ τι—not at all.

ἔργον, -ου, τό—work, deed, "skill."

δέμας, φυήν, φρένας, ἔργα—accusatives of respect: "she [Chryseis] is not inferior to her [Clytemnestra], not with respect to stature or figure or intelligence or skill."

116 καὶ ὥς—even so.

δόμεναι—aorist active infinitive of δίδωμι.

πάλιν—back.

ἐθέλω [κούρην] δόμεναι πάλιν.

ἀμείνων, -ον—better.

εἰ τό γ' ἄμεινόν [ἐστιν].

117 βούλομ' = βούλομαι. Notice the number of first-person verbs expressing the idea of wanting that Agamemnon uses—ἔθελον (line 112), προβέβουλα (line 113), ἐθέλω (line 116), βούλομ' (line 117)—as he stresses the importance of his own wishes and saves face by asserting that his wishes are paramount. He is not being forced to give Chryseis back. He *wants* to.

σόος, -η, -ον—safe.

ἔμμεναι = εἶναι—infinitive of εἰμί.

ἤ—"rather than."

ἀπόλλυμι, ἀπολέσσω, ἀπώλεσα—destroy; *middle*—be destroyed, perish; ἀπολέσθαι—aorist middle infinitive.

Scanning Notes

108 The last syllable of εἶπας is scanned long because ἔπος was originally spelled Ϝέπος, putting two consonants after the short α.

111 The υ in Χρυσηΐδος is long.

113 You would expect ῥα to be scanned long because it is followed by two consonants. However, if the first consonant is a mute or stop (π, β, φ, κ, γ, χ, τ, δ, or θ) and the second is either λ or ρ, the preceding syllable can be scanned short, as it is here.

117 The α in λαόν is long.

αὐτὰρ ἐμοὶ γέρας αὐτίχ᾿ ἑτοιμάσατ᾿, ὄφρα μὴ οἶος   118
᾿Αργείων ἀγέραστος ἔω, ἐπεὶ οὐδὲ ἔοικε·   119
λεύσσετε γὰρ τό γε πάντες, ὅ μοι γέρας ἔρχεται ἄλλη."   120

Achilles asks Agamemnon where they will find him another prize. He suggests Agamemnon give the priest's daughter back now and be repaid later when they capture Troy.

Τὸν δ᾿ ἠμείβετ᾿ ἔπειτα ποδάρκης δῖος ᾿Αχιλλεύς·   121
" ᾿Ατρεΐδη κύδιστε, φιλοκτεανώτατε πάντων,   122
πῶς γάρ τοι δώσουσι γέρας μεγάθυμοι ᾿Αχαιοί;   123
οὐδέ τί που ἴδμεν ξυνήϊα κείμενα πολλά·   124
ἀλλὰ τὰ μὲν πολίων ἐξεπράθομεν, τὰ δέδασται,   125
λαοὺς δ᾿ οὐκ ἐπέοικε παλίλλογα ταῦτ᾿ ἐπαγείρειν.   126
ἀλλὰ σὺ μὲν νῦν τήνδε θεῷ πρόες· αὐτὰρ ᾿Αχαιοὶ   127
τριπλῇ τετραπλῇ τ᾿ ἀποτείσομεν, αἴ κέ ποθι Ζεὺς   128

---

118 **γέρας, -αος, τό**—prize, gift of honor. (These prizes were regarded as marks of status, which explains Agamemnon's unwillingness to be without one.)

αὐτίχ᾿ = αὐτίκα—immediately.

ἑτοιμάζω, (aor.) **ἡτοίμασα**—prepare, make ready; ἑτοιμάσατ᾿ = ἑτοιμάσατε—aorist imperative.

ὄφρα—in order that.

οἶος, -η, -ον—alone.

119 **ἀγέραστος, -η, -ον**—without a prize of honor.

ἔω—present subjunctive of εἰμί, 1st pers. sing.; ὄφρα μὴ οἶος / ᾿Αργείων ἀγέραστος ἔω (lines 118–19)—a purpose clause.

ἔοικα (perfect; translate as present)—be fitting, be suitable; ἐπεὶ οὐδὲ ἔοικε— "since [that] is not right." (The Greeks have been raiding and sacking cities near Troy for the past nine years. Whenever they captured booty and slaves, each warrior received a γέρας (prize). After the raid on Chryse, Chryseis had been Agamemnon's γέρας. As supreme commander of the Greeks, he argues, it would not be seemly for him to be without a prize.)

120 **λεύσσω**—see.

πάντες—modifies the subject of λεύσσετε: "you all see . . ."

ὅ = ὅτι—that, the fact that.

μοι—dative of interest; μοι γέρας—"my prize."

ἄλλη—elsewhere.

The intense concern Agamemnon (and Achilles) show for their war prizes (which may seem almost childish to us) is the result of the Homeric hero's belief that loss of property meant loss of personal honor.

121 ἀμείβω, ἀμείψω, ἤμειψα—exchange; *middle*—answer, reply; ἠμείβετ᾽ = ἠμείβετο.

ποδάρκης, -ες—swift-footed.

122 Ἀτρεΐδη—vocative sing.

κύδιστος, -η, -ον—most glorious; κύδιστε—vocative sing.

φιλοκτεανώτατος, -η, -ον—most greedy (for other men's possessions).

123 πῶς—how?

μεγάθυμος, -ον—great-hearted, high-spirited.

124 οὐδέ τι—not at all, none whatever.

που—anywhere.

ἴδμεν—1st pers. plur. of οἶδα.

ξυνήϊος, -η, -ον—common; ξυνήϊα—"common property."

κεῖμαι, κείσομαι—lie, be placed.

"We know of no large amounts of common property lying about anywhere."

125 πολίων—refers to the cities near Troy that the Greeks had captured and plundered during the preceding nine years.

ἐκπέρθω, ἐκπέρσω, ἐξέπερσα or ἐξέπραθον—sack, plunder, carry off from (+ gen.).

δατέομαι, δάσ(σ)ομαι, ἐδα(σ)σάμην, δέδασμαι—divide up, allot.

τὰ μὲν πολίων ἐξεπράθομεν, τὰ δέδασται—"the things we plundered from the cities, [these things] have been divided up."

126 ἐπέοικε (impersonal)—it is proper, it is right, it is seemly (with accusative and infinitive).

παλίλλογος, -ον—gathered together again, collected again.

ταῦτ᾽ = ταῦτα.

ἐπαγείρω—bring together.

"It is not right for the army to bring these things together again."

127 τήνδε = Chryseis.

προΐημι, προήσω, προέηκα—give up; πρόες—aorist imperative.

αὐτάρ—Marks a contrast with the immediately preceding sentence, containing μέν.

128 τριπλῇ—threefold, triply.

τετραπλῇ—fourfold, quadruply.

ἀποτίνω, ἀποτείσω, ἀπέτεισα—pay back, repay.

αἴ—if, if only (+ κε[ν] + subjunctive).

ποθι—ever.

Scanning Notes

122 The υ in κύδιστε is long.

123 The υ in μεγάθυμοι is long.

124 The υ in ξυνήϊα is long.

126 The α in λαούς is long.

δῶσι πόλιν Τροίην εὐτείχεον ἐξαλαπάξαι."   129

Agamemnon insists that he must be given another prize or he will take one from one of the other leaders.

Τὸν δ᾽ ἀπαμειβόμενος προσέφη κρείων Ἀγαμέμνων·   130
"μὴ δὴ οὕτως, ἀγαθός περ ἐών, θεοείκελ᾽ Ἀχιλλεῦ,   131
κλέπτε νόῳ, ἐπεὶ οὐ παρελεύσεαι οὐδέ με πείσεις.   132
ἦ ἐθέλεις, ὄφρ᾽ αὐτὸς ἔχῃς γέρας, αὐτὰρ ἔμ᾽ αὔτως   133
ἦσθαι δευόμενον, κέλεαι δέ με τήνδ᾽ ἀποδοῦναι;   134
ἀλλ᾽ εἰ μὲν δώσουσι γέρας μεγάθυμοι Ἀχαιοί,   135
ἄρσαντες κατὰ θυμόν, ὅπως ἀντάξιον ἔσται·   136
εἰ δέ κε μὴ δώωσιν, ἐγὼ δέ κεν αὐτὸς ἕλωμαι   137
ἢ τεὸν ἢ Αἴαντος ἰὼν γέρας, ἢ Ὀδυσῆος   138

---

129   **δῶσι**—aorist subjunctive of δίδωμι, 3rd pers. sing.; subjunctive in the protasis of a future-more-vivid condition.
       δῶσι [ἡμῖν].
       Τροίη, -ης, ἡ—Troy.
       εὐτείχεος, -ον—well-walled, well-fortified.
       ἐξαλαπάζω, ἐξαλαπάξω, ἐξηλάπαξα—sack, utterly destroy.
130   **κρείων**—"the ruler."
       Compare this line to line 84. What is the difference in the scansion of the two lines?
131   **οὕτως**—thus, in this way.
       ἀγαθός, -ή, -όν—brave, valiant, noble.
       περ—although.
       ἐών—present participle of εἰμί, nom. sing. masc.; ἀγαθός περ ἐών—"even though you are brave."
       θεοείκελος, -ον—godlike; θεοείκελ᾽ = θεοείκελε.
132   **κλέπτω**—hide, steal, deceive.
       νόος, -ου, ὁ—mind, understanding; νόῳ—dative of place.
       μὴ ... κλέπτε νόῳ (lines 131–32)—"do not hide [things] in your mind," i.e., "do not deceive me" or "do not try to trick me."
       παρέρχομαι, παρελεύσομαι—go by, pass by, outwit; παρελεύσεαι = Attic παρελεύσει (originally παρελεύσεσαι)—future, 2nd pers. sing.
       πείσεις—future of πείθω.
133   **ἦ**—indicates a question.
       ὄφρ᾽= ὄφρα.
       αὐτός—modifies the 2nd pers. sing. subject of ἔχῃς; αὐτὸς ἔχῃς—"you yourself may keep."

αὐτάρ—emphasizes the contrast between Achilles having a prize and Agamemnon being without one.

ἔμ᾽ = ἐμέ.

αὕτως—thus, so.

In scanning this line, notice how the syllable αὐτ- is repeated three times and always receives the ictus. This repeatedly stressed sound may demonstrate Agamemnon's rising anger.

134 ἧμαι—sit; ἧσθαι—present infinitive.

δεύομαι—lack, be without.

κέλεαι = κέλει—present, 2nd pers. sing.

τήνδ᾽ = τήνδε.

ἀποδοῦναι—aorist active infinitive of ἀποδίδωμι.

"Indeed, do you wish me to sit here thus without a prize so that you yourself may keep [your] prize, and do you tell me to give this girl back?" (lines 133–34)

136 ἀραρίσκω, (aor.) ἦρσα—join, fit, suit.

κατὰ θυμόν—"to [my] wish."

ὅπως—so that, that.

ἀντάξιος, -η, -ον—equivalent, of equal value.

ἔσται—future of εἰμί.

The conclusion to the condition expressed in lines 135–36 must be understood: "But if the great-hearted Greeks will give [me] a prize that will be of equal value, suiting [it] to my wish, [I will be satisfied]."

137 αἱρέω, αἱρήσω, εἷλον or ἕλον—take, seize.

δώωσιν, ἕλωμαι—subjunctives; translate as futures. (It is not uncommon for subjunctives to be used to indicate future time in Homer.)

138 τεός, -ή, -όν—your, yours.

Αἴας, -αντος, ὁ—Ajax, one of the leading Greek warriors.

ἰών—present active participle of εἶμι, nom. sing. masc.; modifies ἐγὼ . . . αὐτός from the previous line: "I, myself, going out, will . . ."

Ὀδυσ(σ)εύς, -ῆος, ὁ—Odysseus, king of Ithaca, Greek leader renowned for his craftiness.

Scanning Notes

131 By synizesis (two vowels run together and pronounced as one long syllable), δή and the first syllable of οὕτως are run together to form one syllable. Pronounce as though it were written δ᾽ οὕτως.

135 The υ in μεγάθυμοι is long.

136 The υ in θυμόν is long.

ἄξω ἑλών· ὁ δέ κεν κεχολώσεται ὅν κεν ἵκωμαι.   139

Agamemnon sets aside the question of replacing his prize and arranges for the return of Chryseis.

ἀλλ' ἤτοι μὲν ταῦτα μεταφρασόμεσθα καὶ αὖτις,   140
νῦν δ' ἄγε νῆα μέλαιναν ἐρύσσομεν εἰς ἅλα δῖαν,   141
ἐν δ' ἐρέτας ἐπιτηδὲς ἀγείρομεν, ἐς δ' ἑκατόμβην   142
θείομεν, ἂν δ' αὐτὴν Χρυσηΐδα καλλιπάρῃον   143
βήσομεν· εἰς δέ τις ἀρχὸς ἀνὴρ βουληφόρος ἔστω,   144
ἢ Αἴας ἢ Ἰδομενεὺς ἢ δῖος Ὀδυσσεὺς   145
ἠὲ σύ, Πηλεΐδη, πάντων ἐκπαγλότατ' ἀνδρῶν,   146
ὄφρ' ἡμῖν ἑκάεργον ἱλάσσεαι ἱερὰ ῥέξας."   147

Achilles is now angry. He reminds Agamemnon that he has no quarrel with the Trojans and that he and his men are only fighting to help Agamemnon and Menelaus.

Τὸν δ' ἄρ' ὑπόδρα ἰδὼν προσέφη πόδας ὠκὺς Ἀχιλλεύς·   148
"ὤ μοι, ἀναιδείην ἐπιειμένε, κερδαλεόφρον,   149

---

139 **ἑλών**—aorist active participle from αἱρέω, nom. sing. masc.

κεχολώσεται—future middle; κεν κεχολώσεται—κεν indicates that κεχολώσεται is contingent on something, in this case, the following clause. It is not unusual for Homer to use a future indicative verb with κε(ν) to indicate some type of limitation or condition.

ἵκωμαι—aorist subjunctive in a future-more-vivid conditional relative clause.

ὁ δέ κεν κεχολώσεται ὅν κεν ἵκωμαι—"and he to whom I [will] come will be angry."

140 **ἤτοι**—conveys an emphatic affirmative: "indeed," "to be sure," "definitely," "certainly."

μεταφράζομαι—consider later, consider by and by; μεταφρασόμεσθα = μεταφρασόμεθα—future.

καὶ αὖτις—later, by and by; repeats and emphasizes the idea of "at a later time" already present in μεταφρασόμεσθα.

141 **νῆα**—from νηῦς; νῆα μέλαιναν—The pitch (pine tar) that was smeared on the ships to keep them watertight made them look dark or black.

ἐρύω, ἐρύω, εἴρυσ(σ)α—drag; ἐρύσσομεν (a short-vowel subjunctive) = ἐρύσωμεν—aorist subjunctive; this is a hortatory subjunctive: "let us drag." (Watch for several examples of this type of subjunctive in the next three lines.)

ἅλς, ἁλός, ἡ—sea.

142 **ἐν**—(adv.) therein, "in it."

ἐρέτης, -αο, ὁ—rower, oarsman.

ἐπιτηδές—as are needed, in sufficient number.

ἀγείρομεν = ἀγείρωμεν—aorist subjunctive.

ἐς—(adv.) into [something], in.

ἑκατόμβην—"the animals for the sacrifice."

143   θείομεν = θέωμεν—aorist subjunctive of τίθημι.

ἄν—goes with βήσομεν in the next line (tmesis).

καλλιπάρῃος, -ov—fair-cheeked, with beautiful cheeks.

144   ἀναβαίνω, ἀναβήσω, ἀνέβησα or ἀνέβην—take on board; ἄν . . . βήσομεν = ἄν . . . βήσωμεν.

εἷς, μία, ἕν—one.

ἀρχός, -οῦ, ὁ—leader, commander.

βουληφόρος, -ου, ὁ—leader, member of the βουλή (the council of the most important leaders).

ἔστω—imperative of εἰμί.

ἀνὴρ βουληφόρος—in apposition to εἷς . . . τις. Understand in the order εἷς τις, ἀνὴρ βουληφόρος, ἔστω ἀρχός: "Let someone, a man [who is] an important leader, be the commander."

145   Ἰδομενεύς, -ῆος, ὁ—Idomeneus, king of Crete.

146   ἠέ = ἤ—or.

Πηλεΐδης, -εω, ὁ—son of Peleus (= Achilles); Πηλεΐδη—vocative.

ἔκπαγλος, -ov—terrible; ἐκπαγλότατ᾿ = ἐκπαγλότατε.

147   ἡμῖν—dative of advantage: "for us."

ἑκάεργος, -ου, ὁ—far-worker, far-shooter (a name given to Apollo).

ἱλάσσεαι = ἱλάσῃ—aorist middle subjunctive, 2nd pers. sing.

ὄφρ᾿ . . . ἱλάσσεαι—purpose clause.

ἱερόν, -οῦ, τό—sacrifice.

ῥέζω, ῥέξω, ἔρεξα—perform, make, do; ῥέξας—aorist active participle, nom. sing. masc.

148   ὑπόδρα—darkly, grimly, sternly; ὑπόδρα ἰδών—"frowning" (literally, "looking grimly"); although ἰδών is an aorist participle, translate it as a present. In Homer, an aorist participle often indicates something happening at the same time as the main verb.

149   ὤ μοι—oh! alas!

ἀναιδείη, -ης, ἡ—shamelessness.

ἐπιέννυμι—clothe in; ἐπιειμένε—perfect passive participle, vocative.

κερδαλεόφρων, -ov—crafty, sly; κερδαλεόφρον—vocative.

Scanning Notes

143   The υ in Χρυσηΐδα is long.

145   The second α in Αἴας and the ι in Ἰδομενεύς are long.

147   The ι in ἱερά is long.

πῶς τίς τοι πρόφρων ἔπεσιν πείθηται Ἀχαιῶν   150
ἢ ὁδὸν ἐλθέμεναι ἢ ἀνδράσιν ἶφι μάχεσθαι;   151
οὐ γὰρ ἐγὼ Τρώων ἕνεκ᾽ ἤλυθον αἰχμητάων   152
δεῦρο μαχησόμενος, ἐπεὶ οὔ τί μοι αἴτιοί εἰσιν·   153
οὐ γάρ πώ ποτ᾽ ἐμὰς βοῦς ἤλασαν οὐδὲ μὲν ἵππους,   154
οὐδέ ποτ᾽ ἐν Φθίῃ ἐριβώλακι βωτιανείρῃ   155
καρπὸν ἐδηλήσαντ᾽, ἐπεὶ ἦ μάλα πολλὰ μεταξὺ   156
οὔρεά τε σκιόεντα θάλασσά τε ἠχήεσσα·   157

---

150   **πρόφρων**—"cheerfully."
      ἔπεσιν—dat. plur. of ἔπος.
      πείθηται—present middle subjunctive; a deliberative subjunctive: πῶς τίς . . .
         πείθηται—"how is anyone to obey . . . ?"
151   **ὁδός, -οῦ, ἡ**—journey, expedition, road.
      ἐλθέμεναι—aorist infinitive of ἔρχομαι.
      ὁδὸν ἐλθέμεναι—"to go on a journey," referring to the journey Agamemnon has
         just proposed, to return Chryseis.
      ἀνδράσιν—dat. plur. of ἀνήρ.
152   **Τρῶες, -ων, οἱ**—Trojans.
      ἕνεκ᾽= ἕνεκα.
      ἤλυθον = ἦλθον.
      αἰχμητής, -ᾶο, ὁ—spearman, warrior (αἰχμή = spear).
153   **δεῦρο**—to this place, here.
      μαχησόμενος—future participle of purpose.
      οὔ τι—not at all, by no means.
      μοι—dative of disadvantage: "in my eyes," "in regard to me."
      αἴτιος, -η, -ον—to blame, guilty, at fault.
154   **ποτ᾽**= ποτε.
      βοῦς, βοός, ὁ, ἡ—cow, bull, ox.
      ἐλάω, ἐλάσω, ἤλασα—drive away, rustle.
155   **Φθίη, -ης, ἡ**—Phthia, region in Thessaly that was Achilles' home.
      ἐριβῶλαξ, -ακος—with large clods, fertile.
      βωτιάνειρα—(fem. adj.) hero-nourishing.
156   **καρπός, -οῦ, ὁ**—crop.
      δηλέομαι, δηλήσομαι, ἐδηλησάμην—lay waste, destroy; ἐδηλήσαντ᾽ =
         ἐδηλήσαντο.
      μάλα—very.
      μεταξύ—between (i.e., between Troy and Phthia).
      μάλα πολλὰ μεταξύ—Supply "are" or "lie" as a verb.
157   **οὖρος, -εος, τό**—mountain.

Fig. 2. Achilles. Painting on an Attic red-figure amphora attributed to the
Achilles Painter, ca. 450 B.C. Rome, Vatican. (Photograph from the Vatican
Museums.)

σκιόεις, -εσσα, -εν—shady.

ἠχήεις, -εσσα, -εν—roaring, echoing; ἠχήεσσα—hear the sound of the roaring
sea in this onomatopoetic word.

Scanning Notes

152   The second α in αἰχμητάων is long.

153   The last syllable of μαχησόμενος is scanned long. A short final syllable that receives the ictus can be scanned long. What is the sense pause after this syllable
called?

155   The ι in Φθίη is long.

ἀλλὰ σοί, ὦ μέγ᾽ ἀναιδές, ἅμ᾽ ἑσπόμεθ᾽, ὄφρα σὺ χαίρῃς,   158
τιμὴν ἀρνύμενοι Μενελάῳ σοί τε, κυνῶπα,   159
πρὸς Τρώων· τῶν οὔ τι μετατρέπῃ οὐδ᾽ ἀλεγίζεις·   160

Achilles complains that he does the greater share of the fighting but never
receives as much loot as Agamemnon. He threatens to sail home.

καὶ δή μοι γέρας αὐτὸς ἀφαιρήσεσθαι ἀπειλεῖς,   161
ᾧ ἔπι πολλὰ μόγησα, δόσαν δέ μοι υἷες Ἀχαιῶν.   162
οὐ μὲν σοί ποτε ἶσον ἔχω γέρας, ὁππότ᾽ Ἀχαιοὶ   163
Τρώων ἐκπέρσωσ᾽ εὖ ναιόμενον πτολίεθρον·   164
ἀλλὰ τὸ μὲν πλεῖον πολυάϊκος πολέμοιο   165
χεῖρες ἐμαὶ διέπουσ᾽· ἀτὰρ ἤν ποτε δασμὸς ἵκηται,   166
σοὶ τὸ γέρας πολὺ μεῖζον, ἐγὼ δ᾽ ὀλίγον τε φίλον τε   167

---

158   μέγ᾽= μέγα.
        ἀναιδής, -ές—shameless; ἀναιδές—voc. sing. masc.
        ἅμ᾽= ἅμα—along with, together with (+ dat.).
        ἕπομαι, ἕψομαι, ἑσπόμην—follow (+ dat.); ἑσπόμεθ᾽ = ἑσπόμεθα; ἅμ᾽
            ἑσπόμεθ᾽—"we accompanied."
        χαίρω, χαιρήσω, κεχαρόμην—be glad, be happy; χαίρῃς—subjunctive verb
            in a purpose clause (ὄφρα σὺ χαίρῃς).
159   τιμή, -ῆς, ἡ—honor; in this context, perhaps "retribution" or "satisfaction."
        ἄρνυμαι—win, achieve, gain.
        Μενέλαος, -ου, ὁ—Menelaus, king of Sparta, the brother of Agamemnon. (The
            Trojan War was fought because the Trojan prince Paris stole Menelaus's wife,
            Helen.)
        κυνώπης—dog-faced, shameless (κύων, κυνός—dog; ὤψ, ὠπός—face); κυ-
            νῶπα—vocative. (This is an insult, an expression of contempt. While it is usu-
            ally translated as "shameless," it has also been suggested that it means "greedy"
            or "acquisitive.")
        σοί, σύ, σοί (lines 158–59)—The repeated forms of σύ emphasize Achilles'
            point that the other Greeks have done so much for Agamemnon.
160   πρός—from (+ gen.).
        τῶν—neut.: "these things" (i.e., the fact that the other Greeks came to Troy to help
            Menelaus and Agamemnon).
        μετατρέπομαι—consider (+ gen.); μετατρέπῃ—present, 2nd pers. sing.
        ἀλεγίζω—care for (+ gen.).
161   μοι—dative of disadvantage: "from me."
        ἀφαιρέω, ἀφαιρήσω, ἀφεῖλον—take away; ἀφαιρήσεσθαι—future middle
            infinitive.

ἀπειλέω—threaten; αὐτός strengthens the subject of ἀπειλεῖς: "you yourself threaten."

162 ᾧ ἔπι—"for which." (ἐπί is normally accented on the final syllable, the *ultima,* but when it follows its object, the accent moves to the next-to-the-last syllable, the *penult.*)

μογέω, (aor.) ἐμόγησα—suffer, struggle; μόγησα = ἐμόγησα.

δόσαν = ἔδοσαν—aorist active of δίδωμι, 3rd pers. plur.

υἱός, a second-declension noun that also has some third-declension forms, such as the nominative plural υἷες in this line; υἷες Ἀχαιῶν = the Greeks.

163 ἴσος, -η, -ον—equal.

ὁππότ' = ὁππότε—whenever.

164 ἐκπέρσωσ' = ἐκπέρσωσι—aorist subjunctive of ἐκπέρθω, 3rd pers. plur.; subjunctive verb in the protasis of a present general condition.

ναίω—be situated, dwell, inhabit; ναιόμενον—present middle participle.

πτολίεθρον, -ου, τό—city, town.

ὁππότ' Ἀχαιοὶ / Τρώων ἐκπέρσωσ' εὖ ναιόμενον πτολίεθρον (lines 163–64)—"whenever the Greeks sack a well-situated town of the Trojans"; Achilles is not referring to Troy itself, but to the towns near Troy that the Greeks captured and plundered.

165 πλείων, -ον—more, greater, the greater part (comparative of πολύς).

πολυάϊξ, -ϊκος—rushing, impetuous.

Note the alliteration in πλεῖον πολυάϊκος πολέμοιο.

166 διέπω—attend to, accomplish; διέπουσ' = διέπουσι.

ἀτάρ—but.

ἤν ποτε—if ever, whenever.

δασμός, -οῦ, ὁ—division (of booty or loot).

ἵκηται—aorist subjunctive of ἱκνέομαι; subjunctive verb in the protasis of a present general condition.

167 πολύ—much, by far.

μείζων, -ον—comparative of μέγας.

σοὶ τὸ γέρας πολὺ μεῖζόν [ἐστι].

ὀλίγος, -η, -ον—little, small, few.

ὀλίγον τε φίλον τε—"[a prize] small but dear to me."

Scanning Notes
159 The ι in τιμήν and the α in Μενελάῳ are long.
165 The ι in πολυάϊκος is long.

ἔρχομ᾽ ἔχων ἐπὶ νῆας, ἐπεί κε κάμω πολεμίζων.   168
νῦν δ᾽ εἶμι Φθίηνδ᾽, ἐπεὶ ἦ πολὺ φέρτερόν ἐστιν   169
οἴκαδ᾽ ἴμεν σὺν νηυσὶ κορωνίσιν, οὐδέ σ᾽ ὀΐω   170
ἐνθάδ᾽ ἄτιμος ἐὼν ἄφενος καὶ πλοῦτον ἀφύξειν."   171

Agamemnon urges Achilles to leave if he wants to.

Τὸν δ᾽ ἠμείβετ᾽ ἔπειτα ἄναξ ἀνδρῶν Ἀγαμέμνων·   172
"φεῦγε μάλ᾽, εἴ τοι θυμὸς ἐπέσσυται, οὐδέ σ᾽ ἔγωγε   173
λίσσομαι εἵνεκ᾽ ἐμεῖο μένειν· πάρ᾽ ἔμοιγε καὶ ἄλλοι   174
οἵ κέ με τιμήσουσι, μάλιστα δὲ μητίετα Ζεύς.   175
ἔχθιστος δέ μοί ἐσσι διοτρεφέων βασιλήων·   176
αἰεὶ γάρ τοι ἔρις τε φίλη πόλεμοί τε μάχαι τε·   177
εἰ μάλα καρτερός ἐσσι, θεός που σοὶ τό γ᾽ ἔδωκεν·   178
οἴκαδ᾽ ἰὼν σὺν νηυσί τε σῆς καὶ σοῖς ἑτάροισι   179

---

168   **ἔρχομ᾽** = ἔρχομαι.

     ἐπὶ νῆας—"to the camp" (where the ships were pulled up on the shore).

     ἐπεί κε—whenever.

     κάμνω, καμέομαι, ἔκαμον—grow tired; **κάμω**—aorist subjunctive; subjunctive verb in the protasis of a present general condition.

     πολεμίζω—fight.

     ἐπεί κε κάμω πολεμίζων—"whenever I am worn out from fighting."

169   **Φθίηνδ᾽** = Φθίηνδε—What does the suffix -δε add to the meaning of Φθίην?

     φέρτερος, -η, -ον—better (comparative of ἀγαθός).

170   **οἴκαδ᾽** = οἴκαδε—home(ward), to home.

     ἴμεν—present infinitive of εἶμι.

     κορωνίς, -ίδος—curved (refers to the upward curve at the ends of ancient Greek ships).

     σ᾽ = σοι; dative of advantage.

     ὀΐω—intend.

171   **ἐνθάδ᾽** = ἐνθάδε—here.

     ἄτιμος, -ον—unhonored, slighted, dishonored.

     ἄφενος, -εος, τό—riches, wealth.

     πλοῦτος, -ου, ὁ—wealth.

     ἀφύσσω, ἀφύξω, ἤφυσα—accumulate, draw up (as water from a well), dip out (as wine from a jar). (This word suggests the image of a slave drawing water from a well or dipping wine from a jar. Achilles is stating that he will not serve as Agamemnon's slave.)

172   Compare this line with line 121. Do they have the same scansion pattern?

173   **φεῦγε**—What does Agamemnon's choice of this word imply about Achilles?

μάλ' = μάλα—by all means.

θυμός, -οῦ, ὁ—heart, soul.

ἐπισσεύομαι—hurry, urge on, be eager; ἐπέσσυται—perfect; translate as present.

εἴ τοι θυμὸς ἐπέσσυται—"if your heart is so moved" or "if you want to."

ἔγωγε = ἐγώ γε—"I, at any rate," "I , at least." (The suffix -γε strengthens or emphasizes the word to which it is attached. See ἔμοιγε in the next line.)

174   λίσσομαι, (aor.) ἐλισάμην—beg, beseech.

εἵνεκα—on account of, for the sake of (+ gen.).

ἐμεῖο—gen. sing. of ἐγώ.

πάρ'= παρά—beside, by (+ dat.).

πάρ' ἔμοιγε καὶ ἄλλοι [εἰσίν].

175   οἵ—relative pronoun referring to ἄλλοι.

κε—"in that case," "under the circumstances" (i.e., "if you leave").

τιμάω, τιμήσω, ἐτίμησα—honor.

μητίετα, -αο, ὁ—counselor (one of the few first-declension masculine nouns). Agamemnon's confidence that Zeus will honor him is based on the belief that, as a king, his power comes from Zeus. It is ironic that Zeus will take Achilles' side in this quarrel and bring defeat and humiliation to Agamemnon.

176   ἔχθιστος, -η, -ον—most hated, most odious, most hostile.

ἐσσι = εἶ—2nd pers. sing., present tense of εἰμί.

διοτρεφής, -ές—cherished by Zeus, Zeus-nurtured.

διοτρεφέων βασιλήων—i.e., the Greek leaders.

177   ἔρις, -ιδος, ἡ—strife, quarrel, contention, rivalry.

ἔρις τε φίλη [ἐστίν]—φίλη agrees with ἔρις but also should be understood with πόλεμοι and μάχαι.

μάχη, -ης, ἡ—battle, fight.

178   μάλα—very.

καρτερός, -ή, -όν—powerful, strong, mighty.

που—"doubtless," "I suppose."

179   σός, σή, σόν—your.

ἕταρος, -ου, ὁ—companion.

Scanning Notes

169   The ι in Φθίηνδ' is long.

170   The ι in ὀΐω is long.

171   The ι in ἄτιμος is long.

173   The υ in θυμός is long.

175   The first ι in τιμήσουσι is long.

Μυρμιδόνεσσιν ἄνασσε, σέθεν δ᾽ ἐγὼ οὐκ ἀλεγίζω,   180
οὐδ᾽ ὄθομαι κοτέοντος·

Since Apollo is taking Chryseis, Agamemnon says that he will take Briseis,
the woman who is Achilles' prize.

ἀπειλήσω δέ τοι ὧδε·   181
ὡς ἔμ᾽ ἀφαιρεῖται Χρυσηΐδα Φοῖβος Ἀπόλλων,   182
τὴν μὲν ἐγὼ σὺν νηΐ τ᾽ ἐμῇ καὶ ἐμοῖς ἑτάροισι   183
πέμψω, ἐγὼ δέ κ᾽ ἄγω Βρισηΐδα καλλιπάρῃον   184
αὐτὸς ἰὼν κλισίηνδε, τὸ σὸν γέρας, ὄφρ᾽ ἐῢ εἰδῇς   185
ὅσσον φέρτερός εἰμι σέθεν, στυγέῃ δὲ καὶ ἄλλος   186
ἶσον ἐμοὶ φάσθαι καὶ ὁμοιωθήμεναι ἄντην."   187

Achilles, about to draw his sword on Agamemnon, is stopped by the goddess
Athena.

"Ὣς φάτο· Πηλεΐωνι δ᾽ ἄχος γένετ᾽, ἐν δέ οἱ ἦτορ   188
στήθεσσιν λασίοισι διάνδιχα μερμήριξεν,   189

180 **Μυρμιδών, -όνος, ὁ**—Myrmidon. (The Myrmidons were the followers of Achilles.
The name *Myrmidon* comes from μύρμηξ, "ant." Achilles' grandfather, Aeachus,
ruled the island of Aegina. When a plague wiped out the population, Zeus created
people out of ants to repopulate the island. Hence his subjects [and those of his
son, Peleus, and his grandson, Achilles] were known as Myrmidons.)
ἀνάσσω—be king over, rule over (+ dat.); ἄνασσε—present active imperative.
σέθεν—gen. sing. of σύ.
ἀλεγίζω—care about (+ gen.).
Note the emphatic position of the word Μυρμιδόνεσσιν at the beginning of line
180. Agamemnon is stressing to Achilles that though Achilles may rule the
Myrmidons, he should not think he can rule all the Greeks.
181 **ὄθομαι**—care about, trouble oneself (+ gen.).
κοτέω—be angry; κοτέοντος—present active participle, gen. sing. masc. (This
participle agrees with an understood σεῖο, gen. sing. of σύ.)
τοι—dative with ἀπειλήσω.
ὧδε—thus, in this way, in the following way.
182 **ἔμ᾽ ἀφαιρεῖται Χρυσηΐδα**—Both the person being taken away (Χρυσηΐδα) and
the person being deprived (ἔμ᾽) are in the accusative.
183 Agamemnon, with his emphasis (ἐμῇ, ἐμοῖς) on his ship and his companions,
stresses that he is doing this voluntarily and not because he is being forced by
Achilles. His point is rather like a child's "I'm doing this because I want to, not
because you tell me to." The parallels between lines 179 and 183–84 stress the

contrast between what Achilles will be doing with his ships and companions (οἴκαδ᾿ ἰὼν σὺν νηυσί τε σῆς καὶ σοῖς ἑτάροισι) and what Agamemnon will do with his (τὴν μὲν ἐγὼ σὺν νηΐ τ᾿ ἐμῇ καὶ ἐμοῖς ἑτάροισι / πέμψω).

184 πέμπω, πέμψω, ἔπεμψα—send, send home.

ἄγω—subjunctive used to express a future idea; translate as though ἄξω.

Βρισηΐς, -ίδος, ἡ—Briseis, the woman who had previously been allotted to Achilles as his prize.

Ancient commentators pointed out that in lines 182–84, Agamemnon manages to imply that he is superior to Achilles in the way Apollo is superior to him.

185 αὐτός—adds emphasis to ἐγώ in the preceeding line: "I myself."

κλισίη, -ης, ἡ—hut, shelter. (Although it has been frequently translated as "tent," the κλισίη was most likely a small single-roomed wooden hut with a thatched roof, a temporary dwelling for a soldier. Achilles' κλισίη, more elaborate than that of an ordinary soldier, is larger and includes a courtyard and a front porch, according to the description in book 24, lines 449–56.)

τὸ σὸν γέρας—"that prize of yours" (in apposition to Βρισηΐδα, line 184).

εἰδῇς—perfect subjunctive of οἶδα.

186 ὅσσον—by how much, how much.

σέθεν—genitive of comparison: "than you."

στυγέω—be afraid, fear; στυγέῃ—present subjunctive, 3rd pers. sing.

Why are εἰδῇς (line 185) and στυγέῃ (line 186) subjunctive?

187 ἶσον—equally, "as an equal," "on equal terms."

φάσθαι—present middle infinitive of φημί; translate as active.

ὁμοιόω—compare, liken; ὁμοιωθήμεναι—aorist passive infinitive; translate as middle: "to compare himself."

ἄντην—openly.

188 φάτο = ἔφατο.

Πηλεΐων, -ωνος, ὁ—son of Peleus (= Achilles).

ἄχος, -εος, τό—distress, pain, anguish.

γένετ᾿ = ἐγένετο.

ἐν—translate with στήθεσσιν in the next line.

ἦτορ, -ορος, τό—heart.

οἱ ἦτορ—"his heart"; οἱ is a dative of interest.

189 λάσιος, -η, -ον—hairy, shaggy.

διάνδιχα—between two ways, between two courses.

μερμηρίζω, (aor.) ἐμερμήριξα—ponder, think over, consider, "waver," "be torn"; μερμήριξεν = ἐμερμήριξεν.

Scanning Notes

182 The υ in Χρυσηΐδα is long.

The α in Ἀπόλλων is long, but the first syllable is scanned short. A long vowel that does not receive the ictus can be scanned short.

184 The first ι in Βρισηΐδα is long.

ἢ ὅ γε φάσγανον ὀξὺ ἐρυσσάμενος παρὰ μηροῦ   190
τοὺς μὲν ἀναστήσειεν, ὁ δ' Ἀτρεΐδην ἐναρίζοι,   191
ἦε χόλον παύσειεν ἐρητύσειέ τε θυμόν.   192
ἦος ὁ ταῦθ' ὥρμαινε κατὰ φρένα καὶ κατὰ θυμόν,   193
ἕλκετο δ' ἐκ κολεοῖο μέγα ξίφος, ἦλθε δ' Ἀθήνη   194
οὐρανόθεν· πρὸ γὰρ ἦκε θεὰ λευκώλενος Ἥρη,   195
ἄμφω ὁμῶς θυμῷ φιλέουσά τε κηδομένη τε·   196
στῆ δ' ὄπιθεν, ξανθῆς δὲ κόμης ἕλε Πηλεΐωνα   197
οἴῳ φαινομένη· τῶν δ' ἄλλων οὔ τις ὁρᾶτο·   198

---

190   **ἢ**—whether.

    φάσγανον, -ου, τό—sword.

    ὀξύς, -εῖα, -ύ—sharp.

    ἐρύω, ἐρύω, εἴρυσ(σ)α—draw.

    παρά—from (+ gen.).

    μηρός, -οῦ, ὁ—thigh; παρὰ μηροῦ—i.e., from the sheath that hung beside his thigh. Assuming that he was right-handed, his sword would have been in a sheath on his left side, hanging from a strap that passed over his right shoulder (rather than from a belt around the waist).

191   **τούς**—the other Greeks seated with Agamemnon.

    ἀναστήσειεν—aorist optative of ἀνίστημι, 3rd pers. sing.; optative verb in an indirect question.

    There is disagreement over how to translate τοὺς μὲν ἀναστήσειεν. While several scholars argue for "make the others stand up [so Achilles can get to Agamemnon]", others have suggested "dismiss or break up the meeting," "push through the crowd," or "rouse his own men [against Agamemnon]." An ancient commentator, probably the second century B.C. Alexandrian scholar Aristarchus, suggested "rouse the other Greeks [against Agamemnon]."

    ἐναρίζω—kill; ἐναρίζοι—optative verb in an indirect question. While ἐναρίζω was used to mean "kill," its actual meaning was "strip a slain enemy of his weapons and armor." By using this word here, Homer may be suggesting that Achilles is considering a way to take material possessions from Agamemnon to get back at Agamemnon for taking away his property (Briseis).

192   **ἦε**—or.

    παύω, παύσω, ἔπαυσα—stop, restrain; παύσειεν—optative verb in an indirect question.

    ἐρητύω, (aor.) ἠρήτυσα—hold back, restrain; ἐρητύσειε—optative verb in an indirect question.

    θυμόν—"feelings," "emotions."

193   **ἦος**—while.

    ταῦθ'= ταῦτα.

ὁρμαίνω, (aor.) ὥρμηνα—debate, turn over (in the mind), ponder; ὥρμαινε—imperfect.

κατά—"down through," "in."

194 ἕλκω—draw; ἕλκετο—imperfect.

κολεόν, -οῦ, τό—sheath or scabbard (of a sword).

ξίφος, -εος, τό—sword.

δ᾽—"then."

Ἀθήνη, -ης, ἡ—Athena, goddess of the arts and war. (She supports the Greeks in the Trojan War.)

195 οὐρανός, -οῦ, ὁ—the heavens, the sky; οὐρανόθεν—from the sky. (The suffix -θεν indicates "place from": οἴκοθεν—from home; Τροίηθεν—from Troy.)

πρό—(adv.) forth.

ἵημι, ἥσω, ἧκα—send.

The selection of tenses in lines 193–95 is most effective. The imperfect tenses describing Achilles' actions (ὥρμαινε, ἕλκετο) and aorists (ἦλθε, ἧκε) used in connection with Athena's arrival paint a picture of Achilles in the process of pondering and drawing his sword when Athena suddenly and dramatically arrives.

196 ἄμφω—(acc. dual) both; refers to Agamemnon and Achilles. It is the object of both φιλέουσα and κηδομένη. Its case is governed by φιλέουσα, since κηδομένη would take a genitive object.

ὁμῶς—together, alike, equally.

θυμῷ—What use of the dative is this?

φιλέω, φιλήσω, ἐφίλησα—love, hold dear; φιλέουσα—present active participle, nom. sing. fem.

197 ἵστημι, στήσω, ἔστησα or ἔστην—stand; στῆ = ἔστη.

ὄπιθεν—behind.

ξανθός, -ή, -όν—blond, reddish yellow.

κόμη, -ης, ἡ—hair; κόμης—"by his hair"; partitive genitive, indicating the part touched, seized, etc.

ἕλε—from αἱρέω.

198 οἴῳ—"to [him] alone."

φαίνω—show, reveal, shine; *middle and passive*—appear, be visible, shine.

ὁρᾶτο—imperfect middle; translate as active.

Scanning Notes

192 The υ in ἐρητύσειε is long.

193 The υ in θυμόν is long.

195 The α in θεά is long.

196 The υ in θυμῷ is long.

Achilles tells Athena he intends to kill Agamemnon.

θάμβησεν δ᾽ Ἀχιλεύς, μετὰ δ᾽ ἐτράπετ᾽, αὐτίκα δ᾽ ἔγνω   199
Παλλάδ᾽ Ἀθηναίην· δεινὼ δέ οἱ ὄσσε φάανθεν·   200
καί μιν φωνήσας ἔπεα πτερόεντα προσηύδα·   201
"τίπτ᾽ αὖτ᾽, αἰγιόχοιο Διὸς τέκος, εἰλήλουθας;   202
ἦ ἵνα ὕβριν ἴδῃ Ἀγαμέμνονος Ἀτρεΐδαο;   203
ἀλλ᾽ ἔκ τοι ἐρέω, τὸ δὲ καὶ τελέεσθαι ὀΐω·   204
ἧς ὑπεροπλίῃσι τάχ᾽ ἄν ποτε θυμὸν ὀλέσσῃ."   205

Athena urges Achilles not to resort to violence.

Τὸν δ᾽ αὖτε προσέειπε θεὰ γλαυκῶπις Ἀθήνη·   206
"ἦλθον ἐγὼ παύσουσα τὸ σὸν μένος, αἴ κε πίθηαι,   207
οὐρανόθεν· πρὸ δέ μ᾽ ἧκε θεὰ λευκώλενος Ἥρη   208

---

199   **θαμβέω, θαμβήσω, ἐθάμβησα**—wonder, be astonished, be amazed; θάμβησεν
       = ἐθάμβησεν.

       μετατρέπομαι—turn around, turn toward; μετὰ . . . ἐτράπετ᾽ = μετὰ . . .
       ἐτράπετο—aorist. (What is this "splitting" of a compound verb called? Why is
       it an inappropriate name?)

       γιγνώσκω, γνώσομαι, ἔγνων—know, recognize; ἔγνω—aorist active, 3rd pers.
       sing.

200   **Παλλάς, -άδος, ἡ**—Pallas, a name given to Athena; Παλλάδ᾽ = Παλλάδα. (The
       name *Pallas* is perhaps derived from πάλλω ["wield" or "brandish," as a spear
       or a shield]. It may be an older word for "maiden" or "virgin," virginity being
       one of Athena's attributes. Or it may come from Pallas, a friend whom Athena
       accidentally killed and whose name she took in her friend's honor.)

       Ἀθηναίη = Ἀθήνη.

       δεινώ—nom. dual.

       οἱ—"her" (What use of the dative is this?)

       φάανθεν = ἐφάνθησαν—aorist passive of φαίνω, 3rd pers. plur.

       δεινὼ δέ οἱ ὄσσε φάανθεν—"her eyes flashed dreadfully" (literally, "her ter-
       rible eyes shone"). (A dual subject [ὄσσε] may have a plural verb.)

201   **μιν**—"her."

       φωνέω, φωνήσω, ἐφώνησα—raise the voice, speak; φωνήσας—aorist active
       participle, nom. plur. masc.

       πτερόεις, -εσσα, -εν—winged.

       προσαυδάω—speak to, address (can take two accusatives, as here: he spoke
       ἔπεα πτερόεντα to μιν); προσηύδα—imperfect active, 3rd pers. sing.

       ἔπεα πτερόεντα—"winged words"; poetic phrase conveying the idea of words
       flying through the air from the speaker to the listener.

202   τίπτ'= τίπτε—why?

αὖτ'= αὖτε—but (can express a feeling of irritation, vexation, or impatience).

αἰγίοχος, -η, -ον—aegis-holding, aegis-bearing. (The aegis is Zeus's shield, which he often allows Athena to carry. With the head of the Gorgon Medusa [the monstrous woman with snakes for hair whose look turned men to stone and who was killed by Perseus] mounted on it, the aegis creates terror among men.)

τέκος, -εος, τό—child, offspring.

εἰλήλουθας—perfect active of ἔρχομαι, 2nd pers. sing.

203   ἦ—indicates a question.

ἵνα—so that, in order that.

ὕβρις, -ιος, ἡ—arrogance, insolence.

ἴδη—aorist middle subjunctive of ὁράω, 2nd pers. sing.; ἵνα . . . ἴδη—purpose clause.

204   ἐξερέω (future)—speak out, say, tell; ἔκ . . . ἐρέω—tmesis.

τελέεσθαι—future middle infinitive of τελείω; translate as passive.

τὸ δὲ καὶ τελέεσθαι ὀΐω—"and I think that it will be accomplished."

205   ὅς, ἥ, ὅν—his own, her own, its own.

ὑπεροπλίαι, -ῶν, αἱ—arrogance, arrogant behavior, presumption; ἧς ὑπεροπλίησι—dative of cause: "because of his arrogant behavior."

τάχ'= τάχα—soon, quickly.

θυμόν—"life."

ὄλλυμι, ὀλέσ(σ)ω, ὤλεσ(σ)α—lose; ὀλέσσῃ—aorist active subjunctive, 3rd pers. sing.; a subjunctive with ἄν used to convey a future idea.

206   γλαυκῶπις, -ιδος—gleaming-eyed, bright-eyed (possibly "gray-eyed," "green-eyed," or "owl-eyed").

207   παύσουσα—What idea does the future participle express here?

τὸ σὸν μένος—"this anger of yours."

αἴ κε—if only, in the hope that (+ subjunctive).

πίθηαι = πίθῃ (originally πίθησαι)—aorist middle subjunctive of πείθω, 2nd pers. sing.

208–9   Compare lines 208–9 to lines 195–96.

Scanning Notes

201   The α in φωνήσας is long.

You would expect the final syllable of πτερόεντα to be scanned long because it is followed by two consonants. However, if the first consonant is a mute or stop (π, β, φ, κ, γ, χ, τ, δ, or θ) and the second is either λ or ρ, the preceding syllable can be scanned short, as it is here.

203   The second α in Ἀτρεῖδαο is long.

204   The ι in ὀΐω is long.

205   The ι in ὑπεροπλίησι and the υ in θυμόν are long.

206   The α in θεά is long.

208   The α in θεά is long.

ἄμφω ὁμῶς θυμῷ φιλέουσά τε κηδομένη τε· 209
ἀλλ' ἄγε λῆγ' ἔριδος, μηδὲ ξίφος ἕλκεο χειρί· 210
ἀλλ' ἤτοι ἔπεσιν μὲν ὀνείδισον ὡς ἔσεταί περ· 211
ὧδε γὰρ ἐξερέω, τὸ δὲ καὶ τετελεσμένον ἔσται· 212
καί ποτέ τοι τρὶς τόσσα παρέσσεται ἀγλαὰ δῶρα 213
ὕβριος εἵνεκα τῆσδε· σὺ δ' ἴσχεο, πείθεο δ' ἡμῖν." 214

Achilles agrees to be guided by the goddess, and Athena returns to Olympus.

Τὴν δ' ἀπαμειβόμενος προσέφη πόδας ὠκὺς Ἀχιλλεύς· 215
"χρὴ μὲν σφωΐτερόν γε, θεά, ἔπος εἰρύσσασθαι 216
καὶ μάλα περ θυμῷ κεχολωμένον· ὣς γὰρ ἄμεινον· 217
ὅς κε θεοῖς ἐπιπείθηται, μάλα τ' ἔκλυον αὐτοῦ." 218
Ἦ καὶ ἐπ' ἀργυρέῃ κώπῃ σχέθε χεῖρα βαρεῖαν, 219
ἂψ δ' ἐς κουλεὸν ὦσε μέγα ξίφος, οὐδ' ἀπίθησε 220
μύθῳ Ἀθηναίης· ἡ δ' Οὐλυμπόνδε βεβήκει 221
δώματ' ἐς αἰγιόχοιο Διὸς μετὰ δαίμονας ἄλλους. 222

---

210 **λήγω**—stop, cease, leave off (+ gen.); λῆγ' = λῆγε—present active imperative.

ἕλκω—draw; ἕλκεο—present middle imperative: "continue to draw"; ἕλκεο = ἕλκου (originally ἕλκεσο). (Watch for -εο rather than -ου as a present middle imperative ending in Homer.)

χειρί—dative of means.

211 **ἔπεσιν**—dative of means.

ὀνειδίζω, (aor.) **ὠνείδισα**—reproach; ὀνείδισον—aorist active imperative.

ὡς—how.

ἔσεται = ἔσται—future of εἰμί.

περ—adds emphasis to ὡς ἔσεται.

ἔπεσιν μὲν ὀνείδισον ὡς ἔσεταί περ—"reproach [him] with words [telling him] how it will be."

212 **ὧδε**—thus, so, in this way.

καί—"too," "also."

τετελεσμένον—perfect passive participle.

Compare this line with line 204. How do they differ?

213 **τρίς**—three times, thrice.

τόσσος, -η, -ον—so many.

πάρειμι, παρέσσομαι—be present, be at hand.

δῶρον, -ου, τό—gift.

214 **ἴσχω**—hold back, restrain; ἴσχεο—present middle imperative.

πείθεο—present middle imperative of πείθω.

ἡμῖν—refers to Athena and Hera.

215 Compare this line with line 84. What's the only difference?

216 χρή—(impersonal) there is need, [one] ought.

σφῶϊτερος, -η, -ον—of you two, of you both.

ἔπος—"command."

ἐρύομαι, (aor.) εἰρυσσάμην—respect.

217 καὶ μάλα περ—"even though very."

ὡς γὰρ ἄμεινόν [ἐστιν].

218 ὅς—"he who," "whoever."

ἐπιπείθομαι—obey (+ dat.); ἐπιπείθηται—present subjunctive in a present general conditional relative clause.

μάλα—certainly.

τ'—τε is not translated; it marks this clause as a common or proverbial statement.

ἔκλυον—the gods are the subject of this verb. (ἔκλυον is a gnomic aorist, i.e., an aorist verb used in a statement of a general truth; translate as present tense.)

219 ἦ—he spoke.

ἀργυρέη—i.e., silver-studded or decorated with silver.

κώπη, -ης, ἡ—handle, hilt [of a sword].

σχέθε = ἔσχεθε—aorist active of ἔχω, 3rd pers. sing.: "kept," "held," "restrained."

220 ἄψ—back, back again.

ἐς—into, to (+ acc.).

κουλεόν, -οῦ, τό—sheath or scabbard (of a sword).

ὠθέω, (aor.) ἔωσα—push, thrust; ὦσε = ἔωσε.

ἀπιθέω, (aor.) ἠπίθησα—disobey (+ dat.); ἀπίθησε—unaugmented aorist.

221 βεβήκει = ἐβεβήκει—pluperfect of βαίνω; "she had set out" = "she was gone."

222 δώματ'= δώματα; plural but translate singular.

μετά—to, into the midst of, to join (+ acc.).

δαίμων, -ονος, ὁ, ἡ—god, goddess.

Athena's intervention has been interpreted in different ways. Some suggest she is merely a symbol of Achilles' better judgment, which prevents him from killing Agamemnon. Others see the goddess's actions (pulling Achilles' hair and persuading him not to attack Agamemnon) as literal actions vital for the plot. According to this view, Achilles' judgment has led him to the decision to attack Agamemnon, and Athena must stop him to avoid disaster for the Greeks.

Scanning Notes

209 The υ in θυμῷ is long.

216 The α in θεά is long.

217 The υ in θυμῷ is long.

221 The υ in μύθῳ is long.

Achilles taunts Agamemnon, accusing him of cowardice and greed.

Πηλεΐδης δ᾽ ἐξαῦτις ἀταρτηροῖς ἐπέεσσιν   223
Ἀτρεΐδην προσέειπε, καὶ οὔ πω λῆγε χόλοιο·   224
"οἰνοβαρές, κυνὸς ὄμματ᾽ ἔχων, κραδίην δ᾽ ἐλάφοιο,   225
οὔτε ποτ᾽ ἐς πόλεμον ἅμα λαῷ θωρηχθῆναι   226
οὔτε λόχονδ᾽ ἰέναι σὺν ἀριστήεσσιν Ἀχαιῶν   227
τέτληκας θυμῷ· τὸ δέ τοι κῆρ εἴδεται εἶναι.   228
ἦ πολὺ λώϊόν ἐστι κατὰ στρατὸν εὐρὺν Ἀχαιῶν   229
δῶρ᾽ ἀποαιρεῖσθαι ὅς τις σέθεν ἀντίον εἴπῃ·   230
δημοβόρος βασιλεύς, ἐπεὶ οὐτιδανοῖσιν ἀνάσσεις·   231
ἦ γὰρ ἄν, Ἀτρεΐδη, νῦν ὕστατα λωβήσαιο.   232

Achilles swears that the Greeks will one day miss him, when they are being slaughtered by Hector, and that Agamemnon will deeply regret treating him so poorly.

ἀλλ᾽ ἔκ τοι ἐρέω καὶ ἐπὶ μέγαν ὅρκον ὀμοῦμαι·   233
ναὶ μὰ τόδε σκῆπτρον, τὸ μὲν οὔ ποτε φύλλα καὶ ὄζους   234

---

223 **ἐξαῦτις**—again.
      ἀταρτηρός, -ή, -όν—harsh, abusive.
      ἐπέεσσιν = ἔπεσιν—dative of means.
225 **οἰνοβαρής, -ές**—wine guzzler, drunk (οἶνος, "wine," + βαρύς, "heavy"); οἰνο-
      βαρές—vocative.
      κύων, κυνός, ὁ—dog. (The dog is used here as an insult, as in line 159, when
      Achilles called Agamemnon κυνῶπα, "dog-face.")
      ὄμμα, -ατος, τό—eye; ὄμματ᾽ = ὄμματα.
      κραδίη, -ης, ἡ—heart.
      ἔλαφος, -ου, ὁ, ἡ—deer. (The deer is used as a symbol of cowardice.)
226 **ἐς πόλεμον**—"for battle."
      θωρήσσω, (aor.) **ἐθώρηξα**, (aor. pass.) **ἐθωρήχθην**—arm; *middle and passive*—
      arm oneself, put on a breastplate (θώρηξ); θωρηχθῆναι—aorist passive infini-
      tive.
227 **λόχος, -ου, ὁ**—ambush; λόχονδ᾽ = λόχονδε—"into an ambush."
      ἰέναι—present infinitive of εἶμι.
      ἀριστεύς, -ῆος, ὁ—best man, chief, leader.
228 **τέτληκα** (perfect; translate as present)—dare, venture, have the courage.
      κῆρ, κηρός, ἡ—death, destruction.
      εἴδομαι—seem.
      "This [i.e., arming for battle and going into an ambush] seems dangerous [liter-
      ally, "to be destruction"] to you."

229 πολύ—much, by far.

λωΐων, -ον—better, preferable.

εὐρύς, -εῖα, -ύ—wide, broad.

230 δῶρ᾽= δῶρα.

ἀποαιρεῖσθαι—present middle infinitive of ἀφαιρέω.

ὅς τις—"whoever."

δῶρ᾽ ἀποαιρεῖσθαι ὅς τις . . .—"to take gifts [from] whoever . . ."

σέθεν—gen. sing. of σύ.

ἀντίον—against (+ gen.).

231 δημοβόρος, -ον—devouring the people's goods, devouring the people's property (literally, "people-devouring").

δημοβόρος βασιλεύς—nominative used for vocative.

οὐτιδανός, -ή, -όν—good-for-nothing, worthless.

"You king who devours the property of others, since you are the ruler of worthless men [who let you get away with it]."

232 ἦ γὰρ ἄν—"otherwise".

ὕστατος, -η, -ον—last; ὕστατα—neuter adjective used as an adverb.

λωβάομαι, (aor.) ἐλωβησάμην—maltreat, outrage, wrong; λωβήσαιο—aorist optative, 2nd pers. sing.; a potential optative, which expresses something that, in the opinion of the speaker, is a future possibility or likelihood. "Otherwise, son of Atreus, you might now have committed this outrage for the last time."

233 ἐκ . . . ἐρέω—tmesis.

ἐπόμνυμι, ἐπομοῦμαι—swear; ἐπὶ . . . ὀμοῦμαι—tmesis.

ὅρκος, -ου, ὁ—oath.

234 ναί—yes.

σκῆπτρον—This is not Achilles' staff but the one that the person addressing the assembly held, signifying that he "had the floor" or perhaps that he had something especially important to say.

τό—"this one [which]."

φύλλον, -ου, τό—leaf.

ὄζος, -ου, ὁ—branch, twig, shoot.

Scanning Notes

226 The last syllable of πόλεμον is scanned long. A short final syllable that receives the ictus can be scanned long.

The α in λαῷ is long.

Line 226 is a spondaic line. What does that mean? How do you think this scansion pattern could contribute to the effectiveness of the line?

228 The υ in θυμῷ is long.

233 The last syllable of ἐπί is scanned long. A short final syllable that ends in a vowel and is followed by a word beginning with μ can be scanned long.

76 *Iliad*, Book 1

φύσει, ἐπεὶ δὴ πρῶτα τομὴν ἐν ὄρεσσι λέλοιπεν,   235
οὐδ' ἀναθηλήσει· περὶ γάρ ῥά ἑ χαλκὸς ἔλεψε   236
φύλλα τε καὶ φλοιόν· νῦν αὖτέ μιν υἷες Ἀχαιῶν   237
ἐν παλάμῃς φορέουσι δικασπόλοι, οἵ τε θέμιστας   238
πρὸς Διὸς εἰρύαται· ὁ δέ τοι μέγας ἔσσεται ὅρκος·   239
ἦ ποτ' Ἀχιλλῆος ποθὴ ἵξεται υἷας Ἀχαιῶν   240
σύμπαντας· τότε δ' οὔ τι δυνήσεαι ἀχνύμενός περ   241
χραισμεῖν, εὖτ' ἂν πολλοὶ ὑφ' Ἕκτορος ἀνδροφόνοιο   242
θνήσκοντες πίπτωσι· σὺ δ' ἔνδοθι θυμὸν ἀμύξεις   243
χωόμενος ὅ τ' ἄριστον Ἀχαιῶν οὐδὲν ἔτισας."   244

Nestor, the aged king of Pylos and a renowned orator, gets up to speak.

Ὣς φάτο Πηλεΐδης, ποτὶ δὲ σκῆπτρον βάλε γαίῃ   245
χρυσείοις ἥλοισι πεπαρμένον, ἕζετο δ' αὐτός·   246

---

235 **φύω, φύσω**—produce, put forth, grow.
    τομή, -ῆς, ἡ—stump, the end left after cutting.
    ὄρος, -εος, τό—mountain.
    λείπω, λείψω, ἔλιπον, λέλοιπα—leave.
236 **ἀναθηλέω, ἀναθηλήσω**—bloom again.
    περιλέπω, περιλέψω—strip off all around from (+ two accusatives); περὶ . . .
    ἔλεψε—tmesis.
    ῥά = ἄρα.
    ἑ—acc. sing. of εἷο—"it."
    χαλκός, -οῦ, ὁ—bronze, "a bronze knife," "a bronze ax."
237 **φλοιός, -οῦ, ὁ**—bark.
    ἑ χαλκὸς ἔλεψε / φύλλα τε καὶ φλοιόν (lines 236–37)—"the bronze knife
    stripped it [of] its leaves and bark."
238 **παλάμη, -ης, ἡ**—palm, hand.
    φορέω—carry.
    δικασπόλος, -ου, ὁ—judge.
    θέμις, θέμιστος, ἡ—law, right.
239 **ἐρύομαι**, (aor.) **εἰρυσσάμην**, (perf.) **εἴρυμαι**—preserve, defend; εἰρύαται =
    εἴρυνται—perfect, 3rd pers. plur.; translate as present.
    "But now the sons of the Achaeans [who act as] the judges who preserve the laws
    [which come] from Zeus carry it in their hands." (lines 237–39)
    τοι—certainly, you may be sure.
    ἔσσεται—future of εἰμί.
240 **ποθή, -ῆς, ἡ**—longing for, yearning for (+ gen.).
    ἵξεται—future of ἱκνέομαι.

υἷας—acc. plur., another third-declension form of υἱός.

241 οὔ τι—"not at all."

δύναμαι, δυνήσομαι—be able; δυνήσεαι = δυνήσει (originally δυνήσεσαι)—future, 2nd pers. sing.

ἀχνύμενος—"even though [you are] distressed."

περ—very (adds emphasis, usually to what comes just before it).

242 χραισμέω—help. (Agamemnon used the same word when threatening Chryses [line 28]. Now he is the one being threatened.)

εὖτ᾽= εὖτε—when; εὖτ᾽ ἄν—whenever.

ὑφ᾽= ὑπό—at the hands of, by (+ gen.).

Ἕκτωρ, -ορος, ὁ—Hector, son of King Priam of Troy and leader of the Trojan forces.

ἀνδροφόνος, -ον—man-slaying.

243 πίπτω—fall, perish, die; πίπτωσι—subjunctive verb in the protasis of a future-more-vivid condition; translate as future.

ἔνδοθι—within; equivalent to ἐν φρεσί—"within [your] breast."

ἀμύσσω, ἀμύξω—tear, scratch.

Ironically, in predicting Greek deaths at Hector's hands, Achilles is also predicting the death of his dear friend Patroclus. Agamemnon may, as he says, tear at the heart within his breast, but so will Achilles in his grief at the death of his friend.

244 ὅ τ᾽= ὅ τε = ὅτι—because, that.

οὐδέν—not at all.

τίω, τίσω, ἔτισα—honor, esteem.

245 ποτί—at, "to" (+ dat.).

As the staff represents the authority of the community, Achilles, by hurling it to the ground, is powerfully emphasizing his rejection of that community (which he feels has treated him unjustly) and his withdrawal from it. Throwing the staff to the ground is an especially abrupt way to conclude an oath and indicates the strength of Achilles' feelings.

246 χρύσειος, -η, -ον—made of gold, golden.

ἧλος, -ου, ὁ—nail, ornamental stud.

πείρω, (aor.) ἔπειρα, (perf. mid./pass.) πέπαρμαι—pierce; πεπαρμένον—perfect passive participle describing σκῆπτρον (line 245).

Scanning Notes

235 The υ in φύσει is long.
243 The υ in θυμόν is long.
244 The ι in ἔτισας is long.
246 The υ in χρυσείοις is long.

Ἀτρεΐδης δ' ἑτέρωθεν ἐμήνιε· τοῖσι δὲ Νέστωρ   247
ἡδυεπὴς ἀνόρουσε, λιγὺς Πυλίων ἀγορητής,   248
τοῦ καὶ ἀπὸ γλώσσης μέλιτος γλυκίων ῥέεν αὐδή·   249
τῷ δ' ἤδη δύο μὲν γενεαὶ μερόπων ἀνθρώπων   250
ἐφθίαθ', οἵ οἱ πρόσθεν ἅμα τράφεν ἠδ' ἐγένοντο   251
ἐν Πύλῳ ἠγαθέῃ, μετὰ δὲ τριτάτοισιν ἄνασσεν·   252
ὅ σφιν ἐϋφρονέων ἀγορήσατο καὶ μετέειπεν·   253

*Nestor points out how happy the quarrel between Agamemnon and Achilles
would make the Trojans if they knew about it.*

"ὦ πόποι, ἦ μέγα πένθος Ἀχαιΐδα γαῖαν ἱκάνει·   254
ἦ κεν γηθήσαι Πρίαμος Πριάμοιό τε παῖδες   255
ἄλλοι τε Τρῶες μέγα κεν κεχαροίατο θυμῷ,   256
εἰ σφῶϊν τάδε πάντα πυθοίατο μαρναμένοιϊν,   257
οἳ περὶ μὲν βουλὴν Δαναῶν, περὶ δ' ἐστὲ μάχεσθαι.   258

---

247   **ἑτέρωθεν**—from the other side, on the other side.
       μηνίω, μηνίσω, ἐμήνισα—be angry.
       τοῖσι—"before them."
       Νέστωρ, -ορος, ὁ—Nestor, king of Pylos and the oldest of the Greek leaders.
248   **ἡδυεπής, -ές**—sweet-speaking.
       ἀνορούω, (aor.) **ἀνόρουσα**—spring up, jump up.
       λιγύς, -εῖα, -ύ—clear-voiced.
       Πύλιοι, -ων, οἱ—Pylians, people of Pylos (a kingdom on the southwest coast of
       the Peloponnese).
       ἀγορητής, -οῦ, ὁ—speaker, orator.
249   **τοῦ**—the article used as a relative pronoun (= οὗ)—"whose."
       γλῶσσα, -ης, ἡ—tongue; τοῦ καὶ ἀπὸ γλώσσης—"from whose tongue."
       μέλι, -ιτος, τό—honey; μέλιτος—genitive of comparison.
       γλυκύς, -εῖα, -ύ—sweet; γλυκίων, -ον—comparative.
       ῥέω—flow, run, pour; ῥέεν—unaugmented imperfect, 3rd pers. sing.
       αὐδή, -ῆς, ἡ—speech, voice.
250   **τῷ**—"for him."
       ἤδη—already.
       γενεή, -ῆς, ἡ—generation (a time period of about thirty years).
       μέροψ, -οπος—a word of unknown meaning; possibly "endowed with speech."
251   **φθίνω, φθίσω, ἔφθισα, ἔφθιμαι**—die, perish; ἐφθίαθ' = ἐφθίατο—pluperfect,
       3rd pers. plur.
       οἵ—relative pronoun, refers to ἀνθρώπων (line 250).
       οἱ—him (dat. with ἅμα).

πρόσθεν—before, formerly.

τρέφω, (aor.) ἔτραφον, (aor. pass.) ἐτράφην—nurture, bring up; τράφεν = ἐτράφησαν—aorist passive, 3rd pers. plur.

Logically, men would have to be born (ἐγένοντο) before they were brought up (τράφεν). Here, the verbs are reversed in a figure of speech called *hysteron proteron* (literally, "the latter the former"), which puts the more significant word first. Translate: "who were born and brought up with him . . ."

252   Πύλος, -ου, ἡ—Pylos, the kingdom of Nestor.

ἠγάθεος, -η, -ον—very sacred, very holy.

μετά—among (+ dat.).

τρίτατος, -η, -ον—third; μετὰ . . . τριτάτοισιν—"among the third [generation]."

ἄνασσεν = ἤνασσεν—imperfect.

If he has outlived two generations and is ruling in the third, this makes Nestor over sixty years old.

254   πόποι—alas! for shame!

πένθος, -εος, τό—grief, sadness.

Ἀχαΐς, -ΐδος—(fem. adj.) Achaean.

ἱκάνω—come to.

255   γηθέω, (aor.) ἐγήθησα—rejoice, be glad; γηθήσαι—aorist optative, 3rd pers. sing. (agrees with Πρίαμος but also goes with Πριάμοιό τε παῖδες).

256   κεχαροίατο = κεχάροιντο—aorist optative, 3rd pers. plur.

θυμῷ—"in their hearts."

257   σφῶϊν—gen. dual of σύ: "you two."

τάδε πάντα—accusative of respect.

πεύθομαι, (aor.) ἐπυθόμην—learn, hear (the person or thing heard or learned about is in the genitive); πυθοίατο = πύθοιντο—aorist optative, 3rd pers. plur.

μάρναμαι—fight; μαρναμένοιϊν—present middle participle, gen. dual.

εἰ σφῶϊν τάδε πάντα πυθοίατο μαρναμένοιϊν—"if they should learn of the two of you fighting about all this."

ἦ κεν γηθήσαι . . . μαρναμένοιϊν (lines 255–57)—a future-less-vivid condition.

258   οἵ—relative pronoun: "you who."

περίειμι—be superior, excel; περὶ . . . ἐστέ—tmesis; present, 2nd pers. plur. (the person[s] excelled will be in the genitive).

βουλή, -ῆς, ἡ—counsel, advice; βουλήν—accusative of respect.

μάχεσθαι—an infinitive used as an accusative of respect: "in battle," "in fighting."

Scanning Notes

254   The α in ἱκάνει is long.

256   The υ in θυμῷ is long.

Nestor says that better men than Agamemnon and Achilles have taken his advice in the past.

ἀλλὰ πίθεσθ'· ἄμφω δὲ νεωτέρω ἐστὸν ἐμεῖο· 259
ἤδη γάρ ποτ' ἐγὼ καὶ ἀρείοσιν ἠέ περ ὑμῖν 260
ἀνδράσιν ὡμίλησα, καὶ οὔ ποτέ μ' οἵ γ' ἀθέριζον. 261
οὐ γάρ πω τοίους ἴδον ἀνέρας οὐδὲ ἴδωμαι, 262
οἷον Πειρίθοόν τε Δρύαντά τε, ποιμένα λαῶν, 263
Καινέα τ' Ἐξάδιόν τε καὶ ἀντίθεον Πολύφημον, 264
Θησέα τ' Αἰγεΐδην, ἐπιείκελον ἀθανάτοισι· 265
κάρτιστοι δὴ κεῖνοι ἐπιχθονίων τράφεν ἀνδρῶν· 266
κάρτιστοι μὲν ἔσαν καὶ καρτίστοις ἐμάχοντο, 267
φηρσὶν ὀρεσκῴοισι, καὶ ἐκπάγλως ἀπόλεσσαν. 268
καὶ μὲν τοῖσιν ἐγὼ μεθομίλεον ἐκ Πύλου ἐλθών, 269
τηλόθεν ἐξ ἀπίης γαίης· καλέσαντο γὰρ αὐτοί· 270

259 **πίθεσθ'**= πίθεσθε—aorist middle imperative, 2nd pers. plur.: "be persuaded."
   ἄμφω—both (nom. dual).
   νέος, -η, -ον—young; νεωτέρω—comparative; nom. dual.
   ἐστόν—2nd pers. dual of εἰμί.
   ἐμεῖο—What use of the genitive is this?
260 **ἤδη ... ποτ'**—"before," "previously."
   καί—even.
   ἀρείων, -ον—better, superior; ἀρείοσιν—dat. plur.
   ἠέ—than.
   ὑμῖν—dative by attraction to ἀρείοσιν ... ἀνδράσιν; ἠέ περ ὑμῖν = ἠέ περ ὑμεῖς ἐστε.
261 **ὁμιλέω**, (aor.) **ὡμίλησα**—associate with (+ dat.).
   ἀθερίζω—disregard, treat with disrespect; ἀθέριζον = ἠθέριζον.
262 **τοῖος, -η, -ον**—such.
   ἀνέρας = ἄνδρας (acc. plur. of ἀνήρ).
   ἴδωμαι—aorist subjunctive of ὁράω; translate as future.
263 **οἷος, -η, -ον**—such as.
   Πειρίθοος, -ου, ὁ—Pirithous, king of the Lapiths (a people of northern Thessaly) and a friend of the Athenian hero Theseus.
   Δρύας, -αντος, ὁ—Dryas, a Lapith leader.
   ποιμήν, -ένος, ὁ—shepherd, guardian.
264 **Καινεύς, -ῆος, ὁ**—Caeneus, a Lapith leader.
   Ἐξάδιος, -ου, ὁ—Exadius, a Lapith leader.
   ἀντίθεος, -η, -ον—godlike.
   Πολύφημος, -ου, ὁ—Polyphemus, a Lapith leader.

265   Θησεύς, -ῆος, ὁ—Theseus, a great Athenian hero.

Αἰγεΐδης, -αο, ὁ—son of Aegeus (= Theseus).

ἐπιείκελος, -ον—like (+ dat.).

ἀθάνατος, -η, -ον—immortal.

Line 265 is not contained in the best manuscripts of the *Iliad,* nor is it referred to in the scholia (annotations and explanations of classical texts written by ancient scholars and copied with the texts in manuscripts). Some scholars suspect that it was not originally part of the *Iliad* but was interpolated or added later, perhaps by or for Athenians, so as to include mention of the great Athenian hero Theseus.

266   κάρτιστος, -η, -ον—strongest, mightiest, best. Nestor's repetition of this word three times in this line and the next adds emphasis to his point.

κεῖνος, -η, -ο (= ἐκεῖνος, -η, -ο)—that, that one; *plur.*—those.

ἐπιχθόνιος, -ον—upon the earth, earthly; ἐπί + χθών (earth). "Those [were] the best earthly men [i.e., mortals, rather than gods] [ever] brought up."

267   μέν = μήν—indeed.

ἔσαν = ἦσαν—imperfect of εἰμί.

268   φήρ, φηρός, ὁ, ἡ—wild animal, beast.

ὀρεσκῷος, -ον—having mountain lairs (ὄρος means "mountain").

φηρσὶν ὀρεσκῴοισι—in apposition to καρτίστοις (line 267) and referring to the centaurs, creatures who were half man and half horse. Nestor is talking about the fight between the Lapiths and the centaurs (a subject portrayed in sculptures on the temple of Zeus at Olympia and on the Parthenon in Athens). At the wedding feast of the Lapith king Pirithous, the centaurs got drunk and tried to rape the bride and other Lapith women. The human heroes who were there for the wedding fought and defeated the centaurs.

ἐκπάγλως—exceedingly, terribly.

ἀπόλεσσαν = ἀπώλεσαν.

καὶ ἐκπάγλως ἀπόλεσσαν—"and they destroyed [them] utterly."

269   μεθομιλέω—associate with (+ dat.); μεθομίλεον = μεθωμίλουν—imperfect.

270   τηλόθεν—far, from far away.

ἄπιος, -η, -ον—distant.

καλέσαντο = ἐκαλέσαντο.

Scanning Notes

260   The υ in ὑμῖν is long.

261   The ι in ὡμίλησα is long.

262   The first α in ἀνέρας is long.

263   The α in λαῶν is long.

265   The first α in ἀθανάτοισι is long.

269   The ι in μεθομίλεον is long.

καὶ μαχόμην κατ᾿ ἔμ᾿ αὐτὸν ἐγώ· κείνοισι δ᾿ ἂν οὔ τις   271
τῶν οἳ νῦν βροτοί εἰσιν ἐπιχθόνιοι μαχέοιτο·   272
καὶ μέν μευ βουλέων ξύνιεν πείθοντό τε μύθῳ·   273

Nestor urges Agamemnon not to take Briseis from Achilles, and he urges
Achilles to respect Agamemnon's position as king.

ἀλλὰ πίθεσθε καὶ ὔμμες, ἐπεὶ πείθεσθαι ἄμεινον·   274
μήτε σὺ τόνδ᾿ ἀγαθός περ ἐὼν ἀποαίρεο κούρην,   275
ἀλλ᾿ ἔα, ὥς οἱ πρῶτα δόσαν γέρας υἷες Ἀχαιῶν·   276
μήτε σύ, Πηλεΐδη, ἔθελ᾿ ἐριζέμεναι βασιλῆϊ   277
ἀντιβίην, ἐπεὶ οὔ ποθ᾿ ὁμοίης ἔμμορε τιμῆς   278
σκηπτοῦχος βασιλεύς, ᾧ τε Ζεὺς κῦδος ἔδωκεν.   279
εἰ δὲ σὺ καρτερός ἐσσι, θεὰ δέ σε γείνατο μήτηρ,   280
ἀλλ᾿ ὅ γε φέρτερός ἐστιν, ἐπεὶ πλεόνεσσιν ἀνάσσει.   281
Ἀτρεΐδη, σὺ δὲ παῦε τεὸν μένος· αὐτὰρ ἔγωγε   282

---

271 **μαχόμην** = ἐμαχόμην.
   κατ᾿ ἔμ᾿ αὐτόν—"by myself." (This may mean Nestor fought as a leader in his
      own right, not as a retainer of another hero.)
   κείνοισι—"with them" (refers to the centaurs); dative with μαχέοιτο in line 272.
272 **βροτός, -οῦ, ὁ**—mortal, mortal man.
   μαχέοιτο—present optative; a potential optative: "could fight."
273 **ξυνίημι**—hear, take heed of (+ gen.); ξύνιεν = ξυνίεσαν—imperfect, 3rd pers.
      plur.
   πείθοντο = ἐπείθοντο.
   μύθῳ—"counsel," "advice."
274 **καί**—"also."
   ὔμμες = ὑμεῖς.
   ἐπεὶ πείθεσθαι ἄμεινόν [ἐστιν].
275 **μήτε**—and not; μήτε . . . μήτε—neither . . . nor.
   σύ—refers to Agamemnon.
   ἀγαθός—"noble" (and therefore powerful).
   περ—although.
   ἐών—present participle of εἰμί, nom. sing. masc.
   ἀποαίρεο—present middle imperative (ἀφαιρέω). (Both the person being taken
      away [κούρην] and the person being deprived [τόνδ᾿] are in the accusative.)
276 **ἐάω**—permit, allow, let, leave, let alone, let be; ἔα = ἔαε—present active imper-
      ative, 2nd pers. sing.; ἔα [κούρην] or ἔα [Ἀχιλλῆα ἔχειν κούρην].
   ὥς—"since."
   οἱ—dat. sing. of εἷο.

δόσαν = ἔδοσαν—aorist active of δίδωμι, 3rd pers. plur.
277 Πηλεΐδη—vocative.
ἔθελ᾿ = ἔθελε—imperative.
ἐρίζω—quarrel with, contend with (+ dat.); ἐριζέμεναι—present active infinitive.
μήτε ... ἔθελ᾿ ἐριζέμεναι—"don't quarrel with."
278 ἀντιβίην—hostilely, antagonistically.
ποθ᾿= ποτε.
ὁμοῖος, -η, -ον—equal, similar.
μείρομαι, (perf.) ἔμμορα—share, receive (+ gen.).
279 σκηπτοῦχος, -ον—scepter-holding, scepter-bearing.
οὔ ποθ᾿ ὁμοίης ἔμμορε τιμῆς / σκηπτοῦχος βασιλεύς (lines 278–79)—i.e., Agamemnon has received greater honor than any other king.
κῦδος, -εος, τό—glory.
280 καρτερός, -ή, -όν—powerful, strong, mighty.
ἐσσι—present of εἰμί, 2nd pers. sing.
γείνομαι, (aor.) ἐγεινάμην—bear, give birth to; γείνατο = ἐγείνατο.
θεά ... μήτηρ—refers to Thetis, Achilles' mother, a sea goddess who will appear shortly.
281 ἀλλ᾿—"yet."
ὅ = Agamemnon.
φέρτερος—"more powerful," "of higher rank."
πλέων, -ον—more (comparative of πολύς).
282 τεός, -ή, -όν—your.
αὐτὰρ ἔγωγε—"indeed, even I myself."

Scanning Notes
273 The -εων in βουλέων is scanned as one long syllable (synizesis).
The υ in μύθῳ is long.
277 The last syllable of Πηλεΐδη and the first syllable of ἔθελ᾿ are scanned together as one long syllable (synizesis). Pronounce as though it were written Πηλεΐδ᾿ ἔθελ᾿.
278 The ι in τιμῆς is long.
280 The α in θεά is long.

λίσσομ' Ἀχιλλῆϊ μεθέμεν χόλον, ὃς μέγα πᾶσιν   283
ἕρκος Ἀχαιοῖσιν πέλεται πολέμοιο κακοῖο."   284

Agamemnon complains that Achilles is arrogant and rude.

Τὸν δ' ἀπαμειβόμενος προσέφη κρείων Ἀγαμέμνων·   285
"ναὶ δὴ ταῦτά γε πάντα, γέρον, κατὰ μοῖραν ἔειπες·   286
ἀλλ' ὅδ' ἀνὴρ ἐθέλει περὶ πάντων ἔμμεναι ἄλλων,   287
πάντων μὲν κρατέειν ἐθέλει, πάντεσσι δ' ἀνάσσειν,   288
πᾶσι δὲ σημαίνειν, ἅ τιν' οὐ πείσεσθαι ὀΐω·   289

---

283 **λίσσομ'** = λίσσομαι; λίσσομ' [σε]. (Homer earlier used the same word when he described Chryses begging the Greeks for his daughter [λίσσετο πάντας Ἀχαιούς, line 15]. Agamemnon also used it when he said he would not beg Achilles to stay [οὐδέ σ' ἔγωγε / λίσσομαι εἵνεκ' ἐμεῖο μένειν, lines 173–74]. Now Nestor is willing to play the suppliant for the sake of harmony among the Greeks.)

Ἀχιλλῆϊ—dative of disadvantage: "against Achilles," "with Achilles."

μεθίημι, μεθήσω, μεθέηκα—give up, dismiss; μεθέμεν = μεθεῖναι—aorist active infinitive.

284 **ἕρκος, -εος, τό**—defense against, barrier, hedge; ἕρκος ... πολέμοιο κακοῖο—"a defense against disastrous war."

πέλομαι—be; πέλεται = ἐστί.

πᾶσιν ... Ἀχαιοῖσιν—dative of advantage: "for all the Greeks."

Nestor's advice seems extremely sensible. Yet neither Agamemnon nor Achilles will do as he suggests. Neither feels he can yield, because that would mean loss of honor. The world of the Homeric heroes is highly competitive, what is called an agonistic society (from ἀγών, "contest" or "struggle"). The goal of the competition is to win honor (τιμή), which is measured in public recognition and visible marks of respect, as shares of booty or prizes or gifts. Acquiring and keeping such possessions is a way to increase fame and glory. To be dishonored or not to be honored would be an unendurable insult. Loss of prestige, power, or property is shameful and anyone who suffers such a loss is judged to be of lesser value. Despite the consequences, Achilles and Agamemnon must maintain their honor. Who is "right" and who is "wrong" in this quarrel have been much debated. Some argue that Achilles is acting like a spoiled child, others that although he is indeed wronged by Agamemnon, his temper and injured pride lead him to forget the duty he owes to the commander of the Greek forces and to take actions that end tragically in the death of his best friend. Still others argue that Achilles is totally justified, does the only thing he can do, and is the only Greek willing to speak out against Agamemnon's injustice. Another suggestion is that Achilles is suffering from combat trauma after nine years of fighting and "loses it," so to speak, when he feels betrayed by his commander.

A key factor in trying to judge Achilles' actions is how one views Agamemnon. Agamemnon's character, his position among the Greeks (supreme king, commander in chief, or simply the organizer of a cooperative effort who happens to have brought more troops than anyone else?), and his role in the *Iliad* are much debated. He has been described as weak, vacillating, insecure, unfair, arrogant, cruel, easily deceived, prone to despair, incompetent, brave, overburdened with leadership, devoted to his brother, imperious, greedy, and unscrupulous. In the Homeric world, the number of followers a leader has is a measure of status, so the fact that Agamemnon has brought the largest number of troops to Troy earns him the position of leader of the entire army (see *Il.* 1.281: ἀλλ᾽ ὅ γε φέρτερός ἐστιν, ἐπεὶ πλεόνεσσιν ἀνάσσει). A good leader, though, would also be valiant in war, leading his men into battle, and generous with gifts and rewards. Achilles questions Agamemnon in both these areas. A leader who is both brave and generous should be able to persuade his men to follow him, something Agamemnon is failing to do with Achilles. But Agamemnon himself is suffering dishonor from the loss of Chryseis, so who is "right" or perhaps "less" wrong here is indeed a thorny question.

286   ναί—yes, in truth, indeed.

     γέρον—vocative. (Agamemnon also addressed Chryses as γέρον (line 26) when he rejected his request.)

     μοῖρα, -ης, ἡ—share, portion, lot, fate; κατὰ μοῖραν—properly, rightly.

     ἔειπες—2nd pers. sing. of εἶπον.

287   ὅδ᾽ ἀνήρ—Agamemnon is so angry or so contemptuous that he cannot even say Achilles' name.

     περίειμι—be superior to (+ gen.); περὶ . . . ἔμμεναι—tmesis; present infinitive.

288   πάντεσσι = πᾶσι—dat. plur.

289   σημαίνω—command, give orders to (+ dat.).

     ἅ—"in which" (accusative of respect; literally, "in respect to which things" [i.e., Achilles' wanting to be in charge]).

     τιν᾽ = τινά—"someone," i.e., Agamemnon.

     πείσεσθαι—future middle infinitive.

     ἅ τιν᾽ οὐ πείσεσθαι ὀΐω—"[and] in this regard I think that someone [meaning himself] will not obey [him]."

     From line 287 to 289, Agamemnon repeats a similar idea four times, using forms of πᾶς in each clause. Several modern scholars have suggested that such repetition shows his extreme, perhaps even out-of-control, anger. As the note in the ancient scholia says: οὐδέποτε γὰρ οἴονται ἱκανῶς εἰρηκέναι οἱ θυμούμενοι [angry men [οἱ θυμούμενοι] never think they have spoken enough].

Scanning Notes

283   The last syllable of Ἀχιλλῆϊ is scanned long. A short final syllable that ends in a vowel and is followed by a word beginning with μ can be scanned long.

289   The ι in ὀΐω is long.

εἰ δέ μιν αἰχμητὴν ἔθεσαν θεοὶ αἰὲν ἐόντες,   290
τοὔνεκά οἱ προθέουσιν ὀνείδεα μυθήσασθαι;"   291

*Achilles declares that he will no longer obey Agamemnon and that while he
will not fight to retain Briseis, he will fight if Agamemnon ever tries to take
anything else away from him.*

Τὸν δ᾽ ἄρ᾽ ὑποβλήδην ἠμείβετο δῖος Ἀχιλλεύς·   292
"ἦ γάρ κεν δειλός τε καὶ οὐτιδανὸς καλεοίμην,   293
εἰ δὴ σοὶ πᾶν ἔργον ὑπείξομαι ὅττι κεν εἴπῃς·   294
ἄλλοισιν δὴ ταῦτ᾽ ἐπιτέλλεο, μὴ γὰρ ἔμοιγε   295
σήμαιν᾽· οὐ γὰρ ἔγωγ᾽ ἔτι σοὶ πείσεσθαι ὀΐω.   296
ἄλλο δέ τοι ἐρέω, σὺ δ᾽ ἐνὶ φρεσὶ βάλλεο σῇσι·   297
χερσὶ μὲν οὔ τοι ἔγωγε μαχήσομαι εἵνεκα κούρης   298
οὔτε σοὶ οὔτε τῳ ἄλλῳ, ἐπεί μ᾽ ἀφέλεσθέ γε δόντες·   299
τῶν δ᾽ ἄλλων ἅ μοί ἐστι θοῇ παρὰ νηΐ μελαίνῃ,   300
τῶν οὐκ ἄν τι φέροις ἀνελὼν ἀέκοντος ἐμεῖο·   301
εἰ δ᾽ ἄγε μὴν πείρησαι, ἵνα γνώωσι καὶ οἵδε·   302

---

290 **αἰχμητής, -ᾶο, ὁ**—warrior, spearman (αἰχμή = spear). The word Agamemnon
      chooses for Achilles (αἰχμητήν, "warrior") is much weaker than the words
      Nestor used to describe him (μέγα πᾶσιν / ἕρκος Ἀχαιοῖσιν [a great defense
      for all the Greeks], lines 283–84). Is Agamemnon trying to downplay Achilles'
      status as a heroic fighter?
      ἔθεσαν = ἔθηκαν.
      αἰέν = αἰεί.
      ἐόντες—present participle (εἰμί).
291 **τοὔνεκα** = τοῦ ἕνεκα.
      οἱ—dat. sing. of εἷο: "for him."
      προθέω—rush forward.
      ὄνειδος, -εος, τό—words of abuse, insult, reproach.
      A literal translation of lines 290–91 would be, "If the always-being gods made
      him a warrior, do insults therefore rush forward for him to speak?" The impli-
      cation is, "Just because the eternal gods made him a warrior, does that give him
      the right to be insulting?"
292 **ὑποβλήδην**—interrupting.
293 **δειλός, -ή, -όν**—cowardly.
      οὐτιδανός, -ή, -όν—good-for-nothing, worthless.
      καλεοίμην—present optative: "I should be called."
294 **πᾶν ἔργον** = everything (accusative of respect).
      ὑπείκω, ὑπείξω—yield, submit.

ὅττι—that.

295 ἐπιτέλλω—order, command (+ dat. and acc.); ἐπιτέλλεο—present middle imperative, 2nd pers. sing.; translate as active.

γάρ—adds emphasis to this clause: "DO NOT . . ."

ἔμοιγε = ἔμοι γε. (The suffix -γε strengthens or emphasizes the word to which it is attached.)

296 σήμαιν' = σήμαινε.

ἔγωγ' = ἔγωγε = ἐγώ γε—"I, at any rate," "I , at least."

οὐ . . . ἔτι—no longer.

Compare Achilles' words here with Agamemnon's in line 289. How are they similar and how different?

297 ἄλλο—"another thing."

εἴρω, ἐρέω—tell, say.

βάλλεο—present middle imperative of βάλλω.

σὺ δ' ἐνὶ φρεσὶ βάλλεο σῇσι—"take it to heart," "turn it over in your mind" (literally, "throw [it] in your heart").

298 χερσί—dative of means.

τοι—certainly, you may be sure.

299 τῷ = τινί—dative sing. of τις.

δόντες—aorist active participle (δίδωμι).

ἐπεί μ' ἀφέλεσθέ γε δόντες—"since you who gave [me the girl] took [her] from me."

300 μοι—dative of possession.

τῶν δ' ἄλλων ἅ μοί ἐστι—"as for the other things that are mine."

θοός, -ή, -όν—swift.

301 τῶν—refers to the τῶν . . . ἄλλων in line 300.

οὐκ ἄν . . . φέροις—"you will not carry [off]. (φέροις is a potential optative used with the force of a threat.)

ἀναιρέω, ἀναιρήσω, ἀνεῖλον—take, seize; ἀνελών—aorist active participle, nom. sing. masc.

ἀέκων, -ουσα, -ον—unwilling.

ἀέκοντος ἐμεῖο—What use of the genitive is this?

302 εἰ δ' ἄγε—come! come on!

μήν—indeed.

πειράω, πειρήσω, ἐπειρησάμην—try; πείρησαι—aorist middle imperative.

γνώωσι—aorist active subjunctive, 3rd pers. plur. from γιγνώσκω; ἵνα γνώωσι—purpose clause.

οἴδε—"these men" (referring to the rest of the Greeks).

Scanning Notes

291 The υ in μυθήσασθαι is long.

296 The ι in ὀΐω is long.

αἶψά τοι αἷμα κελαινὸν ἐρωήσει περὶ δουρί." 303

Following the end of the assembly, Chryseis is sent home, and the army
makes a sacrifice to Apollo.

Ὣς τώ γ᾽ ἀντιβίοισι μαχεσσαμένω ἐπέεσσιν 304
ἀνστήτην, λῦσαν δ᾽ ἀγορὴν παρὰ νηυσὶν Ἀχαιῶν· 305
Πηλεΐδης μὲν ἐπὶ κλισίας καὶ νῆας ἐΐσας 306
ἤϊε σύν τε Μενοιτιάδῃ καὶ οἷς ἑτάροισιν· 307
Ἀτρεΐδης δ᾽ ἄρα νῆα θοὴν ἅλαδε προέρυσσεν, 308
ἐν δ᾽ ἐρέτας ἔκρινεν ἐείκοσιν, ἐς δ᾽ ἑκατόμβην 309
βῆσε θεῷ, ἀνὰ δὲ Χρυσηΐδα καλλιπάρῃον 310
εἷσεν ἄγων· ἐν δ᾽ ἀρχὸς ἔβη πολύμητις Ὀδυσσεύς. 311
    Οἱ μὲν ἔπειτ᾽ ἀναβάντες ἐπέπλεον ὑγρὰ κέλευθα, 312
λαοὺς δ᾽ Ἀτρεΐδης ἀπολυμαίνεσθαι ἄνωγεν· 313
οἱ δ᾽ ἀπελυμαίνοντο καὶ εἰς ἅλα λύματα βάλλον, 314
ἔρδον δ᾽ Ἀπόλλωνι τεληέσσας ἑκατόμβας 315
ταύρων ἠδ᾽ αἰγῶν παρὰ θῖν᾽ ἁλὸς ἀτρυγέτοιο· 316

---

303 **αἶψα**—at once, immediately.
    τοι—you may be sure.
    αἷμα, -ατος, τό—blood.
    κελαινός, -ή, -όν—dark.
    ἐρωέω, ἐρωήσω—flow, rush forth.
    περί—around (+ dat.).
    δόρυ, δουρός, τό—spear.
    How ironic it is that the Greeks, who came to Troy to fight for a stolen woman
(Helen), are now fighting among themselves over another stolen woman (Briseis).
304 **τώ**—nom. dual of ὁ: "these two men."
    ἀντίβιος, -η, -ον—hostile.
    μαχεσσαμένω—aorist participle, nom. dual.
    ἐπέεσσιν = ἔπεσιν.
305 **ἀνστήτην** = ἀνεστήτην—aorist active of ἀνίστημι, 3rd pers. dual.
    λῦσαν = ἔλυσαν—"they dismissed," "they caused [the assembly] to disperse."
306 **ἐπί**—to (+ acc.).
    ἐΐσος, -η, -ον—well-balanced, trim.
307 **Μενοιτιάδης, -αο, ὁ**—son of Menoetius (= Patroclus). (Patroclus is Achilles'
    closest friend. Notice how he alone of Achilles' companions is singled out by
    name, indicating his importance.)
308 **ἅλαδε**—"into the sea."

προερύω, (aor.) προέρυσσα—drag forward, launch; προέρυσσεν—"he caused to be launched." (Agamemnon did not do it personally.)

309   ἐν—in, therein, "in it."

ἐρέτης, -αο, ὁ—rower, oarsman.

κρίνω, κρινέω, ἔκρινα—pick, choose, select.

ἐείκοσι(ν)—twenty.

ἐς—"into it."

310   βῆσε = ἔβησε—"he moved" or "he caused to go."

311   ἕζομαι, (aor.) εἷσα—sit; *with* ἀνά—put on board a ship.

ἀρχός, -οῦ, ὁ—leader.

πολύμητις, -ιος—crafty, shrewd.

ἐν δ᾽ ἀρχὸς ἔβη πολύμητις Ὀδυσσεύς—"and shrewd Odysseus went along as the leader."

312   ἀναβαίνω, ἀναβήσω, ἀνέβησα or ἀνέβην—embark, go on board; ἀναβάντες—aorist active participle.

ἐπιπλέω—sail over.

ὑγρός, -ή, -όν—wet, liquid, watery.

κέλευθος, -ου, ἡ (plural: κέλευθα, -ων, τά)—path, way; ὑγρὰ κέλευθα— "watery ways" (= the sea).

313   ἀπολυμαίνομαι—purify or cleanse oneself of pollution (by washing).

ἀνώγω, ἀνώξω, ἤνωξα—order, command; ἄνωγεν—unaugmented imperfect; translate as aorist.

314   λῦμα, -ατος, τό—dirt, defilement, filth, what is washed off.

The army is literally washing and symbolically cleansing itself of the pollution of the plague.

315   ἔρδω, ἔρξω, ἔρξα—do, make, sacrifice.

τελήεις, -εσσα, -εν—perfect, unblemished.

316   θίς, θινός, ἡ—shore; θῖν᾽ = θῖνα; παρὰ θῖν᾽—"along the shore."

ἀτρύγετος, -ον—There is uncertainty about the meaning of this word. It is usually translated "barren," "unfruitful," or "unharvested" (contrasting the sea to the earth). Other suggested meanings are "tireless," "restless," "noisy," "enduring," or "never runs dry" (in contrast to pools or rivers, which can dry up).

Scanning Notes

306   The ι in ἐΐσας is long.

309   The α in ἐρέτας and the ι in ἔκρινεν are long.

310   The υ in Χρυσηΐδα is long.

313   The α in λαούς and the υ in ἀπολυμαίνεσθαι are long.

314   The υ in ἀπελυμαίνοντο and the υ in λύματα are long.

315   The α in Ἀπόλλωνι and the α in τελήεσσας are long.

κνίση δ᾿ οὐρανὸν ἷκεν ἑλισσομένη περὶ καπνῷ.   317

Agamemnon sends the heralds Talthybius and Eurybates to take Briseis from Achilles.

Ὣς οἱ μὲν τὰ πένοντο κατὰ στρατόν· οὐδ᾿ Ἀγαμέμνων   318
λῆγ᾿ ἔριδος, τὴν πρῶτον ἐπηπείλησ᾿ Ἀχιλῆϊ,   319
ἀλλ᾿ ὅ γε Ταλθύβιόν τε καὶ Εὐρυβάτην προσέειπε,   320
τώ οἱ ἔσαν κήρυκε καὶ ὀτρηρὼ θεράποντε·   321
"ἔρχεσθον κλισίην Πηληϊάδεω Ἀχιλῆος·   322
χειρὸς ἑλόντ᾿ ἀγέμεν Βρισηΐδα καλλιπάρῃον·   323
εἰ δέ κε μὴ δώῃσιν, ἐγὼ δέ κεν αὐτὸς ἕλωμαι   324
ἐλθὼν σὺν πλεόνεσσι· τό οἱ καὶ ῥίγιον ἔσται."   325

Going to Achilles' camp, the two heralds find Achilles and stand silent before him.

Ὣς εἰπὼν προΐει, κρατερὸν δ᾿ ἐπὶ μῦθον ἔτελλε·   326
τὼ δ᾿ ἀέκοντε βάτην παρὰ θῖν᾿ ἁλὸς ἀτρυγέτοιο,   327
Μυρμιδόνων δ᾿ ἐπί τε κλισίας καὶ νῆας ἱκέσθην.   328
τὸν δ᾿ εὗρον παρά τε κλισίῃ καὶ νηῒ μελαίνῃ   329

---

317   **κνίση, -ης, ἡ**—odor of roast meat, steam or smell of burnt offerings. (When an animal was sacrificed, it was the smell of the burning bones and fat that the gods were thought to enjoy.)

     ἵκω—reach, come to; ἷκεν—imperfect.

     ἑλίσσω—curl, wind.

     καπνός, -οῦ, ὁ—smoke.

     ἑλισσομένη περὶ καπνῷ—"whirling around in the smoke." The smell of the burning fat from the animals sacrificed is rising heavenward toward the gods.

318   **πένομαι**—work at, labor at; πένοντο = ἐπένοντο.

319   **λῆγ᾿** = ἔληγε.

     τήν—"which" (relative pronoun referring to ἔριδος).

     ἐπαπειλέω, (aor.) **ἐπηπείλησα**—threaten against (+ dat.); ἐπηπείλησ᾿ = ἐπηπείλησε.

     "And Agamemnon did not put aside the threats he previously made against Achilles" (literally, "and Agamemnon did not give up the quarrel that he first threatened against Achilles" [lines 318–19]).

320   **Ταλθύβιος, -ου, ὁ**—Talthybius.

     Εὐρυβάτης, -αο, ὁ—Eurybates.

321   **τώ**—relative pronoun, nom. dual.

     οἱ—dative of possession.

ἔσαν = ἦσαν.

κῆρυξ, -υκος, ὁ—herald; κήρυκε—nom. dual. (Heralds were general assistants
   to leaders. They kept order at meetings, made proclamations, assisted at
   sacrifices, and served as messengers. Considered to be under the protection of
   a god (perhaps Zeus or Hermes), they were inviolable.)

ὀτρηρός, -ή, -όν—ready, busy; ὀτρηρώ—nom. dual. masc.

θεράπων, -οντος, ὁ—attendant, companion; θεράποντε—nom. dual.

322 ἔρχεσθον—dual present imperative of ἔρχομαι.

   κλισίην—"to the hut" (accusative of the goal of motion).

323 χειρός—"by the hand"; partitive genitive, indicating the part touched, seized, etc.

   ἑλόντ' = ἑλόντε—aorist active participle of αἱρέω, nom. dual.

   ἀγέμεν = ἄγειν (infinitive used as imperative).

324 δώῃσιν—aorist subjunctive, 3rd pers. sing.

   δώῃσιν and ἕλωμαι—subjunctives; translate as futures.

   Compare this line with line 137. What is the difference between them?

325 σὺν πλεόνεσσι [ἀνδράσι].

   οἱ—"for him."

   καί—"even."

   ῥίγιον—(neut. comp. adj.) more horrible, more terrible, worse.

326 προΐημι—send forth; προΐει—imperfect.

   ἐπὶ . . . ἔτελλε—tmesis.

   κρατερὸν δ' ἐπὶ μῦθον ἔτελλε—"he commanded [them] harshly."

327 τώ—"the two of them" (nom. dual).

   ἀέκοντε—nom. dual masc. of ἀέκων.

   βάτην = ἐβάτην = ἐβήτην—aorist active, 3rd pers. dual.

328 ἱκέσθην—aorist of ἱκνέομαι, 3rd pers. dual.

329 τόν—"him" (i.e., Achilles).

   εὑρίσκω, (aor.) εὗρον—find.

Scanning Notes

317 The ι in κνίση is long.

322 The -δεω in Πηληϊάδεω is scanned as one long syllable. What is it called when
   two vowels are run together like this?

323 The first ι in Βρισηΐδα is long.

325 The first ι in ῥίγιον is long.

ἤμενον· οὐδ᾿ ἄρα τώ γε ἰδὼν γήθησεν Ἀχιλλεύς.   330
τὼ μὲν ταρβήσαντε καὶ αἰδομένω βασιλῆα   331
στήτην, οὐδέ τί μιν προσεφώνεον οὐδ᾿ ἐρέοντο·   332
αὐτὰρ ὁ ἔγνω ᾗσιν ἐνὶ φρεσὶ φώνησέν τε·   333

Achilles greets the heralds, assuring them that he blames not them but
Agamemnon. He then tells his friend Patroclus to bring out Briseis and hand
her over to them.

"χαίρετε, κήρυκες, Διὸς ἄγγελοι ἠδὲ καὶ ἀνδρῶν,   334
ἆσσον ἴτ᾿· οὔ τί μοι ὔμμες ἐπαίτιοι, ἀλλ᾿ Ἀγαμέμνων,   335
ὃ σφῶϊ προΐει Βρισηΐδος εἵνεκα κούρης.   336
ἀλλ᾿ ἄγε, διογενὲς Πατρόκλεες, ἔξαγε κούρην   337
καί σφωϊν δὸς ἄγειν· τὼ δ᾿ αὐτὼ μάρτυροι ἔστων   338
πρός τε θεῶν μακάρων πρός τε θνητῶν ἀνθρώπων,   339
καὶ πρὸς τοῦ βασιλῆος ἀπηνέος, εἴ ποτε δὴ αὖτε   340
χρειὼ ἐμεῖο γένηται ἀεικέα λοιγὸν ἀμῦναι   341

---

330   **ἤμενον** (from ἧμαι)—describes τόν (line 329).
       τώ—"the two of them" (acc. dual).
       ἰδών—aorist active participle of ὁράω, nom. sing. masc.
       γηθέω, (aor.) **ἐγήθησα**—rejoice, be glad; γήθησεν = ἐγήθησεν.
       οὐδ᾿ ἄρα τώ γε ἰδὼν γήθησεν Ἀχιλλεύς—a figure of speech called *litotes,* an
       ironic understatement in which an idea is expressed by negating a contrary idea.
       Saying that Achilles "did not rejoice" is putting it mildly, to say the least, empha-
       sizing all the more how very unhappy he would have been to see the two heralds.
331   **τώ**—"the two of them" (nom. dual).
       ταρβέω, (aor.) **ἐτάρβησα**—fear, be afraid; ταρβήσαντε—aorist active par-
       ticiple, nom. dual: "seized with fear."
       αἴδομαι—respect, have regard for; αἰδομένω—present participle, nom. dual.
       βασιλῆα = Achilles.
332   **στήτην** = ἐστήτην—aorist active of ἵστημι, 3rd pers. dual.
       οὐδέ τι—not at all.
       προσφωνέω—speak to, address; προσεφώνεον—imperfect.
       ἐρέω—ask; ἐρέοντο—unaugmented imperfect.
333   **ὁ**—"he" (i.e., Achilles).
       ἔγνω—aorist active of γιγνώσκω, 3rd pers. sing.
       ᾗσιν—dat. plur. fem.
334   **χαίρετε**—welcome! hail!
       ἄγγελος, -ου, ὁ—messenger.
335   **ἆσσον**—nearer.

ἴτ᾽ = ἴτε—imperative of εἶμι, 2nd pers. plur.

οὔ τι—not at all, by no means.

ἐπαίτιος, -ον—to blame, blameworthy.

οὔ τί μοι ὔμμες ἐπαίτιοί [ἐστε], ἀλλ᾽ Ἀγαμέμνων [ἐπαίτιός ἐστι].

336 ὄ = ὅς.

σφῶϊ—acc. dual of σύ.

337 διογενής, -ές—descended from Zeus, divine (a word used to describe heroes).

Πάτροκλος, -ου, ὁ—Patroclus; διογενὲς Πατρόκλεες—vocative.

ἐξάγω—bring out, lead out.

338 σφῶϊν—dat. dual of εἷο.

δός—aorist active imperative, 2nd pers. sing.

ἄγειν—"to take away" (infinitive used to express purpose).

τὼ δ᾽ αὐτώ—"these two themselves."

μάρτυρος, -ου, ὁ—witness.

ἔστων—imperative of εἰμί, 3rd pers. dual.

339 πρός—before, in the sight of (+ gen.).

μάκαρ, -αρος—blessed, happy.

θνητός, -ή, -όν—mortal.

340 ἀπηνής, -ές—harsh, unfeeling.

αὖτε—again, hereafter.

341 χρειώ, -όος, ἡ—need.

γένηται—aorist subjunctive from γίγνομαι; subjunctive verb in the protasis of a future-more-vivid condition.

λοιγόν—The same word was used for the destruction caused by the plague (line 67). Achilles' absence from battle will be just as ruinous for the Greeks.

ἀμύνω, (aor.) ἤμυνα—ward off; ἀμῦναι—aorist active infinitive.

Scanning Notes

334 The υ in κήρυκες is long.

336 The first ι in Βρισηΐδος is long.

337 The ι in διογενές is long.

340 By synizesis, δή and the first syllable of αὖτε are run together to form one syllable. Pronounce as though it were written δ᾽ αὖτε.

τοῖς ἄλλοις· ἦ γὰρ ὅ γ᾽ ὀλοιῇσι φρεσὶ θύει,   342
οὐδέ τι οἶδε νοῆσαι ἅμα πρόσσω καὶ ὀπίσσω,   343
ὅππως οἱ παρὰ νηυσὶ σόοι μαχέονται Ἀχαιοί.᾿   344
   Ὣς φάτο, Πάτροκλος δὲ φίλῳ ἐπεπείθεθ᾽ ἑταίρῳ,   345
ἐκ δ᾽ ἄγαγε κλισίης Βρισηΐδα καλλιπάρῃον,   346
δῶκε δ᾽ ἄγειν· τὼ δ᾽ αὖτις ἴτην παρὰ νῆας Ἀχαιῶν·   347
ἡ δ᾽ ἀέκουσ᾽ ἅμα τοῖσι γυνὴ κίεν·

*Achilles, weeping, sits on the seashore and complains to his mother about
what has happened.*

                                        αὐτὰρ Ἀχιλλεὺς   348
δακρύσας ἑτάρων ἄφαρ ἕζετο νόσφι λιασθείς,   349
θῖν᾽ ἔφ᾽ ἁλὸς πολιῆς, ὁρόων ἐπ᾽ ἀπείρονα πόντον·   350

---

342 τοῖς ἄλλοις—dative of advantage.
   Achilles has called on the heralds to bear witness (lines 338–40) and has indicated
   when they should do it (εἴ ποτε δὴ αὖτε / χρειὼ ἐμεῖο γένηται ἀεικέα λοιγὸν
   ἀμῦναι / τοῖς ἄλλοις), but he does not specify exactly what it is they are to bear
   witness to. How would you express what he has left unsaid?
   ὅ—"he" (i.e., Agamemnon).
   ὀλοιός, -ή, -όν—destructive, deadly.
   θύω—rage.
343 οἶδε—"know how."
   νοέω, νοήσω, ἐνόησα—think, consider, take thought of, direct one's mind.
   ἅμα—(adv.) at the same time.
   πρόσσω—forward.
   ὀπίσσω—backward.
   οὐδέ τι οἶδε νοῆσαι ἅμα πρόσσω καὶ ὀπίσσω—"He does not know how to
   direct his mind at the same time forward and backward." In other words,
   Agamemnon is not considering either the future or the past.
344 ὅππως—so that.
   οἱ—"for him" (i.e., Agamemnon), dative of advantage.
   σόος, -η, -ον—safe.
   μαχέονται = μαχέσονται; future.
345 ἐπεπείθεθ᾽ = ἐπεπείθετο.
   ἑταῖρος, -ου, ὁ—companion, friend.
346 ἄγαγε = ἤγαγε.
347 δῶκε = ἔδωκε.
   τώ—nom. dual.
   ἴτην—imperfect of εἶμι, 3rd pers. dual.

Fig. 3. Briseis led away from Achilles by Agamemnon's heralds. Plaster model
by Bertel Thorvaldsen, 1803. Marble relief by Christian Freund under the
supervision of H. W. Bissen, 1865. Thorvaldsens Museum. Copenhagen,
Denmark. (Photograph by Jonals.)

348   ἀέκουσ' = ἀέκουσα.
      γυνή, γυναικός, ἡ—woman.
      κίω—go; κίεν = ἔκιεν—imperfect.
349   δακρύω, (aor.) ἐδάκρυσα—weep, cry; aorist—"burst into tears"; δακρύσας—
      aorist active participle.
      ἑτάρων—object of νόσφι.
      ἄφαρ—at once, immediately.
      νόσφι—apart from, away from (+ gen.).
      λιάζομαι, (aor. pass.) ἐλιάσθην—withdraw; λιασθείς—aorist passive partici-
      ple, nom. sing. masc.: "having withdrawn."
350   θῖν'—object of ἔφ'(= ἐπί).
      πολιός, -ή, -όν—gray; ἁλὸς πολιῆς refers to the sea near the shore.
      ὁρόων = ὁρῶν—present active participle, nom. sing. masc.: "looking," "gazing."
      ἀπείρων, -ονος—boundless.
      πόντος, -ου, ὁ—sea, the open sea, the deep sea.

Scanning Notes
342   γάρ is scanned as a long syllable. A short final syllable that receives the ictus can
      be scanned long.
      The υ in θύει is long.
346   The first ι in Βρισηΐδα is long.
349   The υ and the second α in δακρύσας are long.

πολλὰ δὲ μητρὶ φίλῃ ἠρήσατο χεῖρας ὀρεγνύς·   351
"μῆτερ, ἐπεί μ' ἔτεκές γε μινυνθάδιόν περ ἐόντα,   352
τιμήν πέρ μοι ὄφελλεν Ὀλύμπιος ἐγγυαλίξαι   353
Ζεὺς ὑψιβρεμέτης· νῦν δ' οὐδέ με τυτθὸν ἔτισεν·   354
ἦ γάρ μ' Ἀτρεΐδης εὐρὺ κρείων Ἀγαμέμνων   355
ἠτίμησεν· ἑλὼν γὰρ ἔχει γέρας, αὐτὸς ἀπούρας."   356

Achilles' mother comes to him from the sea and asks what is troubling him.

Ὣς φάτο δάκρυ χέων, τοῦ δ' ἔκλυε πότνια μήτηρ   357
ἡμένη ἐν βένθεσσιν ἁλὸς παρὰ πατρὶ γέροντι·   358
καρπαλίμως δ' ἀνέδυ πολιῆς ἁλὸς ἠΰτ' ὀμίχλη,   359
καί ῥα πάροιθ' αὐτοῖο καθέζετο δάκρυ χέοντος,   360
χειρί τέ μιν κατέρεξεν, ἔπος τ' ἔφατ' ἔκ τ' ὀνόμαζε·   361
"τέκνον, τί κλαίεις; τί δέ σε φρένας ἵκετο πένθος;   362
ἐξαύδα, μὴ κεῦθε νόῳ, ἵνα εἴδομεν ἄμφω."   363

351 **ἀράομαι, ἀρήσομαι, ἠρησάμην**—pray.

ὀρέγνυμι—stretch out, hold out; **ὀρεγνύς**—present active participle, nom. sing. masc. (Stretching out your hands toward the god (or the cult image of the god) to whom you were praying was a standard gesture for an ancient Greek. If you were praying to a sky god, you raised your hands upward. For prayers to an underworld deity, you stretched your hands, palms down, toward the ground. Achilles' mother is a sea divinity, so he stretches his hands toward the sea.)

352 **μῆτερ**—vocative.

τίκτω, τέξω, ἔτεκον—give birth to, bear.

μινυνθάδιος, -η, -ον—short-lived. (Before Achilles came to Troy, his mother told him that if he took part in the Trojan War, he would die there but would win great glory, whereas if he did not fight at Troy, he would have a long but inglorious life. This is only the first of many allusions in the *Iliad* to Achilles' short life. Although the *Iliad* ends with Achilles triumphant over Hector, he knows he will not live long to enjoy it. This fact may make his treatment by Agamemnon all the harder to bear, for it deprives him of the glory he has chosen over a long life. Achilles' certain knowledge of his own future also makes him different from every other major character in the *Iliad*. No one else can really understand his feelings.)

ἐόντα—present participle of εἰμί.

353 **ὀφέλλω**—ought; **ὄφελλεν** = ὤφελλεν—imperfect.

ἐγγυαλίζω, ἐγγυαλίξω, ἠγγυάλιξα—give, grant, bestow.

354 **ὑψιβρεμέτης, -ου**—high-thundering (adjective used to describe Zeus).

τυτθόν—a little; **οὐδέ . . . τυτθόν**—"not even a little."

ἔτισεν—from τίω.

356 ἑλών—aorist active participle of αἱρέω.

ἀπαυράω—take away, rob, deprive; ἀπούρας—aorist active participle, nom. sing. masc.

ἑλών, αὐτός, ἀπούρας—all refer to Agamemnon, the subject of ἔχει.

357 δάκρυ, -υος, τό—tear.

χέω—pour, shed; δάκρυ χέων = weeping, crying.

πότνια—(fem. adj.) revered, honored.

358 βένθος, -εος, τό—depth.

Achilles' mother, the sea goddess Thetis, is with her father, Nereus, who is known as "the old man of the sea." Homer never refers to Nereus by name, only as "the old man" or "the old man of the sea." Thetis is no longer living with her mortal husband, Peleus, who is Achilles' father.

359 καρπαλίμως—quickly, at once.

ἀναδύομαι, ἀναδύσομαι, ἀνεδυσάμην or ἀνέδυν—rise up from out of, emerge from out of (+ gen.); ἀνέδυ—aorist active, 3rd pers. sing.

ἠΰτ' = ἠΰτε—like, as.

ὁμίχλη, -ης, ἡ—mist.

360 πάροιθ' = πάροιθε—in front of (+ gen.).

καθέζετο = ἐκαθέζετο.

361 χειρί—dative of means.

καταρέζω, (aor.) κατέρεξα—stroked, caress, pat.

ὀνομάζω, ὀνομάσω, ὠνόμασα—call by name (ὄνομα); ὀνόμαζε = ὠνόμαζε.

ἔπος τ' ἔφατ' ἔκ τ' ὀνόμαζε—"addressed."

362 τέκνον, -ου, τό—child.

τί—why?

κλαίω—weep, cry.

σε φρένας—Both accusatives are objects of ἵκετο, σε indicating the person affected and φρένας the specific part affected: "Why has grief come to your heart?"

πένθος, -εος, τό—grief, sadness.

363 ἐξαυδάω—speak out, tell; ἐξαύδα—present active imperative.

κεύθω—hide, conceal.

εἴδομεν = εἴδωμεν—perfect subjunctive of οἶδα; translate as present.

ἄμφω—both.

Scanning Notes

353 The ι in τιμήν is long.

356 The ι in ἠτίμησεν is long.

359 The υ in ἀνέδυ is long.

362 The ι in ἵκετο is long.

363 The second α in ἐξαύδα is long.

Achilles tells his mother what has happened.

Τὴν δὲ βαρὺ στενάχων προσέφη πόδας ὠκὺς Ἀχιλλεύς·   364
"οἶσθα· τίη τοι ταῦτα ἰδυίῃ πάντ᾽ ἀγορεύω;   365
ᾠχόμεθ᾽ ἐς Θήβην, ἱερὴν πόλιν Ἠετίωνος,   366
τὴν δὲ διεπράθομέν τε καὶ ἤγομεν ἐνθάδε πάντα·   367
καὶ τὰ μὲν εὖ δάσσαντο μετὰ σφίσιν υἷες Ἀχαιῶν,   368
ἐκ δ᾽ ἕλον Ἀτρεΐδῃ Χρυσηΐδα καλλιπάρῃον.   369
Χρύσης δ᾽ αὖθ᾽ ἱερεὺς ἑκατηβόλου Ἀπόλλωνος   370
ἦλθε θοὰς ἐπὶ νῆας Ἀχαιῶν χαλκοχιτώνων   371
λυσόμενός τε θύγατρα φέρων τ᾽ ἀπερείσι᾽ ἄποινα,   372
στέμματ᾽ ἔχων ἐν χερσὶν ἑκηβόλου Ἀπόλλωνος   373
χρυσέῳ ἀνὰ σκήπτρῳ, καὶ λίσσετο πάντας Ἀχαιούς,   374
Ἀτρεΐδα δὲ μάλιστα δύω, κοσμήτορε λαῶν.   375
ἔνθ᾽ ἄλλοι μὲν πάντες ἐπευφήμησαν Ἀχαιοὶ   376
αἰδεῖσθαί θ᾽ ἱερῆα καὶ ἀγλαὰ δέχθαι ἄποινα·   377
ἀλλ᾽ οὐκ Ἀτρεΐδῃ Ἀγαμέμνονι ἥνδανε θυμῷ,   378
ἀλλὰ κακῶς ἀφίει, κρατερὸν δ᾽ ἐπὶ μῦθον ἔτελλε·   379

---

364 βαρύ—heavily, deeply.
    στενάχω—groan.
365 τίη—why?
    ταῦτα—object of ἀγορεύω.
    ἰδυίῃ—perfect active participle of οἶδα; translate as present; dat. sing. fem.,
      modifying τοι.
    πάντ᾽= πάντα—object of ἰδυίῃ.
    ἀγορεύω—present subjunctive; deliberative subjunctive.
    τίη τοι ταῦτα ἰδυίῃ πάντ᾽ ἀγορεύω;—"Why should I tell you all these things
      that you already know?" (literally, "Why should I tell all [these things] to you
      knowing these things?"). This is evidently a rhetorical question, as Achilles
      goes on to tell her what happened.
366 οἴχομαι—go, come; ᾠχόμεθ᾽ = ᾠχόμεθα.
    Θήβη, -ης, ἡ—Thebe, a city near Troy.
    Ἠετίων, -ωνος, ὁ—Eetion, king of Thebe. (He is the father of Andromache,
      Hector's wife. In *Il.* 6.414–27, she describes the sack of Thebe, when Achilles
      killed her father and her seven brothers and captured her mother.)
367 διαπέρθω, διαπέρσω, διέπραθον—sack, utterly destroy, devastate.
    ἤγομεν—imperfect of ἄγω.
    ἐνθάδε—here, to this place.
    πάντα—refers to loot and captives.

368 εὖ—"properly," "justly."

δατέομαι, δάσ(σ)ομαι, ἐδασ(σ)άμην, δέδασμαι—divide up, allot; δάσσαντο = ἐδάσσαντο.

σφίσιν—dat. plur. of εἷο.

369 ἐξαιρέω, (aor.) ἔξελον—select, choose; ἐκ . . . ἔλον—tmesis.

Χρυσηΐδα—Why Chryseis, who was from Chryse, was captured at Thebe puz-
zled ancient commentators. Two possible explanations were suggested: (1) she
was visiting Thebe when it was attacked; (2) the Greeks took Chryse on the
same expedition.

370 αὖθ'= αὖτε.

ἐκατηβόλος, -ον—far-shooting.

371 χαλκοχίτων, -ωνος—bronze-clad (refers to either the bronze-plated armor worn
by the soldiers or the bronze-plated shields they carried).

372 ἀπερείσιος, -ον—boundless, immeasurable, unlimited; ἀπερείσι' = ἀπερείσια.

373 στέμματ' = στέμματα.

374 λίσσετο = ἐλίσσετο.

375 Ἀτρεΐδα—acc. dual.

μάλιστα—especially.

κοσμήτωρ, -ορος, ὁ—commander; κοσμήτορε—acc. dual.

Look at lines 372–75. Where did Homer use these same lines earlier in book 1?
Who are the Ἀτρεΐδα . . . κοσμήτορε λαῶν?

376 ἐπευφημέω, ἐπευφημήσω, ἐπευφήμησα—approve, shout assent, speak favorably, agree.

377 αἰδέομαι, αἰδέσομαι, ᾐδεσάμην—respect, have regard for.

378 ἁνδάνω—be acceptable, please; ἥνδανε—imperfect.

379 ἀφίει—imperfect of ἀφίημι.

Look at lines 376–79. Where did Homer use these same lines earlier in book 1?

Scanning Notes

369 The υ in Χρυσηΐδα is long.

370 The υ in Χρύσης and the α in Ἀπόλλωνος are long.

371 The α in θοάς is long.

372 The υ in λυσόμενος is long.

373 The α in Ἀπόλλωνος is long.

374 The υ in χρυσέῳ is long.

The -εῳ in χρυσέῳ is scanned as one syllable (synizesis). When synizesis occurs,
the syllable is usually scanned long. Why is it scanned short in this line?

375 The second α in Ἀτρεΐδα and the α in λαῶν are long.

378 The υ in θυμῷ is long.

χωόμενος δ' ὁ γέρων πάλιν ᾤχετο· τοῖο δ' Ἀπόλλων   380
εὐξαμένου ἤκουσεν, ἐπεὶ μάλα οἱ φίλος ἦεν,   381
ἧκε δ' ἐπ' Ἀργείοισι κακὸν βέλος· οἱ δέ νυ λαοὶ   382
θνῆσκον ἐπασσύτεροι, τὰ δ' ἐπῴχετο κῆλα θεοῖο   383
πάντῃ ἀνὰ στρατὸν εὐρὺν Ἀχαιῶν· ἄμμι δὲ μάντις   384
εὖ εἰδὼς ἀγόρευε θεοπροπίας ἑκάτοιο.   385
αὐτίκ' ἐγὼ πρῶτος κελόμην θεὸν ἱλάσκεσθαι·   386
Ἀτρεΐωνα δ' ἔπειτα χόλος λάβεν, αἶψα δ' ἀναστὰς   387
ἠπείλησεν μῦθον, ὁ δὴ τετελεσμένος ἐστί·   388
τὴν μὲν γὰρ σὺν νηΐ θοῇ ἑλίκωπες Ἀχαιοὶ   389
ἐς Χρύσην πέμπουσιν, ἄγουσι δὲ δῶρα ἄνακτι·   390
τὴν δὲ νέον κλισίηθεν ἔβαν κήρυκες ἄγοντες   391
κούρην Βρισῆος, τήν μοι δόσαν υἷες Ἀχαιῶν.   392

---

380 **χωόμενος**—In line 33, Homer said ἔδεισεν δ' ὁ γέρων. When Achilles describes
the scene here, he says χωόμενος δ' ὁ γέρων. How does Achilles' perception
of Chryses' emotions differ from Homer's original description?

πάλιν—back.

τοῖο—genitive object of ἤκουσεν in line 381.

381 **εὐξαμένου**—aorist participle; translate as "praying." In Homer, an aorist participle often indicates something happening at the same time as the main verb.

ἀκούω, ἀκούσομαι, ἤκουσα—hear (+ gen.).

οἱ—"to him" (refers to Apollo).

ἦεν—imperfect, 3rd pers. sing. (εἰμί). (The subject of ἦεν is the old man,
Chryses.)

382 **ἧκε**—from ἵημι.

βέλος, -εος, τό—arrow, missile.

νυ—indeed.

383 **θνῄσκω, θανέομαι, ἔθανον, τέθνηκα**—die, be killed; θνῆσκον = ἔθνησκον.

ἐπασσύτερος, -η, -ον—in quick succession, one right after another.

ἐποίχομαι—attack.

κῆλον, -ου, τό—arrow.

384 **πάντῃ**—in all directions, everywhere.

ἄμμι = ἡμῖν.

385 **εἰδώς**—perfect active participle of οἶδα, nom. sing. masc.

ἀγόρευε = ἠγόρευε—imperfect.

θεοπροπίη, -ης, ἡ—oracle, prophecy.

ἕκατος, -ου, ὁ—the far-shooter (i.e., Apollo).

386 **πρῶτος, -η, -ον**—first.

κελόμην = ἐκελόμην—imperfect.

κελόμην θεὸν ἱλάσκεσθαι—"I urged [them] to appease the god."
387 Ἀτρεῖων, -ωνος, ὁ = Ἀτρεΐδης.
λαμβάνω, λήψομαι, ἔλαβον—seize, take hold of; λάβεν = ἔλαβεν.
αἶψα—at once, immediately.
ἀναστάς—aorist active participle of ἀνίστημι, nom. sing. masc.
388 ἠπείλησεν μῦθον—"he made a threat" (literally, "he threatened a word"). What about the scansion of ἠπείλησεν gives it an added element of heaviness, perhaps emphasizing Achilles' feelings of sullen anger?
ὁ—"which" (referring to the threat).
τετελεσμένος—What kind of participle is this?
ἠπείλησεν μῦθον, ὁ δὴ τετελεσμένος ἐστί—"he made a threat that has been accomplished."
389 τὴν μέν—the one woman (i.e., Chryseis); contrasted with τὴν δέ in line 391—the other woman (i.e., Briseis).
ἑλίκωψ, -ωπος—(masc. adj.) flashing-eyed; possibly "black-eyed" or "dark-eyed."
390 Χρύσην—the city, not the man.
ἄνακτι—refers to Apollo.
πέμπουσιν and ἄγουσι—present tenses. (These things are happening at the time Achilles is speaking.)
391 νέον—just now.
κλισίηθεν—What does the suffix -θεν add to the meaning of κλισίη?
ἔβαν = ἔβησαν.
392 κούρην—"daughter."
Βρισεύς, -ῆος, ὁ—Briseus, father of Briseis.
τήν—This article is being used as what kind of pronoun?

Scanning Notes
380 The α in Ἀπόλλων is long, but the first syllable is scanned short. A long vowel that does not receive the ictus can be scanned short.
382 The α in λαοί is long.
385 The α in θεοπροπίας is long.
386 The first ι in ἱλάσκεσθαι is long.
390 The υ in Χρύσην is long.
391 The υ in κήρυκες is long.
392 The ι in Βρισῆος is long.

Achilles asks his mother for help. He wants her to remind Zeus that she once
saved him and to ask Zeus to help the Trojans so that Agamemnon will regret
his treatment of her son.

ἀλλὰ σύ, εἰ δύνασαί γε, περίσχεο παιδὸς ἐῆος·   393
ἐλθοῦσ᾿ Οὔλυμπόνδε Δία λίσαι, εἴ ποτε δή τι   394
ἢ ἔπει ὤνησας κραδίην Διὸς ἠὲ καὶ ἔργῳ.   395
πολλάκι γάρ σεο πατρὸς ἐνὶ μεγάροισιν ἄκουσα   396
εὐχομένης, ὅτ᾿ ἔφησθα κελαινεφέϊ Κρονίωνι   397
οἴη ἐν ἀθανάτοισιν ἀεικέα λοιγὸν ἀμῦναι,   398
ὁππότε μιν ξυνδῆσαι Ὀλύμπιοι ἤθελον ἄλλοι,   399
Ἥρη τ᾿ ἠδὲ Ποσειδάων καὶ Παλλὰς Ἀθήνη·   400
ἀλλὰ σὺ τόν γ᾿ ἐλθοῦσα, θεά, ὑπελύσαο δεσμῶν,   401
ᾧχ᾿ ἑκατόγχειρον καλέσασ᾿ ἐς μακρὸν Ὄλυμπον,   402
ὃν Βριάρεων καλέουσι θεοί, ἄνδρες δέ τε πάντες   403

393 **δύνασαι**—present, 2nd pers. sing.
     περιέχομαι—protect (+ gen.); **περίσχεο**—aorist imperative.
     ἐύς, (gen.) **ἐῆος**—good, noble.
394 **ἐλθοῦσ᾿** = ἐλθοῦσα—aorist active participle, nom. sing. fem. (ἔρχομαι).
     λίσαι—aorist imperative of λίσσομαι.
     τι—in any way.
395 **ἔπει**—dative of means.
     ὀνίνημι, ὀνήσω, ὤνησα—help, benefit, be of service to, delight.
     κραδίη, -ης, ἡ—heart.
     ἔργον, -ου, τό—deed; **ἔργῳ**—dative of means.
396 **πολλάκι**—many times, often.
     πατρός—Achilles refers to his father, Peleus, Thetis's husband.
     μέγαρον, -ου, τό—great hall, dining hall; *plur.*—house, palace.
     ἄκουσα = ἤκουσα.
397 **εὐχομένης**—present participle, gen. sing. fem., modifies σεο in line 396: "boast-
     ing."
     ὅτ᾿ = ὅτε—when.
     ἔφησθα—imperfect of φημί, 2nd pers. sing.
     κελαινεφής, -ές—of the dark clouds.
     Κρονίων, -ωνος, ὁ—son of Cronos (= Zeus); κελαινεφέϊ Κρονίωνι—dative of
     advantage.
398 **ἐν ἀθανάτοισιν**—"among the immortals."
     **ὅτ᾿ ἔφησθα κελαινεφέϊ Κρονίωνι / οἴη ἐν ἀθανάτοισιν ἀεικέα λοιγὸν
     ἀμῦναι** (lines 397–98)—"when you said that you alone among the immortals
     warded off grievous destruction from Zeus of the dark clouds."

399 ὁππότε—when.

μιν—refers to Zeus.

ξυνδέω, (aor.) ξυνέδησα—tie up, bind.

Ὀλύμπιοι = Olympians, i.e., the gods.

400 Ποσειδάων, -ωνος, ὁ—Poseidon, god of the sea, brother of Zeus, and a supporter of the Greeks.

401 τόν—"him" (refers to Zeus).

ὑπολύω, ὑπολύσω, ὑπέλυσα—set free, release from; ὑπελύσαο = ὑπελύσω—aorist middle, 2nd pers. sing.; translate as active.

δεσμός, -οῦ, ὁ—restraint, bond, any means of binding; δεσμῶν—genitive of separation: "from the bonds."

402 ὦχ' = ὦκα—quickly.

ἑκατόγχειρος, -ον—hundred-handed; *as a noun*—the hundred-handed one, one of the Hecatoncheires (hundred-handed giants).

καλέσασ'= καλέσασα—aorist active participle of καλέω, nom. sing. fem.

μακρός, -ή, -όν—high, tall, long.

403 ὅν—"whom."

Βριάρεως, -ω, ὁ—Briareus, one of the Hecatoncheires. (There were three Hecatoncheires, sons of Uranus and Gaia. When Zeus fought the Titans, they sided with Zeus. In other versions of the story, Briareus is a son of Poseidon.)

καλέουσι = καλοῦσι.

Scanning Notes

394 The last syllable of Δία is scanned long. A short final vowel followed by a word beginning with λ can be scanned long.

396 The last syllable of ἐνί is scanned long, even though the ι is short. Why?

398 The first α in ἀθανάτοισιν is long.

400 The α in Ποσειδάων is long.

401 The α in θεά and the second υ in ὑπελύσαο are long.

402 The second α in καλέσασ' is long.

403 The -εων in Βριάρεων is scanned as one long syllable. What is this running together of vowels called?

Αἰγαίων'· ὁ γὰρ αὖτε βίην οὗ πατρὸς ἀμείνων·   404
ὅς ῥα παρὰ Κρονίωνι καθέζετο κύδεϊ γαίων·   405
τὸν καὶ ὑπέδεισαν μάκαρες θεοὶ οὐδ' ἔτ' ἔδησαν.   406
τῶν νῦν μιν μνήσασα παρέζεο καὶ λαβὲ γούνων,   407
αἴ κέν πως ἐθέλῃσιν ἐπὶ Τρώεσσιν ἀρῆξαι,   408
τοὺς δὲ κατὰ πρύμνας τε καὶ ἀμφ' ἅλα ἔλσαι Ἀχαιοὺς   409
κτεινομένους, ἵνα πάντες ἐπαύρωνται βασιλῆος,   410
γνῷ δὲ καὶ Ἀτρεΐδης εὐρὺ κρείων Ἀγαμέμνων   411
ἣν ἄτην, ὅ τ' ἄριστον Ἀχαιῶν οὐδὲν ἔτισε."   412

---

404   **Αἰγαίων, -ωνος, ὁ**—Aegaeon; Αἰγαίων' = Αἰγαίωνα.

ὃν Βριάρεων καλέουσι θεοί, ἄνδρες δέ τε πάντες [καλέουσι]/**Αἰγαίων'**
(lines 403–4)—Why Briareus has a divine name and a human name is something of a mystery. This is not the only case of double names in Homer (for example, in *Il.* 20.74, there is a river called Xanthus by the gods and Scamander
by men). Although linguistic theories have been proposed to explain the phe-
nomenon, no explanation seems to cover all cases.

αὖτε—"on his part."

βίη, -ης, ἡ—strength, force, might; βίην—accusative of respect.

ὁ γὰρ αὖτε βίην οὗ πατρὸς ἀμείνων—"who on his part has greater strength
[literally, "[is] greater with respect to strength"] than his father." There is uncertainty about who should be understood as the father of Briareus. Perhaps Poseidon is meant, since he is one of the gods opposing Zeus.

405   **ὅς**—"he."

κῦδος, -εος, τό—glory; κύδεϊ—dative of cause.

γαίω—rejoice, exult.

406   **τόν**—refers to Briareus.

ὑποδείδω, ὑποδείσομαι, ὑπέδεισα—fear, be afraid of, dread, tremble before.

οὐδ' ἔτ'—"and no longer."

δέω, δήσω, ἔδησα—tie up, bind; οὐδ' ἔτ' ἔδησαν [Δία].

οὐδ' ἔτ' ἔδησαν—a pun on ὑπέδεισαν earlier in the line.

These lines in the *Iliad* are the only reference we have to a story of the gods revolt-
ing against Zeus and of Thetis summoning Briareus to save him. Many scholars
suspect that it was not a traditional story but was invented by Homer to put Zeus
in Thetis's debt and therefore more likely to grant her request. However, when
she appeals to Zeus later (lines 503–10), she makes no specific mention of this
incident. Aristotle points this out when he comments on the fact that men do not
like to be reminded of favors they have received (*Nicomachean Ethics* 4.3.24).

407   **μιμνήσκω, μνήσω, ἔμνησα**—remind.

τῶν νῦν μιν μνήσασα—"reminding him now of these things."

παρέζομαι—sit by, sit near; παρέζεο—present middle imperative.

λαβέ—aorist active imperative.

γόνυ, γουνός, τό—knee; γούνων—a partitive genitive, indicating the part touched, grabbed, etc.

καὶ λαβὲ γούνων—"and take hold of him by the knees." (A person coming as a suppliant would grasp the knees of the one being entreated.)

408   ἐθέλῃσιν—present subjunctive, 3rd pers. sing.

ἐπαρήγω, ἐπαρήξω, ἐπήρηξα—help (+ dat.); ἐπὶ . . . ἀρῆξαι—tmesis.

Τρώεσσιν—dat. plur.

409   τούς—with Ἀχαιούς.

κατά—"down by."

πρύμνη, -ης, ἡ—stern (rear part of a ship). (Achilles refers to the ships of the Greeks, which have been pulled out of the water and are on the beach with their sterns toward the land. Up to this point in the war, the fighting has all taken place on the plain in front of Troy. Achilles is asking that Zeus help the Trojans drive the Greeks back to the ships.)

ἀμφ'= ἀμφί—around (+ acc.).

ἀμφ' ἅλα—"around the bay" (literally, "around the sea"). The Greek ships were on the shore of a bay.

εἴλω, (aor.) ἔλσα—hem in, crowd together; ἔλσαι—aorist active infinitive.

410   κτείνω—kill, slay; κτεινομένους—passive participle modifying Ἀχαιούς.

ἐπαυρίσκω, (aor.) ἐπαῦρον—enjoy, appreciate (+ gen.); ἐπαύρωνται—aorist subjunctive.

411   γνῷ—aorist active subjunctive, 3rd pers. sing. of γιγνώσκω.

καί—"even."

412   ἄτη, -ης, ἡ—folly, moral blindness.

ὅ τ' = ὅτι—"in that," "because."

οὐδέν—not at all.

Scanning Notes

405   The υ in κύδεϊ is long.

406   The second syllable of ὑπέδεισαν is scanned long because ὑπέδεισαν was originally spelled ὑπέδϝεισαν.

407   The first α in μνήσασα is long.

412   The α in ἄτην is long.

The ι in ἔτισε is long.

Thetis weeps for her unhappy son. She promises to talk to Zeus, but she must wait until he returns from visiting the Ethiopians.

Τὸν δ᾽ ἠμείβετ᾽ ἔπειτα Θέτις κατὰ δάκρυ χέουσα·   413
"ὤ μοι τέκνον ἐμόν, τί νύ σ᾽ ἔτρεφον αἰνὰ τεκοῦσα;   414
αἴθ᾽ ὄφελες παρὰ νηυσὶν ἀδάκρυτος καὶ ἀπήμων   415
ἧσθαι, ἐπεί νύ τοι αἶσα μίνυνθά περ, οὔ τι μάλα δήν·   416
νῦν δ᾽ ἅμα τ᾽ ὠκύμορος καὶ ὀϊζυρὸς περὶ πάντων   417
ἔπλεο· τῷ σε κακῇ αἴσῃ τέκον ἐν μεγάροισι.   418
τοῦτο δέ τοι ἐρέουσα ἔπος Διὶ τερπικεραύνῳ   419
εἶμ᾽ αὐτὴ πρὸς Ὄλυμπον ἀγάννιφον, αἴ κε πίθηται.   420
ἀλλὰ σὺ μὲν νῦν νηυσὶ παρήμενος ὠκυπόροισι   421
μήνι᾽ Ἀχαιοῖσιν, πολέμου δ᾽ ἀποπαύεο πάμπαν·   422
Ζεὺς γὰρ ἐς Ὠκεανὸν μετ᾽ ἀμύμονας Αἰθιοπῆας   423
χθιζὸς ἔβη κατὰ δαῖτα, θεοὶ δ᾽ ἅμα πάντες ἕποντο·   424
δωδεκάτῃ δέ τοι αὖτις ἐλεύσεται Οὔλυμπόνδε,   425

---

413 Θέτις, -ιδος, ἡ—Thetis, the sea goddess who is Achilles' mother. (This is the first time Homer calls her by name.)
  χέω—pour, shed; κατὰ δάκρυ χέουσα—"weeping."
414 ὤ μοι—oh! alas!
  τρέφω, (aor.) ἔτραφον—bring up, rear.
  αἰνά—calamitously, grievously, for misfortune, for sorrow.
415 αἴθ᾽= αἴθε—introduces a wish.
  ὀφείλω, (aor.) ὤφελον—ought, would that! (+ infinitive); ὄφελες = ὤφελες.
  ἀδάκρυτος, -η, -ον—tearless.
  ἀπήμων, -ον—unharmed, unhurt, safe.
416 ἧσθαι—present infinitive of ἧμαι.
  τοι—dative of possession.
  αἶσα, -ης, ἡ—fate, life span, one's appointed lot.
  μίνυνθα—short, for a short time.
  ἐπεί νύ τοι αἶσα μίνυνθά πέρ [ἐστι].
  δήν—long.
417 νῦν δ᾽—"but as it is."
  ὠκύμορος, -ον—fated to die early, short-lived.
  ὀϊζυρός, -ή, -όν—miserable, unhappy.
  περὶ πάντων—"above all."
418 ἔπλεο—aorist of πέλομαι, 2nd pers. sing.: "you are."
  τῷ—so, therefore, thus.
  κακῇ αἴσῃ—"for an evil fate."
  τέκον = ἔτεκον (aorist of τίκτω).

419 τοῦτο—describes ἔπος.

τοι—"for you."

ἐρέουσα—future participle of εἴρω.

ἔπος—"story".

τερπικέραυνος, -ον—delighting in the thunderbolt; possibly "thunderbolt-hurling," "thunderbolt-wielding."

420 εἴμ' = εἴμι.

ἀγάννιφος, -ον—snowy, snowcapped, snow-covered. (Where the gods live on the summit of Mt. Olympus, the part that rises above the clouds, is not snowy, of course. According to *Odyssey* 6.42–45, it always has cloudless skies and is never shaken by winds or wet by rain or snow.)

πίθηται—aorist middle subjunctive of πείθω, 3rd pers. sing.

421 πάρημαι—sit beside (+ dat.).

ὠκύπορος, -ον—swift, swift-sailing.

422 μῆνι' = μήνιε (imperative).

'Αχαιοῖσιν—"at the Greeks," "against the Greeks."

ἀποπαύω—hinder; *middle*—cease from, refrain from (+ gen.). What kind of imperative is ἀποπαύεο?

πάμπαν—wholly, entirely, completely.

423 Ὠκεανός, -οῦ, ὁ—Oceanus, the river that was believed to circle the flat disc of the earth.

ἀμύμων, -ον—excellent, blameless.

Αἰθιοπεύς, -ῆος, ὁ—Ethiopian. (The Ethiopians were thought to live far to the southeast, near Oceanus. They were much loved by the gods, who frequently visited them.)

424 χθιζός, -ή, -όν—yesterday's; grammatically agrees with Ζεύς in the previous line; translate as an adverb: "yesterday."

δαίς, δαιτός, ἡ—feast, banquet; κατὰ δαῖτα—"for a feast."

ἕποντο—imperfect.

425 δωδέκατος, -η, -ον—twelfth; δωδεκάτη [ἡμέρῃ]—What use of the dative is this?

τοι—you may be sure.

αὖτις—again, back again.

Scanning Notes

415 The υ in ἀδάκρυτος is long.

416 The last syllable of μάλα is scanned long because δήν was originally spelled δϝήν.

417 The υ in ὀϊζυρός is long.

423 The υ in ἀμύμονας is long.

καὶ τότ᾽ ἔπειτά τοι εἶμι Διὸς ποτὶ χαλκοβατὲς δῶ,　　　426
καί μιν γουνάσομαι καί μιν πείσεσθαι ὀΐω."　　　427

Thetis departs, leaving Achilles nursing his anger. In the meantime, Odysseus
and his men arrive in Chryse and return Chryseis to her father.

Ὣς ἄρα φωνήσασ᾽ ἀπεβήσετο, τὸν δὲ λίπ᾽ αὐτοῦ　　　428
χωόμενον κατὰ θυμὸν ἐϋζώνοιο γυναικός,　　　429
τήν ῥα βίῃ ἀέκοντος ἀπηύρων· αὐτὰρ Ὀδυσσεὺς　　　430
ἐς Χρύσην ἵκανεν ἄγων ἱερὴν ἑκατόμβην.　　　431
οἱ δ᾽ ὅτε δὴ λιμένος πολυβενθέος ἐντὸς ἵκοντο,　　　432
ἱστία μὲν στείλαντο, θέσαν δ᾽ ἐν νηῒ μελαίνῃ,　　　433
ἱστὸν δ᾽ ἱστοδόκῃ πέλασαν προτόνοισιν ὑφέντες　　　434
καρπαλίμως, τὴν δ᾽ εἰς ὅρμον προέρεσσαν ἐρετμοῖς.　　　435
ἐκ δ᾽ εὐνὰς ἔβαλον, κατὰ δὲ πρυμνήσι᾽ ἔδησαν·　　　436

426　**τότ᾽ ἔπειτα**—then after that.
　　　τοι—"for you."
　　　ποτί—to (+ acc.).
　　　χαλκοβατής, -ές—with a bronze floor, bronze-floored.
　　　δῶ, τό (indeclinable)—house, home.
427　**γουνάζομαι, γουνάσομαι**—beg, entreat; from γόνυ, "knee." (Recall line 407,
　　　where Achilles told Thetis to take Zeus by the knees [λαβὲ γούνων], the tradi-
　　　tional act of a suppliant.)
　　　μιν πείσεσθαι—indirect statement after ὀΐω.
428　**φωνήσασ᾽** = φωνήσασα.
　　　ἀποβαίνω, ἀποβήσω, ἀπέβησα—depart, go away; ἀπεβήσετο—aorist.
　　　λίπ᾽ = ἔλιπε.
　　　αὐτοῦ—there.
429　**κατὰ θυμόν**—"in his heart," "in his soul."
　　　ἐΰζωνος, -ον—beautifully belted, well-belted (may refer to the trimness of the
　　　woman as the belt, pulling in the fabric of her πέπλος, revealed her waist, rather
　　　than to the beauty of the belt itself); ἐϋζώνοιο γυναικός—genitive of cause.
430　**τήν**—"whom" (refers to γυναικός in the previous line).
　　　βίη, -ης, ἡ—force, strength; βίῃ—dative of manner: "by force."
　　　ἀέκοντος [αὐτοῦ]—"against his will."
　　　ἀπηύρων—imperfect active of ἀπαυράω, 3rd pers. plur.
431　**ἵκανεν**—imperfect, 3rd pers. sing.
432　**ὅτε**—when.
　　　λιμήν, λιμένος, ὁ—harbor.
　　　πολυβενθής, -ές—very deep.

ἐντός—within, inside (+ gen.).

433 ἱστίον, -ου, τό—sail; ἱστία—plural used for singular; the ship had only one sail.

στέλλω, στελέω, ἔστειλα—take in, lower, furl, roll up; στείλαντο = ἐστείλαντο (middle with active meaning).

θέσαν = ἔθεσαν = ἔθηκαν.

θέσαν δ᾽ [ἱστία] ἐν νηῗ μελαίνῃ.

434 ἱστός, -οῦ, ὁ—mast.

ἱστοδόκη, -ης, ἡ—mast receiver, mast hold (a forked piece of wood in the stern [rear] of the ship, in which the mast would lie when it was lowered).

πελάζω, (aor.) ἐπέλασα—bring into (+ dat.); πέλασαν = ἐπέλασαν.

πρότονος, -ου, ὁ—forestay (one of the ropes holding the mast in place); προτόνοισιν—dative of means.

ὑφίημι, ὑφήσω, ὑφῆκα—let down, lower; ὑφέντες—aorist active participle, nom. plur. masc.

The ropes, or forestays (πρότονοι), that held the mast (ἱστός) in place were fastened near the top of the mast and tied to each side of the bow (the front of the ship). To bring the mast down, they untied the lines from the bow and lowered it toward the stern, where its top rested in the mast hold (ἱστοδόκη).

435 καρπαλίμως—quickly.

τήν—refers to the ship.

ὅρμος, -ου, ὁ—anchoring place, landing place.

προερέσσω, (aor.) προήρεσ(σ)α—row forward; προέρεσσαν = προήρεσσαν.

ἐρετμόν, -οῦ, τό—oar; ἐρετμοῖς—What use of the dative is this?

436 εὐνή, -ῆς, ἡ—anchor stone. (Anchor stones were stones attached to ropes and thrown off the front of the ship to hold it in place.)

ἐκβάλλω, (aor.) ἔκβαλον—hurl out, let go, throw out; ἐκ . . . ἔβαλον—tmesis.

πρυμνήσιον, -ου, τό—stern cable (rope for fastening the stern, or rear, of the ship to the shore); πρυμνήσι᾽ = πρυμνήσια.

καταδέω, (aor.) κατέδησα—tie up, tie fast; κατὰ . . . ἔδησαν—tmesis.

The stern of the ship was tied to the shore with cables (πρυμνήσια), and anchor stones (εὐναί) dropped into the water off the bow kept it from swinging. If they had planned to stay a long time, they would have pulled the ship onto the land.

Scanning Notes

427 The ι in ὀίω is long.

428 The α in φωνήσασ᾽ is long.

429 The υ in θυμόν is long.

431 The υ in Χρύσην and the ι and the α in ἵκανεν are long.

436 The α in εὐνάς is long.

ἐκ δὲ καὶ αὐτοὶ βαῖνον ἐπὶ ῥηγμῖνι θαλάσσης,   437
ἐκ δ᾽ ἑκατόμβην βῆσαν ἐκηβόλῳ Ἀπόλλωνι·   438
ἐκ δὲ Χρυσηΐς νηὸς βῆ ποντοπόροιο.   439
τὴν μὲν ἔπειτ᾽ ἐπὶ βωμὸν ἄγων πολύμητις Ὀδυσσεὺς   440
πατρὶ φίλῳ ἐν χερσὶ τίθει, καί μιν προσέειπεν·   441
"ὦ Χρύση, πρό μ᾽ ἔπεμψεν ἄναξ ἀνδρῶν Ἀγαμέμνων   442
παῖδά τε σοὶ ἀγέμεν, Φοίβῳ θ᾽ ἱερὴν ἑκατόμβην   443
ῥέξαι ὑπὲρ Δαναῶν, ὄφρ᾽ ἱλασόμεσθα ἄνακτα,   444
ὃς νῦν Ἀργείοισι πολύστονα κήδε᾽ ἐφῆκεν."   445

Chryses joyfully receives his daughter and prays to Apollo to let the plague cease.

Ὣς εἰπὼν ἐν χερσὶ τίθει, ὁ δὲ δέξατο χαίρων   446
παῖδα φίλην· τοὶ δ᾽ ὦκα θεῷ ἱερὴν ἑκατόμβην   447
ἑξείης ἔστησαν ἐΰδμητον περὶ βωμόν,   448
χερνίψαντο δ᾽ ἔπειτα καὶ οὐλοχύτας ἀνέλοντο.   449
τοῖσιν δὲ Χρύσης μεγάλ᾽ εὔχετο χεῖρας ἀνασχών·   450

---

437   **ἐκβαίνω**—disembark, go forth, step out; *with an object*—set ashore; βαῖνον = ἔβαινον; ἐκ . . . βαῖνον—tmesis.
      ῥηγμίς, -ῖνος, ἡ—the breakers, the edge of the seashore.
438   **ἐκ . . . βῆσαν**—tmesis; "they set ashore"; βῆσαν = ἔβησαν.
439   **ἐκ . . . βῆ**—tmesis; "stepped out"; βῆ = ἔβη.
      νηός—"from the ship."
      ποντοπόρος, -ον—seagoing.
      Lines 436–39 all begin with ἐκ δ᾽ or ἐκ δέ, emphasizing the progression of items and persons leaving the ship, from the inanimate objects (εὐνάς), to the men themselves (αὐτοί) and the sacrificial animals (ἑκατόμβην), and finally to Chryseis herself. Such repetition at the beginning of lines is called *anaphora*.
      It has been suggested that the scansion of line 439 (four spondees, a dactyl, then a final spondee) calls attention to Chryseis as she disembarks from the ship. The first four spondees are her slow cautious steps on the gangplank; the dactyl, her jump down; and the final spondee, the thud of her landing on the ground.
440   **τήν**—her.
      βωμός, -οῦ, ὁ—altar.
      πολύμητις, -ιος—crafty, shrewd.
441   **πατρί**—dative of interest.
      τίθει = ἐτίθει—imperfect active of τίθημι, 3rd pers. sing. (ἐν χερσὶ τίθει probably means "he turned over" or "he gave," rather than literally "he placed [her] in the hands." Compare *Il.* 23.596–97: καὶ ἵππον ἄγων μεγαθύμου Νέστορος

υἱὸς / ἐν χείρεσσι τίθει Μενελάου. What is being placed in Menelaus's
hands?)

442 **Χρύση**—vocative.

προπέμπω—send, dispatch; πρό . . . ἔπεμψεν—tmesis.

443 **ἀγέμεν** = ἄγειν—infinitive expressing purpose.

444 **ῥέζω, ῥέξω, ἔρεξα**—perform, do, make; ῥέξαι—infinitive expressing purpose.

ὑπέρ—on behalf of, for (+ gen.).

ἰλασόμεσθα = ἰλασώμεθα—aorist subjunctive.

ἄνακτα—acc. sing. of ἄναξ; refers to Apollo.

445 **Ἀργείοισι**—"upon the Greeks."

πολύστονος, -ον—causing many groans, grievous.

κῆδος, -εος, τό—suffering, trouble, pain, sorrow; κήδε᾽ = κήδεα.

ἐφίημι, ἐφήσω, ἐφῆκα—send upon, inflict.

446 **ὁ** = Chryses.

447 **τοί** = οἱ—they.

ὦκα—quickly.

448 **ἐξείης**—one after another.

ἐΰδμητος, -ον—well-built.

449 **χερνίπτομαι**, (aor.) **ἐχερνιψάμην**—wash one's hands; χερνίψαντο = ἐχερ-
νίψαντο.

οὐλοχύται, -ῶν, αἱ—barley sprinkled at a sacrifice. (Barley was sprinkled on
the victims before they were sacrificed.)

ἀνέλοντο—aorist middle of ἀναιρέω.

450 **τοῖσιν**—"for them."

μεγάλ᾽ = μεγάλα—loudly.

εὔχετο = ηὔχετο.

ἀνέχω, ἀνέξω, ἀνέσχον—lift up, raise; ἀνασχών—aorist active participle,
nom. sing. masc. (Chryses is raising his hands toward the god, as was customary when praying.)

Scanning Notes

437 The last syllable of ἐπί is scanned long because ῥηγμῖνι was originally spelled
Ϝρηγμῖνι.

438 The α in Ἀπόλλωνι is long.

439 The υ in Χρυσηΐς is long.

442 The υ in Χρύση is long.

444 The ι in ἰλασόμεσθα is long.

449 The α in οὐλοχύτας is long.

450 The υ in Χρύσης is long.

"κλῦθί μευ, ἀργυρότοξ᾽, ὃς Χρύσην ἀμφιβέβηκας   451
Κίλλαν τε ζαθέην Τενέδοιό τε ἶφι ἀνάσσεις·   452
ἠμὲν δή ποτ᾽ ἐμεῦ πάρος ἔκλυες εὐξαμένοιο,   453
τίμησας μὲν ἐμέ, μέγα δ᾽ ἴψαο λαὸν Ἀχαιῶν·   454
ἠδ᾽ ἔτι καὶ νῦν μοι τόδ᾽ ἐπικρήηνον ἐέλδωρ·   455
ἤδη νῦν Δαναοῖσιν ἀεικέα λοιγὸν ἄμυνον."   456

*They make a sacrifice to Apollo, then feast and sing songs of praise to
the god.*

Ὣς ἔφατ᾽ εὐχόμενος, τοῦ δ᾽ ἔκλυε Φοῖβος Ἀπόλλων.   457
αὐτὰρ ἐπεί ῥ᾽ εὔξαντο καὶ οὐλοχύτας προβάλοντο,   458
αὐέρυσαν μὲν πρῶτα καὶ ἔσφαξαν καὶ ἔδειραν,   459
μηρούς τ᾽ ἐξέταμον κατά τε κνίσῃ ἐκάλυψαν   460
δίπτυχα ποιήσαντες, ἐπ᾽ αὐτῶν δ᾽ ὠμοθέτησαν·   461
καῖε δ᾽ ἐπὶ σχίζῃς ὁ γέρων, ἐπὶ δ᾽ αἴθοπα οἶνον   462
λεῖβε· νέοι δὲ παρ᾽ αὐτὸν ἔχον πεμπώβολα χερσίν.   463
αὐτὰρ ἐπεὶ κατὰ μῆρα κάη καὶ σπλάγχνα πάσαντο,   464

---

451   **κλῦθι**—aorist active imperative of κλύω.
      ὅς—[you] who.
452   **ζάθεος, -η, -ον**—very sacred, holy.
453   **ἠμέν**—just as.
      πάρος—before.
      εὐξαμένοιο—aorist participle of εὔχομαι, gen. sing. masc.
454   **τίμησας** = ἐτίμησας.
      ἴπτομαι, ἴψομαι, ἰψάμην—afflict, punish; ἴψαο = ἴψω (originally ἴψασο)—
      aorist, 2nd pers. sing.
455   **ἔτι**—again.
      ἐπικραιαίνω, (aor.) **ἐπεκρήηνα**—grant, fulfill, accomplish; ἐπικρήηνον—
      aorist imperative.
      ἐέλδωρ, τό (indeclinable)—wish.
456   **ἤδη**—at once.
      Δαναοῖσιν—What use of the dative is this?
      ἄμυνον—aorist active imperative of ἀμύνω.
457   As in line 43, to say Apollo "heard" the prayer indicates that he granted it.
      See lines 37–43. Notice that the prayer Chryses makes here began just as his
      earlier prayer did (compare lines 451–52 and lines 37–38) and that the line fol-
      lowing each prayer is identical (compare line 457 and line 43). Such similarities
      draw attention to the very different intents of the two prayers.

458 προβάλλω, προβαλέω, προέβαλον—scatter, sprinkle, throw; προβάλοντο = προεβάλοντο.
459 αὐερύω, (aor.) αὔερυσα—draw up, draw back, pull up (the heads of the victims).
σφάζω, (aor.) ἔσφαξα—cut the throat.
δέρω, (aor.) ἔδειρα—skin, flay.
460 μηρός, -οῦ, ὁ—thigh.
ἐκτάμνω, (aor.) ἐξέταμον—cut out; μηρούς . . . ἐξέταμον—they cut out the thigh(bones).
κατακαλύπτω, κατακαλύψω—cover up; κατά . . . ἐκάλυψαν—tmesis; aorist.
κνίση, -ης, ἡ—fat.
461 δίπτυξ, -υχος—double-folded; δίπτυχα [κνίσην] ποιήσαντες—"making [the fat] double-folded." (They seem to have either placed two layers of fat over the thighbones or put layers of fat both above and below them.)
αὐτῶν—refers to the μηροί.
ὠμοθετέω, (aor.) ὠμοθέτησα—place pieces of raw meat on. (Pieces of raw meat were cut from the rest of the animal and burned with the thighbones and the fat for the gods. The rest of the meat was eaten by those making the sacrifice.)
462 καίω, καύσω, ἔκηα—burn; καῖε [μηρούς]; καῖε = ἔκαιε.
σχίζη, -ης, ἡ—firewood, a piece of split wood.
ὁ γέρων = Chryses.
ἐπιλείβω—pour over; λεῖβε = ἔλειβε; ἐπὶ . . . λεῖβε—tmesis.
αἴθοψ, -οπος—bright, sparkling.
οἶνος, -ου, ὁ—wine.
463 νέος, -η, -ον—young; νέοι—"the young men."
παρ᾽ αὐτόν—"beside him" (i.e., beside Chryses).
ἔχον = εἶχον—imperfect.
πεμπώβολον, -ου, τό—five-pronged fork. (Such forks were used to roast several pieces of meat at one time.)
464 κατακαίω, (aor. pass.) κατεκάην—consume by fire, burn; κατὰ . . . κάη—tmesis.
μῆρα, -ων, τά—thigh pieces.
σπλάγχνα, -ων, τά—entrails (the heart, liver, spleen, etc.).
πατέομαι, (aor.) ἐπασάμην—taste, eat; πάσαντο = ἐπάσαντο.

Scanning Notes
451 The υ in Χρύσην is long.
454 The ι in τίμησας and the α in λαόν are long.
How does the fact that μέγα begins with a μ affect the scansion of ἐμέ ?
456 The υ in ἄμυνον is long.
457 Why is the first syllable of Ἀπόλλων scanned short, when the α is long?
460 The ι in κνίση is long.

μίστυλλόν τ᾽ ἄρα τἆλλα καὶ ἀμφ᾽ ὀβελοῖσιν ἔπειραν,   465
ὤπτησάν τε περιφραδέως, ἐρύσαντό τε πάντα.   466
αὐτὰρ ἐπεὶ παύσαντο πόνου τετύκοντό τε δαῖτα,   467
δαίνυντ᾽, οὐδέ τι θυμὸς ἐδεύετο δαιτὸς ἐΐσης.   468
αὐτὰρ ἐπεὶ πόσιος καὶ ἐδητύος ἐξ ἔρον ἔντο,   469
κοῦροι μὲν κρητῆρας ἐπεστέψαντο ποτοῖο,   470
νώμησαν δ᾽ ἄρα πᾶσιν ἐπαρξάμενοι δεπάεσσιν·   471
οἱ δὲ πανημέριοι μολπῇ θεὸν ἱλάσκοντο   472
καλὸν ἀείδοντες παιήονα κοῦροι Ἀχαιῶν,   473
μέλποντες ἑκάεργον· ὁ δὲ φρένα τέρπετ᾽ ἀκούων.   474

---

465   **μιστύλλω**—cut into small pieces, cut up; μίστυλλον = ἐμίστυλλον.

    τἆλλα = τὰ ἄλλα—the other (parts of the animals).

    ἀμφ᾽ = ἀμφί—(adv.) on both sides, "through."

    ὀβελός, -οῦ, ὁ—spit.

    πείρω, (aor.) **ἔπειρα**—pierce. (They are putting the meat on spits and roasting it, so they can eat it.)

466   **ὀπτάω,** (aor.) **ὤπτησα**—cook, roast.

    περιφραδέως—very carefully, with great care.

    ἐρύω, (aor.) **εἴρυσ(σ)α**—draw off, pull off; ἐρύσαντο = εἰρύσαντο.

    ἐρύσαντό τε πάντα—"they pulled it all off [the spits]."

467   **παύσαντο** = ἐπαύσαντο.

    πόνος, -ου, ὁ—work, toil; παύσαντο πόνου—"they stopped [their] work" (literally, "they ceased from their work").

    τεύχω, τεύξω, ἔτευξα or **τέτυκον**—prepare, make.

468   **δαίνυμι**—give a feast; *middle*—eat, feast; δαίνυντ᾽ = ἐδαίνυντο.

    θυμός—"desire."

    δεύομαι, δευήσομαι, ἐδεύησα—lack, be stinted in the matter of (+ gen.).

    ἔϊσος, -η, -ον—fairly divided.

    οὐδέ τι θυμὸς ἐδεύετο δαιτὸς ἐΐσης—"and no desire went unfulfilled in regard to the fairly divided banquet."

469   **πόσις, -ιος, ἡ**—drink.

    ἐδητύς, -ύος, ἡ—food.

    ἔρος, -ου, ὁ—desire: πόσιος καὶ ἐδητύος . . . ἔρον—"desire for drink and food."

    ἐξίημι—remove, appease, satisfy; ἐξ . . . ἔντο—tmesis; aorist.

470   **κοῦρος, -ου, ὁ**—young man.

    κρητήρ, -ῆρος, ὁ—mixing bowl, krater (the bowl in which the wine was mixed with water before being served; wine was almost always mixed with water before it was drunk).

    ἐπιστέφω, (aor.) **ἐπεστεψάμην**—fill to the brim (+ accusative of the thing filled [κρητῆρας] and genitive of material [ποτοῖο]).

ποτόν, -οῦ, τό—drink (in this case, wine).
471 νωμάω, (aor.) ἐνώμησα—distribute; νώμησαν = ἐνώμησαν.
ἐπάρχομαι—pour the first drops of wine; ἐπαρξάμενοι—aorist participle.
δέπας, -αος, τό—cup; δεπάεσσιν—"into the cups."
"They distributed [the wine] to everyone, having poured the first drops of wine [for the libation ritual] into the cups." (This refers to the ritual of pouring a small portion of wine on the ground as an offering to the gods before beginning to drink.)
472 πανημέριος, -η, -ον—all day long, all the rest of the day (adjective agreeing with the subject where in English you would expect an adverb).
μολπή, -ῆς, ἡ—song, singing.
473 καλόν—well, sweetly.
ἀείδω—sing.
παιήων, παιήονος, ὁ—song of praise, paean.
474 μέλπω—sing the praises of.
ἑκάεργος, -ου, ὁ—far-shooter, far-worker (an epithet of Apollo).
ὁ—he (refers to Apollo).
φρένα—"in his heart." What use of the accusative is this?
τέρπω—delight, please; τέρπετ᾽ = ἐτέρπετο.
    The episode involving Chryses, which ends happily here, has been called a "miniature" *Iliad*. Having lost a woman (his daughter), the old priest was dishonored (by Agamemnon). Weeping, he appealed to a god for help, and anger (Apollo's) brought trouble to the Greeks until the woman was returned and the anger (of the god) appeased. The same pattern applies to Achilles (loss of a woman, dishonor, tearful appeals to a deity [his mother] for help, trouble brought on the Greeks by his anger and subsequent withdrawal from the fighting). But Achilles becomes consumed by his anger, and in book 9, when appeasement in the form of compensation and the return of Briseis are offered, he refuses to accept them. Homer uses the Chryses story to lead his audience to expect a similar resolution to Achilles' story, but he overturns these expectations in book 9.
    The story of Chryses may have been invented to balance the episode with which the *Iliad* ends: Priam coming to the Greek camp to ransom the body of his son, Hector. The *Iliad* thus opens and closes with an old man coming to an enemy camp to ransom a child. Both are successful, although Chryses has his living daughter restored to him, while Priam, who has already lost his son to death, can only bring back Hector's body.

Scanning Notes
468 The υ in θυμός and the ι in ἐΐσης are long.
472 The ι in ἰλάσκοντο is long.
473 The α in καλόν is long.
474 The last syllable of μέλποντες is scanned long because ἑκάεργον was originally spelled Ϝεκάϝεργον.

*The next morning, Odysseus and his men sail back to the Greek camp, where
Achilles, still angry, takes no part in the battles or the assemblies.*

Ἦμος δ' ἠέλιος κατέδυ καὶ ἐπὶ κνέφας ἦλθε,   475
δὴ τότε κοιμήσαντο παρὰ πρυμνήσια νηός·   476
ἦμος δ' ἠριγένεια φάνη ῥοδοδάκτυλος Ἠώς,   477
καὶ τότ' ἔπειτ' ἀνάγοντο μετὰ στρατὸν εὐρὺν Ἀχαιῶν·   478
τοῖσιν δ' ἴκμενον οὖρον ἵει ἑκάεργος Ἀπόλλων·   479
οἱ δ' ἱστὸν στήσαντ' ἀνά θ' ἱστία λευκὰ πέτασσαν,   480
ἐν δ' ἄνεμος πρῆσεν μέσον ἱστίον, ἀμφὶ δὲ κῦμα   481
στείρῃ πορφύρεον μεγάλ' ἴαχε νηὸς ἰούσης·   482
ἡ δ' ἔθεεν κατὰ κῦμα διαπρήσσουσα κέλευθον.   483
αὐτὰρ ἐπεί ῥ' ἵκοντο κατὰ στρατὸν εὐρὺν Ἀχαιῶν,   484
νῆα μὲν οἵ γε μέλαιναν ἐπ' ἠπείροιο ἔρυσσαν   485
ὑψοῦ ἐπὶ ψαμάθοις, ὑπὸ δ' ἔρματα μακρὰ τάνυσσαν·   486
αὐτοὶ δὲ σκίδναντο κατὰ κλισίας τε νέας τε.   487

---

475 **ἦμος**—when.

ἠέλιος, -ου, ὁ—sun (= Attic ἥλιος).

καταδύω, (aor.) **κατέδυν**—go down, set.

κνέφας, -αος, τό—darkness, night.

ἐπέρχομαι, (aor.) **ἐπῆλθον**—come on; ἐπὶ . . . ἦλθε—tmesis.

476 **κοιμάω,** (aor.) **ἐκοίμησα**—lull to sleep; *middle*—lie down to sleep, sleep; κοιμήσαντο = ἐκοιμήσαντο.

πρυμνήσιον, -ου, τό—stern cable (rope used for fastening the stern, or rear, of the ship to the shore). (In other words, they slept on the shore, beside the cables that held the ships in place.)

477 **ἠριγένειος, -α, -ον**—early born.

φαίνω, (aor. pass.) **ἐφάνην**—show; *middle*—appear; φάνη = ἐφάνη—aorist passive used as a middle.

ῥοδοδάκτυλος, -ον—rosy-fingered (referring to the rays of rosy light that appeared in the sky before the sun rose).

Ἠώς, Ἠοῦς, ἡ—Eos, the goddess of dawn.

478 **καὶ τότ' ἔπειτ'**—"then."

ἀνάγω—lead, bring; *middle*—put to sea, sail; ἀνάγοντο = ἀνήγοντο—imperfect.

μετά—"for," "toward"

479 **τοῖσιν**—"for them."

ἴκμενος, -η, -ον—favorable.

οὖρος, -ου, ὁ—wind, breeze.

ἵει—imperfect of ἵημι, 3rd pers. sing.

480 **ἱστός, -οῦ, ὁ**—mast.

στήσαντ᾿ = ἐστήσαντο.

λευκός, -ή, -όν—white.

ἀναπετάννυμι, (aor.) ἀνεπέτασσα—spread out, unfold, unfurl; ἀνά . . . πέτασσαν—tmesis.

481   ἄνεμος, -ου, ὁ—wind.

ἐμπρήθω, ἐμπρήσω, ἐνέπρησα—blow, inflate; ἐν . . . πρῆσεν—tmesis.

μέσος, -η, -ον—middle of.

ἀμφί—(adv.) on both sides, around.

κῦμα, -ατος, τό—wave, waves.

482   στεῖρα, -ης, ἡ—stem, the curved front part of the keel (the beam of wood running down the center of the bottom of the ship) extending up on the end, which cuts through the water.

πορφύρεος, -η, -ον—dark, purple.

ἰάχω—roar; ἴαχε—imperfect.

ἰούσης—present active participle of εἶμι, gen. sing. fem.

ἀμφὶ δὲ κῦμα / στείρῃ πορφύρεον μεγάλ᾿ ἴαχε νηὸς ἰούσης (lines 481–82): "and the purple waves roared loudly round about the stem of the moving ship."

483   ἥ—"it" (refers to the ship).

θέω, θεύσομαι—run; ἔθεεν—imperfect, 3rd pers. sing.

κατά—"down along."

διαπρήσσω—accomplish, traverse.

κέλευθος, -ου, ἡ—journey, voyage, path.

484   κατὰ στρατόν—"off the camp" (i.e., at the landing place).

485   ἐπ᾿= ἐπί—upon, on (+ gen.).

ἤπειρος, -ου, ἡ—land.

ἔρυσσαν = εἴρυσσαν.

486   ὑψοῦ—(adv.) high.

ψάμαθος, -ου, ἡ—sand; ἐπὶ ψαμάθοις—"upon the sand."

ὑπό—(adv.) beneath, under.

ἕρμα, -ατος, τό—prop, beam, support (used to keep ships upright when they were on shore).

τανύω, τανύσω, ἐτάνυσσα—stretch, extend; τάνυσσαν = ἐτάνυσσαν.

487   σκίδναμαι—scatter, disperse; σκίδναντο = ἐσκίδναντο—imperfect.

νέας—acc. plur. of νηῦς.

Scanning Notes

475   The υ in κατέδυ is long.

479   Although the α in Ἀπόλλων is long, the first syllable is scanned short. Why?

482   The ι in ἴαχε is long.

484   The ι in ἵκοντο is long.

Αὐτὰρ ὁ μήνιε νηυσὶ παρήμενος ὠκυπόροισι   488
διογενὴς Πηλῆος υἱός, πόδας ὠκὺς Ἀχιλλεύς·   489
οὔτε ποτ᾽ εἰς ἀγορὴν πωλέσκετο κυδιάνειραν   490
οὔτε ποτ᾽ ἐς πόλεμον, ἀλλὰ φθινύθεσκε φίλον κῆρ   491
αὖθι μένων, ποθέεσκε δ᾽ ἀϋτήν τε πτόλεμόν τε.   492

On the twelfth day, Zeus and the other gods return to Mt. Olympus. Thetis approaches him as a suppliant and begs him to help her son.

Ἀλλ᾽ ὅτε δή ῥ᾽ ἐκ τοῖο δυωδεκάτη γένετ᾽ ἠώς,   493
καὶ τότε δὴ πρὸς Ὄλυμπον ἴσαν θεοὶ αἰὲν ἐόντες   494

488 ὠκύπορος, -ον—swift, swift-sailing.
489 Πηλεύς, -ῆος, ὁ—Peleus, father of Achilles.
    In line 488, the ships are described as swift-sailing (ὠκυπόροισι). In this line, Achilles is πόδας ὠκύς. These references to speed emphasize Achilles' unaccustomed inactivity. The irony of the epithet πόδας ὠκύς to describe Achilles here demonstrates Homer's skill in manipulating formulaic language.
490 πωλέομαι—go; πωλέσκετο—iterative imperfect. (Iterative imperfects and aorists are formed by adding -σκ- and personal endings to the stem; they are usually unaugmented. They indicate repeated past action.)
    κυδιάνειρα—(fem. adj.) bringing honor to men, glory-bringing, making men illustrious.
    οὔτε ποτ᾽ εἰς ἀγορὴν πωλέσκετο κυδιάνειραν—"he never frequented the glory-bringing assembly."
491 οὔτε ποτ᾽ ἐς πόλεμον—"nor [did he go] into battle." Notice the anaphora or repetition at the beginning of lines 490 and 491, emphasizing Achilles' withdrawal from the war.
    φθινύθω—pine away, waste away; φθινύθεσκε—iterative imperfect: "he kept pining away."
    φίλον—"his."
    κῆρ—What use of the accusative is this?
492 αὖθι—there.
    ποθέω, ποθήσω, ἐπόθεσα—long for; ποθέεσκε—iterative imperfect.
    ἀϋτή, -ῆς, ἡ—battle cry, war cry.
    πτόλεμον = πόλεμον.
493 ἐκ τοῖο—"from that time" (refers to the time of Achilles' conversation with Thetis, who told him that all the gods were gone for twelve days, visiting the Ethiopians; see lines 423–25).
    ἠώς, ἠοῦς, ἡ—dawn, morning.
494 ἴσαν—imperfect of εἶμι, 3rd pers. plur.

Fig. 4. Thetis. Painting attributed to either Euthymides or the Berlin Painter on
an Attic red-figure plate, ca. 510–500 B.C. (Courtesy of the Museum of Fine
Arts, Boston. Henry Lillie Pierce Fund, 1900. Reproduced with permission.
© 2000 Museum of Fine Arts, Boston. All Rights Reserved.)

Scanning Notes

489   The ι in διογενής is long.
       The first syllable of υἱός is scanned short. A long vowel or diphthong followed by
          another vowel can be scanned short.
490   The υ in κυδιάνειραν is long.
491   Why is the last syllable of πόλεμον scanned long? Where is the caesura in this
          line?
492   The υ in ἀϋτήν is long.

120   *Iliad*, Book 1

πάντες ἅμα, Ζεὺς δ᾿ ἦρχε· Θέτις δ᾿ οὐ λήθετ᾿ ἐφετμέων 495
παιδὸς ἑοῦ, ἀλλ᾿ ἥ γ᾿ ἀνεδύσετο κῦμα θαλάσσης, 496
ἠερίη δ᾿ ἀνέβη μέγαν οὐρανὸν Οὔλυμπόν τε. 497
εὗρεν δ᾿ εὐρύοπα Κρονίδην ἄτερ ἥμενον ἄλλων 498
ἀκροτάτῃ κορυφῇ πολυδειράδος Οὐλύμποιο· 499
καί ῥα πάροιθ᾿ αὐτοῖο καθέζετο, καὶ λάβε γούνων 500
σκαιῇ, δεξιτερῇ δ᾿ ἄρ᾿ ὑπ᾿ ἀνθερεῶνος ἑλοῦσα 501
λισσομένη προσέειπε Δία Κρονίωνα ἄνακτα· 502
"Ζεῦ πάτερ, εἴ ποτε δή σε μετ᾿ ἀθανάτοισιν ὄνησα 503
ἢ ἔπει ἢ ἔργῳ, τόδε μοι κρήηνον ἐέλδωρ· 504
τίμησόν μοι υἱόν, ὃς ὠκυμορώτατος ἄλλων 505
ἔπλετ᾿· ἀτάρ μιν νῦν γε ἄναξ ἀνδρῶν Ἀγαμέμνων 506
ἠτίμησεν· ἑλὼν γὰρ ἔχει γέρας, αὐτὸς ἀπούρας. 507
ἀλλὰ σύ πέρ μιν τῖσον, Ὀλύμπιε μητίετα Ζεῦ· 508
τόφρα δ᾿ ἐπὶ Τρώεσσι τίθει κράτος, ὄφρ᾿ ἂν Ἀχαιοὶ 509

---

495   **ἄρχω, ἄρξω, ἦρξα**—lead.
     λήθω—escape the notice of; *middle*—forget (+ gen.); λήθετ᾿ = ἐλήθετο.
     ἐφετμή, -ῆς, ἡ—request, command.
496   **ἑός, ἑή, ἑόν**—his, her, its.
     ἀναδύομαι, ἀναδύσομαι, ἀνεδυσάμην or **ἀνέδυν**—rise up from, emerge from; ἀνεδύσετο—aorist.
497   **ἠέριος, -η, -ον**—early in the morning (adjective agreeing with the subject where in English you would expect an adverb).
     μέγαν οὐρανὸν Οὔλυμπόν τε—Aristarchus of Samothrace, a Homeric scholar at the Library of Alexandria during the second century B.C., explained that Thetis went up to the sky because the top of Mt. Olympus was above the clouds.
498   **εὑρίσκω,** (aor.) **εὗρον**—find.
     εὐρύοπα (nom. and acc.)—far-thundering.
     Κρονίδης, -αο, ὁ—son of Cronus (= Zeus).
     ἄτερ—apart from, away from (+ gen.); ἄλλων is its object.
499   **ἄκρος, -η, -ον**—high; ἀκροτάτη—superlative.
     κορυφή, -ῆς, ἡ—peak, summit; κορυφῇ—What use of the dative is this?
     πολυδειράς, -άδος—many-ridged, with many peaks.
500   **πάροιθ᾿** = πάροιθε—in front of (+ gen.).
     λάβε = ἔλαβε.
     γούνων—What use of the genitive is this?
501   **σκαιός, -ή, -όν**—left; σκαιῇ [χειρί]—"with her left hand."
     δεξιτερός, -ή, -όν—right; δεξιτερῇ [χειρί].
     ὑπ᾿= ὑπό—by, under (+ gen.).

ἀνθερεών, -ῶνος, ὁ—chin.

ἑλοῦσα [μιν]—ἑλοῦσα is an aorist active participle from what verb?

καί ῥα πάροιθ'. . . ἑλοῦσα (lines 500–501)—Thetis is assuming the traditional position of a suppliant.

503   πάτερ—vocative. Ζεῦ πάτερ is a conventional way of addressing Zeus; he is not actually Thetis's father.

ὀνίνημι, ὀνήσω, ὤνησα—help; ὄνησα = ὤνησα.

504   κραίνω—accomplish, perform, fulfill; κρήηνον—aorist active imperative.

505   τίμησον—aorist active imperative (τιμάω).

μοι—What use of the dative is this?

ὠκύμορος, -ον—short-lived; ὠκυμορώτατος—superlative.

ἄλλων—"of all," "compared to all others."

How does the scansion of this line emphasize Thetis's pleading tone and the brevity of Achilles' life?

506   ἔπλετ' = ἔπλετο—imperfect of πέλομαι; ὅς . . . ἔπλετ'—"who . . . is."

ἀτάρ—but.

507   ἠτίμησεν—This word is emphatically positioned at the beginning of the line, stressing the dishonor Achilles has suffered and contrasting with τίμησον, also placed emphatically at the beginning of line 505.

ἀπούρας—aorist active participle of ἀπαυράω, nom. sing. masc.

ἑλών, αὐτός, ἀπούρας—all describe Agamemnon, the subject of ἔχει.

Compare lines 506–7 with lines 355–56. How are they different?

508   τῖσον—from τίω. (What kind of imperative is this?)

Ὀλύμπιε—vocative.

μητίετα, -αο, ὁ—counselor, wise one.

509   τόφρα—for so long a time.

ἐπιτίθημι—put into, bestow upon (+ acc. and dat.); ἐπὶ . . . τίθει—tmesis; present active imperative.

κράτος, -εος, τό—might, power, victory.

ὄφρ' = ὄφρα—until (+ subjunctive).

Scanning Notes

495   Synizesis occurs in the last two syllables of ἐφετμέων. How does that affect the scansion and pronunciation?

496   The υ in ἀνεδύσετο is long.

503   The first α in ἀθανάτοισιν is long.

505   The ι in τίμησον is long.

507   The ι in ἠτίμησεν is long.

υἱὸν ἐμὸν τίσωσιν ὀφέλλωσίν τέ ἑ τιμῇ."   510

Zeus says nothing at first. Thetis asks again, and he finally promises to do as she asks, though he knows Hera will not be happy about it.

Ὣς φάτο· τὴν δ᾽ οὔ τι προσέφη νεφεληγερέτα Ζεύς,   511
ἀλλ᾽ ἀκέων δὴν ἧστο· Θέτις δ᾽ ὡς ἥψατο γούνων,   512
ὣς ἔχετ᾽ ἐμπεφυυῖα, καὶ εἴρετο δεύτερον αὖτις·   513
"νημερτὲς μὲν δή μοι ὑπόσχεο καὶ κατάνευσον,   514
ἢ ἀπόειπ᾽, ἐπεὶ οὔ τοι ἔπι δέος, ὄφρ᾽ ἐῢ εἰδῶ   515
ὅσσον ἐγὼ μετὰ πᾶσιν ἀτιμοτάτη θεός εἰμι."   516
Τὴν δὲ μέγ᾽ ὀχθήσας προσέφη νεφεληγερέτα Ζεύς·   517
"ἦ δὴ λοίγια ἔργ᾽ ὅ τέ μ᾽ ἐχθοδοπῆσαι ἐφήσεις   518
Ἥρῃ, ὅτ᾽ ἄν μ᾽ ἐρέθῃσιν ὀνειδείοις ἐπέεσσιν·   519
ἡ δὲ καὶ αὔτως μ᾽ αἰεὶ ἐν ἀθανάτοισι θεοῖσι   520
νεικεῖ, καί τέ μέ φησι μάχῃ Τρώεσσιν ἀρήγειν.   521

---

510   **τίσωσιν**—aorist active subjunctive.
   ὀφέλλω—increase, glorify; ὀφέλλωσιν—present active subjunctive.
   ἑ—acc. sing. of εἷο.
   ὀφέλλωσίν τέ ἑ τιμῇ—"glorify him with honor," perhaps "enrich him with compensation."
   Thetis's request does not go into the detail Achilles had used. Look at lines 407–12. What specifically did he want?
511   **νεφεληγερέτα, -αο, ὁ**—cloud-gatherer.
512   **ἀκέων, -ουσα, -ον**—in silence, silent.
   δήν—for a long time.
   ἧστο—imperfect of ἧμαι, 3rd pers. sing.
   Homer increases the tension in this scene by having Zeus make no response at all to Thetis's request, forcing her to ask again.
   ὡς—as.
   ἅπτω, ἅψω, ἧψα—fasten; *middle*—take hold of, grasp, touch (+ gen.); ἥψατο—"she had taken hold of."
513   **ὣς**—so.
   ἔχετ᾽ = ἔχετο = εἴχετο—"she held on."
   ἐμφύω, ἐμφύσω, ἐνέφυσα, ἐμπέφυκα—cling closely to; ἐμπεφυυῖα = ἐμπεφυκυῖα—perfect active participle, nom. sing. fem.: "clinging."
   εἴρομαι—ask.
   δεύτερον—a second time.
514   **νημερτές**—truly.
   ὑπίσχομαι, ὑποσχήσομαι, ὑπεσχόμην—promise; ὑπόσχεο—aorist imperative.

κατανεύω, κατανεύσω, κατένευσα—nod assent, nod in agreement (literally, "nod down"; to nod the head down meant "yes").

515 ἀποεῖπον (aor.)— refuse; ἀπόειπ᾽ = ἀπόειπε—imperative.

ἔπι = ἔπεστι—is upon.

δέος, δείους, τό—fear.

ἐπεὶ οὔ τοι ἔπι δέος—"since you have nothing to fear" (literally, "since no fear is upon you"—ironic, since Zeus is hesitating precisely because he is, if not afraid of, at least bothered by what he knows Hera's reaction will be).

εἰδῶ—perfect subjunctive of οἶδα, 1st pers. sing.

516 ὅσσον—how much.

ἄτιμος, -ον—unhonored; ἀτιμοτάτη—superlative.

θεός—"goddess."

517 ὀχθέω, (aor.) ὤχθησα—be vexed with, be displeased with.

518 λοίγιος, -η, -ον—dreadful, horrible.

ἔργ᾽= ἔργα.

ἦ δὴ λοίγια ἔργ᾽ [ἔσται]—"truly this will be a bad business."

ὅ τε—seeing that, since, in that.

ἐχθοδοπέω, (aor.) ἠχθοδόπησα—quarrel with (+ dat.).

ἐφίημι, ἐφήσω—cause, drive to, incite.

519 ὅτ᾽= ὅτε—when.

ἐρέθω—provoke, tease, torment; ἐρέθῃσιν—present subjunctive, 3rd pers. sing.; translate as future.

ὀνείδειος, -ον—reproachful, injurious, abusive.

520 καὶ αὔτως—"even as it is," "even now."

ἐν—"among," "in front of."

521 νεικέω—quarrel with, rebuke, taunt.

φησι—present of φημί, 3rd pers. sing.

μάχη, -ης, ἡ—battle; μάχῃ—"in battle."

ἀρήγω—help (+ dat.).

μέ φησι μάχῃ Τρώεσσιν ἀρήγειν—indirect statement; an accusative infinitive construction after the verb φησι.

Scanning Notes

510 The first ι in τίσωσιν is long.

The ι in τιμῇ is long.

515 The word δέος was originally spelled δϝέος. How does that affect the scansion of the last syllable of ἔπι?

516 The ι in ἀτιμοτάτη is long.

520 The first α in ἀθανάτοισι is long.

ἀλλὰ σὺ μὲν νῦν αὖτις ἀπόστιχε, μή τι νοήσῃ   522
Ἥρη· ἐμοὶ δέ κε ταῦτα μελήσεται, ὄφρα τελέσσω·   523
εἰ δ᾽ ἄγε τοι κεφαλῇ κατανεύσομαι, ὄφρα πεποίθῃς·   524
τοῦτο γὰρ ἐξ ἐμέθεν γε μετ᾽ ἀθανάτοισι μέγιστον   525
τέκμωρ· οὐ γὰρ ἐμὸν παλινάγρετον οὐδ᾽ ἀπατηλὸν   526
οὐδ᾽ ἀτελεύτητον, ὅ τί κεν κεφαλῇ κατανεύσω."   527
Ἦ καὶ κυανέῃσιν ἐπ᾽ ὀφρύσι νεῦσε Κρονίων·   528
ἀμβρόσιαι δ᾽ ἄρα χαῖται ἐπερρώσαντο ἄνακτος   529
κρατὸς ἀπ᾽ ἀθανάτοιο· μέγαν δ᾽ ἐλέλιξεν Ὄλυμπον.   530

*Thetis returns to the sea and Zeus to his palace. Hera immediately demands
to know what he and Thetis have been plotting.*

Τώ γ᾽ ὣς βουλεύσαντε διέτμαγεν· ἡ μὲν ἔπειτα   531
εἰς ἅλα ἇλτο βαθεῖαν ἀπ᾽ αἰγλήεντος Ὀλύμπου,   532
Ζεὺς δὲ ἑὸν πρὸς δῶμα· θεοὶ δ᾽ ἅμα πάντες ἀνέσταν   533
ἐξ ἑδέων σφοῦ πατρὸς ἐναντίον· οὐδέ τις ἔτλη   534

---

522   **ἀποστείχω,** (aor.) **ἀπέστιχον**—go away, go back; **ἀπόστιχε**—aorist active im-
      perative.
      νοέω, νοήσω, ἐνόησα—observe; **νοήσῃ**—aorist active subjunctive, 3rd pers.
      sing.
      μή τι νοήσῃ / Ἥρη (lines 522–23)—purpose clause.
523   **μέλω, μελήσω**—be a concern; **μελήσεται**—future middle; translate as active.
      τελέσσω—aorist active subjunctive.
524   **εἰ δ᾽ ἄγε**—come! come now!
      κεφαλή, -ῆς, ἡ—head.
      πεποίθῃς—perfect active subjunctive of πείθω, 2nd pers. sing.; **ὄφρα
      πεποίθῃς**—"so you may trust [me]."
525   **ἐμέθεν**—gen. sing. of ἐγώ.
      μέγιστον—superlative of μέγας.
526   **τέκμωρ, τό** (indeclinable)—sign, pledge.
      τοῦτο ... μέγιστον / τέκμωρ [ἐστίν] (lines 525–26).
      ἐμὸν [τέκμωρ ἐστί].
      παλινάγρετος, -ον—revokable, able to be taken back.
      ἀπατηλός, -ή, -όν—deceitful.
527   **ἀτελεύτητος, -ον**—unaccomplished, unfulfilled.
      ὅ τι—whatever, whatsoever (understand "pledge").
      κατανεύσω—aorist subjunctive.
528   **ἦ**—he spoke.
      κυάνεος, -η, -ον—dark.

ὀφρύς, -ύος, ἡ—brow, eyebrow.

ἐπινεύω, ἐπινεύσω, ἐπένευσα—nod, nod in agreement; ἐπ᾽ . . . νεῦσε—tmesis.

529   ἀμβρόσιος, -η, -ον—ambrosial (ambrosia is the food of the gods; the meaning here seems to be "immortal" or "sweet-smelling").

χαίτη, -ης, ἡ—hair, locks.

ἐπιρρώομαι, (aor.) ἐπερρωσάμην—ripple down, flow down, roll down. (When Zeus nods, his long hair moves with the movement of his head.)

530   κάρη, κρατός, τό—head.

ἐλελίζω, (aor.) ἐλέλιξα—shake, make tremble.

According to Strabo (8.3.30), when the famous sculptor Phidias was asked what model he used for his sculpture of Zeus in the temple at Olympia, he replied that he based it on Homer's description in this passage. The enormous chryselephantine (gold and ivory) statue was considered one of the Seven Wonders of the Ancient World.

531   τώ—"the two of them," i.e., Zeus and Thetis; nom. dual.

βουλεύω, βουλεύσω, ἐβούλευσα—plan; βουλεύσαντε—aorist active participle, nom. dual.

διατμήγω, (aor.) διέτμαγον, (aor. pass.) διετμάγην—separate, part; διέτμαγεν = διετμάγησαν—aorist passive, 3rd pers. plur.; translate as middle.

532   ἅλλομαι, (aor.) ἅλμην—jump, leap; forms like ἆλτο, which lack a thematic vowel, are more common in Homer than in later Greek.

βαθύς, -εῖα, -ύ—deep.

αἰγλήεις, -εσσα, -εν—bright, shining.

533   Ζεὺς δὲ ἑὸν πρὸς δῶμα [ἔβη].

ἀνέσταν = ἀνέστησαν—aorist active of ἀνίστημι, 3rd pers. plur.

534   ἕδος, -εος, τό—seat.

σφός, σφή, σφόν—their own.

ἐναντίον—opposite, facing (+ gen.).

ἔτλην (aor.)—dare, venture.

Scanning Notes

525   The first α in ἀθανάτοισι is long.

527   Why is the last syllable of ἀτελεύτητον scanned long?

528   The υ in κυανέῃσιν and the ι in Κρονίων are long.

530   The α in κρατός and the first α in ἀθανάτοιο are long.

μεῖναι ἐπερχόμενον, ἀλλ᾽ ἀντίοι ἔσταν ἅπαντες.   535
ὣς ὁ μὲν ἔνθα καθέζετ᾽ ἐπὶ θρόνου· οὐδέ μιν Ἥρη   536
ἠγνοίησεν ἰδοῦσ᾽ ὅτι οἱ συμφράσσατο βουλὰς   537
ἀργυρόπεζα Θέτις θυγάτηρ ἁλίοιο γέροντος·   538
αὐτίκα κερτομίοισι Δία Κρονίωνα προσηύδα·   539
"τίς δὴ αὖ τοι, δολομῆτα, θεῶν συμφράσσατο βουλάς;   540
αἰεί τοι φίλον ἐστὶν ἐμεῦ ἀπονόσφιν ἐόντα   541
κρυπτάδια φρονέοντα δικαζέμεν· οὐδέ τί πώ μοι   542
πρόφρων τέτληκας εἰπεῖν ἔπος ὅττι νοήσῃς."   543

*Zeus discloses nothing, but when Hera guesses what he has promised Thetis,
he tells her that she can do nothing about it.*

Τὴν δ᾽ ἠμείβετ᾽ ἔπειτα πατὴρ ἀνδρῶν τε θεῶν τε·   544
"Ἥρη, μὴ δὴ πάντας ἐμοὺς ἐπιέλπεο μύθους   545
εἰδήσειν· χαλεποί τοι ἔσοντ᾽ ἀλόχῳ περ ἐούσῃ·   546

---

535   **μεῖναι**—aorist active infinitive of μένω.
    ἐπέρχομαι—come near, approach.
    οὐδέ τις ἔτλη / μεῖναι ἐπερχόμενον (lines 534–35)—"no one dared to remain
    [seated] as he was approaching."
    ἀντίος, -η, -ον—meeting, to meet.
    ἔσταν = ἔστησαν—aorist of ἵστημι, 3rd pers. plur.
    ἅπας, ἅπασα, ἅπαν = πᾶς, πᾶσα, πᾶν.
536   **ἔνθα**—then.
    καθέζετ᾽ = ἐκαθέζετο.
    θρόνος, -ου, ὁ—chair, seat.
    μιν—object of ἰδοῦσ᾽ in the next line.
537   **ἀγνοιέω**, (aor.) **ἠγνοίησα**—fail to notice, be unaware.
    ἰδοῦσ᾽ = ἰδοῦσα—aorist active participle of ὁράω, nom. sing. fem.
    ὅτι—that.
    οἱ—"him," i.e., Zeus; dat. sing.
    συμφράζομαι, συμφράσσομαι, συνεφρασάμην—make (plans) with, form
    (plans) with (+ dat.); συμφράσσατο = συνεφράσατο.
538   **ἀργυρόπεζος, -α, -ον**—silver-footed (a word frequently used to describe Thetis;
    it may refer to the whiteness of her feet or to the whitecaps of the waves around
    her feet when she rises from the sea).
    ἅλιος, -η, -ον—of the sea.
    ἁλίοιο γέροντος = Nereus, the sea god who is Thetis's father.
    οὐδέ μιν Ἥρη . . . γέροντος (lines 536–38)—"Hera, seeing him, was not un-
    aware that silver-footed Thetis, daughter of the old man of the sea, had been
    making plans with him."

539 κερτόμιος, -ον—cutting, sharp, reproachful; κερτομίοισι [ἔπεσι].

προσαυδάω, προσαυδήσω, προσηύδησα—speak to, address; προσηύδα—imperfect active, 3rd pers. sing.

540 αὖ—again, this time.

τίς δὴ αὖ . . . θεῶν—"who of the gods this time."

τοι—dative with συμφράσσατο.

δολομήτης, -ου, ὁ—deceiver, crafty-minded one; δολομῆτα—vocative.

541 ἀπονόσφιν—apart from, keeping away from (+ gen.).

ἐόντα—agrees with an understood σε, the subject of an accusative/infinitive construction (δικαζέμεν is the infinitive).

542 κρυπτάδιος, -η, -ον—secret; κρυπτάδια—acc. plur. neut.

φρονέω—consider, think about; φρονέοντα—acc. sing. masc.; also agrees with the understood σε.

δικάζω—decide, give decision on; δικαζέμεν = δικάζειν.

αἰεί τοι φίλον ἐστὶν ἐμεῦ ἀπονόσφιν ἐόντα / κρυπτάδια φρονέοντα δικαζέμεν (lines 541–42)—"You always like to consider and make judgments on secret matters when you're apart from me" (literally, "It is always pleasing to you that [you], considering secret things, make decisions being apart from me").

543 πρόφρων—cheerfully, eagerly, "freely."

τέτληκα (perfect; translate as present)—be willing to, venture, bring oneself to.

ἔπος—"plan," "intention."

ὅττι—that.

Are Hera's words here (lines 540–43) asked from true ignorance, or does she actually know what Zeus has just done? Many feel she knows very well what has happened.

545 ἐπιέλπομαι—hope, expect.

μύθους—"thoughts," "plans."

546 εἰδήσειν—future active infinitive of οἶδα.

χαλεπός, -ή, -όν—difficult.

ἔσοντ᾽ = ἔσονται (understand μῦθοι as the subject).

ἄλοχος, -ου, ἡ—wife.

ἐούσῃ—present active participle of εἰμί, dat sing. fem.

"[My plans] will be difficult for you [to know], even though you are my wife" (literally, "even though being my wife").

Scanning Notes

535 Why is the last syllable of ἐπερχόμενον scanned long?

540 By synizesis, δή and αὖ are run together to form one long syllable. Pronounce as though it were written δ᾽ αὖ.

543 The word εἰπεῖν was originally spelled Ϝειπεῖν.

545 The first υ in μύθους is long.

ἀλλ' ὃν μέν κ' ἐπιεικὲς ἀκουέμεν, οὗ τις ἔπειτα   547
οὔτε θεῶν πρότερος τόν γ' εἴσεται οὔτ' ἀνθρώπων·   548
ὃν δέ κ' ἐγὼν ἀπάνευθε θεῶν ἐθέλωμι νοῆσαι,   549
μή τι σὺ ταῦτα ἕκαστα διείρεο μηδὲ μετάλλα."   550
   Τὸν δ' ἠμείβετ' ἔπειτα βοῶπις πότνια Ἥρη·   551
"αἰνότατε Κρονίδη, ποῖον τὸν μῦθον ἔειπες;   552
καὶ λίην σε πάρος γ' οὔτ' εἴρομαι οὔτε μεταλλῶ,   553
ἀλλὰ μάλ' εὔκηλος τὰ φράζεαι ἅσσα θέλησθα.   554
νῦν δ' αἰνῶς δείδοικα κατὰ φρένα μή σε παρείπῃ   555
ἀργυρόπεζα Θέτις θυγάτηρ ἁλίοιο γέροντος·   556
ἠερίη γὰρ σοί γε παρέζετο καὶ λάβε γούνων·   557
τῇ σ' ὀΐω κατανεῦσαι ἐτήτυμον ὡς Ἀχιλῆα   558
τιμήσῃς, ὀλέσῃς δὲ πολέας ἐπὶ νηυσὶν Ἀχαιῶν."   559
   Τὴν δ' ἀπαμειβόμενος προσέφη νεφεληγερέτα Ζεύς·   560
"δαιμονίη, αἰεὶ μὲν ὀΐεαι, οὐδέ σε λήθω·   561

---

547   ὅν—"that which" (in other words, "whatever plan").
      ἐπιεικής, -ές—suitable, proper.
      ἀκουέμεν = ἀκούειν.
      ἀλλ' ὃν μέν κ' ἐπιεικὲς ἀκουέμεν—"but that which [may be] suitable [for anyone] to hear."
548   πρότερος, -η, -ον—sooner; understand σοῦ: "sooner than you."
      τόν—"it" (refers to Zeus's μῦθον).
      εἴσεται—future of οἶδα.
549   ὅν—"whatever [plan, matter, thought]."
      ἀπάνευθε—(prep.) apart from, far from (+ gen.).
      ἐθέλωμι—present active subjunctive of ἐθέλω.
550   μή τι—not at all.
      ἕκαστος, -η, -ον—each, every.
      διείρομαι—ask about.
      μεταλλάω—seek after, inquire about, question; μετάλλα—present imperative.
      "Don't you ask or inquire in any way about each of these things."
551   βοῶπις, -ιδος—(fem. adj.) literally, "ox-eyed." (This is a compliment. It may refer to either the size of the eyes or the calmness of expression and so would be translated into English as "large-eyed" or "calm-eyed" or perhaps simply as "beautiful.")
      πότνια—(fem. adj.) revered, honored.
552   αἰνός, -ή, -όν—terrible, fear-inspiring; αἰνότατε—superlative, vocative sing. masc.
      ποῖος, -η, -ον—what sort of? what kind of?

ἔειπες—2nd pers. sing. of εἶπον.

553   καὶ λίην—assuredly.

πάρος—before, at other times, in the past.

οὔτ᾽ εἴρομαι οὔτε μεταλλῶ—"I have not been in the habit of asking or questioning."

554   εὔκηλος, -ον—quiet, undisturbed, calm.

φράζω—point out, show; *middle*—consider; φράζεαι = φράζει—present middle, 2nd pers. sing.

ἄσσα—whatever things (acc. plur. neut. of ὅς τις).

θέλῃσθα = ἐθέλῃσθα—present subjunctive of ἐθέλω, 2nd pers. sing.

555   αἰνῶς—greatly, terribly.

δείδω, δείσομαι, ἔδεισα, δέδοικα—fear; δείδοικα = δέδοικα—perfect; translate as present.

μή—After a verb of fearing, μή introduces the clause that expresses what is feared.

παρεῖπον (aor.)—persuade, beguile, win over; παρείπῃ—aorist subjunctive, 3rd pers. sing.

557   ἠέριος, -η, -ον—early in the morning.

σοί—"beside you"

558   τῇ—"to her" (i.e., Thetis).

σ᾽... κατανεῦσαι—accusative and infinitive after ὀΐω.

ἐτήτυμον—truly, actually.

ὡς—that.

559   τιμήσῃς—aorist subjunctive of τιμάω; translate as future.

ὄλλυμι, ὀλέσ(σ)ω, ὤλεσ(σ)α—destroy, kill; ὀλέσῃς—aorist subjunctive; translate as future.

πολέας—acc. plur. masc. of πολύς.

There cannot be any doubt after lines 555–59 that Hera either knows exactly what is going on or is a remarkably astute guesser.

561   δαιμόνιος, -η, -ον—literally, "possessed by a divine being" and hence acting foolishly, unreasonably, or inexplicably; translate as "fool" or "what possesses you?" or "misguided woman." (Homer may be making a joke here, since the word would normally be applied to a human, not a goddess.)

ὀΐομαι—think, imagine, suspect; ὀΐεαι—present, 2nd pers. sing.

λήθω—escape the notice of, escape the observation of.

οὐδέ σε λήθω—"you are always watching me" (literally, "I do not escape the notice of you").

Scanning Notes

553   The ι in λίην is long.

559   The ι in τιμήσῃς is long.

      Synizesis occurs in the last two syllables of πολέας.

561   The first ι in ὀΐεαι is long.

πρῆξαι δ᾽ ἔμπης οὔ τι δυνήσεαι, ἀλλ᾽ ἀπὸ θυμοῦ   562
μᾶλλον ἐμοὶ ἔσεαι· τὸ δέ τοι καὶ ῥίγιον ἔσται.   563
εἰ δ᾽ οὕτω τοῦτ᾽ ἐστίν, ἐμοὶ μέλλει φίλον εἶναι·   564
ἀλλ᾽ ἀκέουσα κάθησο, ἐμῷ δ᾽ ἐπιπείθεο μύθῳ,   565
μή νύ τοι οὐ χραίσμωσιν ὅσοι θεοί εἰσ᾽ ἐν Ὀλύμπῳ   566
ἆσσον ἰόνθ᾽, ὅτε κέν τοι ἀάπτους χεῖρας ἐφείω."   567

Hephaestus urges his mother, Hera, not to quarrel with Zeus. He reminds her of the time Zeus, displeased with him, threw him off Mt. Olympus.

Ὣς ἔφατ᾽, ἔδεισεν δὲ βοῶπις πότνια Ἥρη,   568
καί ῥ᾽ ἀκέουσα καθῆστο, ἐπιγνάμψασα φίλον κῆρ·   569
ὄχθησαν δ᾽ ἀνὰ δῶμα Διὸς θεοὶ Οὐρανίωνες·   570
τοῖσιν δ᾽ Ἥφαιστος κλυτοτέχνης ἦρχ᾽ ἀγορεύειν,   571
μητρὶ φίλῃ ἐπὶ ἦρα φέρων, λευκωλένῳ Ἥρῃ·   572

---

562 **πρήσσω, πρήξω, ἔπρηξα**—do, act, accomplish.
    ἔμπης—nevertheless.
    δυνήσεαι = δυνήσει (originally δυνήσεσαι)—future, 2nd pers. sing.
    ἀπὸ θυμοῦ . . . ἐμοί (lines 562–63)—"away from my heart," i.e., "out of my
    favor."
563 **μᾶλλον**—more.
    ἔσεαι—future of εἰμί, 2nd pers. sing.
    τό—this (refers to being out of his favor).
    καί—"even."
    ῥίγιον—(neut. comp. adj.) more terrible, worse.
    Compare this line with line 325, where Agamemnon uttered the same threat.
    What seemed bluster from Agamemnon will be taken decidedly more seriously
    when spoken by Zeus.
564 **οὕτω**—so, thus.
    τοῦτ᾽—this (i.e., what Hera has accused him of—plotting with Thetis to help
    Achilles and hurt the Greeks).
    μέλλει (impersonal)—it is likely.
    In other words, Zeus tells Hera that if he is doing as she suspects, it is because
    that is what he wants to do.
565 **κάθημαι**—sit, sit down; κάθησο—imperative.
    ἐπιπείθομαι—obey (+ dat.).
566 **μή**—lest.
    χραισμέω, χραισμήσω, ἔχραισμον—keep off, help against (the person helped
    is in the dative); χραίσμωσιν—aorist active subjunctive, 3rd pers. plur.
    ὅσοι, -αι, -α—as many as, all that.

εἰσ᾽= εἰσί.
567 ἆσσον—nearer.

ἰόνθ᾽ = ἰόντα [με].

μή νύ τοι οὐ χραίσμωσιν ὅσοι θεοί εἰσ᾽ ἐν Ὀλύμπῳ / ἆσσον ἰόνθ᾽ [με] (lines
566–67)—this clause depends on the understood idea that Hera should be
afraid: "[be afraid] lest all the gods [there] are on Mt. Olympus not [be able to]
help you against [me] when I approach."

τοι—"on you."

ἄαπτος, -ον—invincible.

ἐφίημι—lay on; ἐφείω—aorist subjunctive.

Is Hera a nagging, scolding, interfering wife, or someone who truly cares for
the Greeks and is genuinely worried about Zeus's plans for them, or both? However she is viewed, she can do little against the greater power of Zeus.

568 ὣς ἔφατ᾽, ἔδεισεν δέ—This is another echo of the Agamemnon/Chryses scene
(see line 33). The human conflict leads to plague, suffering, and death, but the
gods' argument is swiftly resolved and followed by a feast and merriment. The
lives of the gods, while similar in many ways to the lives of men, are also completely different. Homer, by showing the gods on Mt. Olympus, allows us to
contrast their deathless existence with that of humans, who cannot escape suffering and death. Mortals have only a short time to accomplish what they will
and the consequences of their actions are much more serious.

569 καθῆστο—imperfect.

ἐπιγνάμπτω, (aor.) ἐπέγναμψα—restrain, repress.

570 ὀχθέω, (aor.) ὤχθησα—be distressed, be troubled; ὄχθησαν = ὤχθησαν.

Οὐρανίων, -ωνος—heaven-dwelling.

571 Ἥφαιστος, -ου, ὁ—Hephaestus, lame son of Zeus and Hera; god of fire and all
arts that use fire, especially metalworking.

κλυτοτέχνης, -ου, ὁ—renowned artisan.

ἄρχω, ἄρξω, ἦρξα—begin; ἦρχ᾽ = ἦρχε.

572 ἐπιφέρω—lay on, lay upon; ἐπὶ . . . φέρων—tmesis.

ἦρα (acc. sing.)—what is pleasing or agreeable, kindness.

ἐπὶ ἦρα φέρων—"making himself agreeable," "doing kind service."

Scanning Notes

562 The first υ in θυμοῦ is long.
563 The first ι in ῥίγιον is long.
565 The υ in μύθῳ is long.
568 The word ἔδεισεν was originally spelled ἔδϝεισεν.
569 The second α in ἐπιγνάμψασα is long.

132 *Iliad*, Book 1

"ἦ δὴ λοίγια ἔργα τάδ' ἔσσεται οὐδ' ἔτ' ἀνεκτά, 573
εἰ δὴ σφὼ ἕνεκα θνητῶν ἐριδαίνετον ὧδε, 574
ἐν δὲ θεοῖσι κολῳὸν ἐλαύνετον· οὐδέ τι δαιτὸς 575
ἐσθλῆς ἔσσεται ἦδος, ἐπεὶ τὰ χερείονα νικᾷ. 576
μητρὶ δ' ἐγὼ παράφημι, καὶ αὐτῇ περ νοεούσῃ, 577
πατρὶ φίλῳ ἐπὶ ἦρα φέρειν Διί, ὄφρα μὴ αὖτε 578
νεικείῃσι πατήρ, σὺν δ' ἡμῖν δαῖτα ταράξῃ. 579
εἴ περ γάρ κ' ἐθέλῃσιν Ὀλύμπιος ἀστεροπητὴς 580
ἐξ ἑδέων στυφελίξαι· ὁ γὰρ πολὺ φέρτατός ἐστιν· 581
ἀλλὰ σὺ τόν γ' ἐπέεσσι καθάπτεσθαι μαλακοῖσιν· 582
αὐτίκ' ἔπειθ' ἵλαος Ὀλύμπιος ἔσσεται ἡμῖν." 583

Ὣς ἄρ' ἔφη, καὶ ἀναΐξας δέπας ἀμφικύπελλον 584
μητρὶ φίλῃ ἐν χειρὶ τίθει, καί μιν προσέειπε· 585
"τέτλαθι, μῆτερ ἐμή, καὶ ἀνάσχεο κηδομένη περ, 586
μή σε φίλην περ ἐοῦσαν ἐν ὀφθαλμοῖσιν ἴδωμαι 587

---

573 **λοίγιος, -η, -ον**—dreadful, horrible; **λοίγια ἔργα τάδ'**—"these horrible things," "this bad business." Look at line 518. Zeus used the same words when he predicted that Thetis's request would lead to a quarrel with Hera, as indeed it has. Now Hephaestus tries to smooth things over.
οὐδ' ἔτ'—no longer.
ἀνεκτός, -όν—endurable.
574 **σφώ**—the two of you (nom. dual of σύ).
ἐριδαίνω—quarrel; **ἐριδαίνετον**—present, 2nd pers. dual.
ὧδε—thus, in this way.
575 **κολῳός, -οῦ, ὁ**—quarrel, disturbance.
ἐλαύνω—stir up, set in motion; **ἐλαύνετον**—present, 2nd pers. dual.
576 **ἐσθλός, -ή, -όν**—good, excellent, fine.
ἦδος, -εος, τό—enjoyment, pleasure.
χερείων, -ον—worse; **τὰ χερείονα**—"worse matters."
νικάω—prevail, be victorious; **νικᾷ**—present, 3rd pers. sing.
577 **παράφημι**—urge, advise (+ dat. and infinitive).
καὶ ... περ—although.
νοεούσῃ—present active participle of νοέω, dat. sing. fem.
καὶ αὐτῇ περ νοεούσῃ—"although she herself perceives this."
578 **αὖτε**—again.
579 **νεικείῃσι**—present subjunctive, 3rd pers. sing.
συνταράσσω, συνταράξω—disturb, spoil; **σὺν ... ταράξῃ**—tmesis; aorist subjunctive, 3rd pers. sing.
ἡμῖν—"for us." What use of the dative is this?

ὄφρα μὴ αὖτε / νεικείῃσι πατήρ, σὺν δ' ἡμῖν δαῖτα ταράξῃ (lines 578–79)—What kind of a clause is this?

580   εἴ περ—"just suppose," "at any rate, if."
ἐθέλῃσιν—present subjunctive, 3rd pers. sing.; subjunctive verb in the protasis of a future-more-vivid condition.
ἀστεροπητής, -αο, ὁ—lightning hurler; Ὀλύμπιος ἀστεροπητής = Zeus.
581   ἕδος, -εος, τό—seat.
στυφελίζω, (aor.) ἐστυφέλιξα—hurl, thrust; στυφελίξαι—aorist active infinitive.
εἴ περ γάρ κ' ἐθέλῃσιν Ὀλύμπιος ἀστεροπητὴς / ἐξ ἑδέων στυφελίξαι [ἡμᾶς] (lines 580–81)—The understood conclusion is something like "he could easily do it" or "what could we do?" This is an example of a figure of speech called *aposiopesis*, wherein a sentence is broken off and its completion is left to the imagination.
πολύ—much, by far.
φέρτατος, -η, -ον—best, strongest, most powerful.
582   καθάπτομαι—address, approach; καθάπτεσθαι—infinitive used as an imperative.
μαλακός, -ή, -όν—soft, gentle.
583   ἔπειθ'= ἔπειτα.
ἵλαος, -η, -ον—propitious, kind.
Ὀλύμπιος—the Olympian = Zeus.
ἡμῖν—"to us," "toward us."
584   ἔφη—imperfect of φημί, 3rd pers. sing.
ἀναΐσσω, ἀναΐξω, ἀνήϊξα—spring up, leap up.
ἀμφικύπελλος, -ον—double, two-handled; δέπας ἀμφικύπελλον may be a double cup, i.e., one forming a cup both on the top and the bottom, or a two-handled cup.
585   μητρὶ φίλῃ—"of his mother," "his mother's."
τίθει = ἐτίθει (imperfect).
586   τέτλαθι—perfect active imperative.
ἀνέχω, ἀνέξω, ἀνέσχον—lift up, hold up; *middle*—bear up, endure, hold up under; ἀνάσχεο—aorist middle imperative.
κήδω—trouble, distress.
587   φίλην περ ἐοῦσαν—"who are very dear [to me]" (literally, "being very dear").
ὀφθαλμός, -οῦ, ὁ—eye; ἐν ὀφθαλμοῖσιν—"before my eyes."
μή . . . ἴδωμαι—What kind of a clause is this?

Scanning Notes

576   The ι in νικᾷ is long.
583   The ι and the α in ἵλαος are long.
584   The second α in ἀναΐξας is long.

θεινομένην, τότε δ᾽ οὔ τι δυνήσομαι ἀχνύμενός περ　　588
χραισμεῖν· ἀργαλέος γὰρ Ὀλύμπιος ἀντιφέρεσθαι·　　589
ἤδη γάρ με καὶ ἄλλοτ᾽ ἀλεξέμεναι μεμαῶτα　　590
ῥῖψε ποδὸς τεταγὼν ἀπὸ βηλοῦ θεσπεσίοιο,　　591
πᾶν δ᾽ ἦμαρ φερόμην, ἅμα δ᾽ ἡελίῳ καταδύντι　　592
κάππεσον ἐν Λήμνῳ, ὀλίγος δ᾽ ἔτι θυμὸς ἐνῆεν·　　593
ἔνθα με Σίντιες ἄνδρες ἄφαρ κομίσαντο πεσόντα."　　594

The gods feast until sundown, then return to their homes for the night.

Ὣς φάτο, μείδησεν δὲ θεὰ λευκώλενος Ἥρη,　　595
μειδήσασα δὲ παιδὸς ἐδέξατο χειρὶ κύπελλον·　　596
αὐτὰρ ὁ τοῖς ἄλλοισι θεοῖς ἐνδέξια πᾶσιν　　597
οἰνοχόει γλυκὺ νέκταρ ἀπὸ κρητῆρος ἀφύσσων·　　598
ἄσβεστος δ᾽ ἄρ᾽ ἐνῶρτο γέλως μακάρεσσι θεοῖσιν,　　599

588　**θείνω**—beat, strike, hit; **θεινομένην**—present passive participle, acc. sing. fem.

589　**ἀργαλέος, -η, -ον**—difficult, hard.

　　ἀντιφέρομαι—set oneself against, oppose.

　　ἀργαλέος γὰρ Ὀλύμπιος ἀντιφέρεσθαι—"for the Olympian [is] difficult to oppose."

590　**ἤδη**—already.

　　ἄλλοτ᾽ = **ἄλλοτε**—on another occasion.

　　ἀλέξω—aid, defend; **ἀλεξέμεναι**—present active infinitive (understand σε as the object).

　　μέμονα (perfect; translate as present)—desire, be eager; **μεμαῶτα**—perfect active participle, acc. sing. masc.; describes με.

591　**ῥίπτω, ῥίψω, ἔρριψα**—hurl, throw, fling; **ῥῖψε** = **ἔρριψε**.

　　ποδός—"by the foot."

　　τέταγον (aor.)—seize, grasp; **τεταγών**—aorist active participle.

　　βηλός, -οῦ, ὁ—threshold.

　　θεσπέσιος, -η, -ον—divine.

　　ἀπὸ βηλοῦ θεσπεσίοιο—in other words, from the threshold of a palace on Mt. Olympus.

592　**ἦμαρ, ἤματος, τό**—day; **πᾶν δ᾽ ἦμαρ**—accusative of extent of time.

　　φέρω—carry; **φερόμην** = **ἐφερόμην**—imperfect passive: "I fell," "I was falling" (literally, "I was carried").

　　ἅμα—at the time of (+ dat.).

　　καταδύντι—aorist active participle, dat. sing. masc.

593　**καταπίπτω**, (aor.) **κάππεσον**—fall down.

　　Λῆμνος, -ου, ἡ—Lemnos, an island in the Aegean Sea. (Worship of Hephaestus seems to have been of special importance on Lemnos. As the god of fire, he may have been associated with Lemnos because of the volcanic nature of the island.)

ὀλίγος, -η, -ον—little.

θυμός—"breath," "life."

ἔνειμι—be in; ἐνῆεν—imperfect.

594 Σίντιες, -ων, οἱ—Sintians, inhabitants of Lemnos; Σίντιες ἄνδρες—Sintian men.

ἄφαρ—at once, immediately.

κομίζω, κομιῶ, ἐκόμισα—care for, attend to; *middle*—rescue, come to the relief of; κομίσαντο = ἐκομίσαντο.

πίπτω, (aor.) ἔπεσον—fall; πεσόντα—aorist active participle, acc. sing. masc. (modifies με).

Hephaestus refers to an earlier occasion when Zeus, angry at Hera, suspended her with anvils hanging from her feet. When Hephaestus tried to help her, Zeus hurled him to the earth. See *Il.* 15.18–24.

595 μειδάω, (aor.) ἐμείδησα—smile, laugh; μείδησεν = ἐμείδησεν.

596 παιδός—"from her son."

χειρί—"in her hand," "with her hand."

κύπελλον, -ου, τό—cup.

597 ἐνδέξια—from left to right (from left to right was considered the propitious direction).

598 οἰνοχοέω—pour, pour wine; οἰνοχόει = ᾠνοχόει—imperfect.

γλυκύς, -εῖα, -ύ—sweet.

νέκταρ, -αρος, τό—nectar (the drink of the gods).

ἀφύσσω—dip out; Hephaestus is using a ladle to dip the nectar out of the mixing bowl and pour it into cups.

599 ἄσβεστος, -η, -ον—unquenchable, inextinguishable, ceaseless.

ἐνόρνυμι, ἐνόρσω, ἐνῶρσα—arouse, stir up; *middle*—arise, rise among; ἐνῶρτο—aorist middle.

γέλως, γέλωτος, ὁ—laughter.

μακάρεσσι θεοῖσιν—"among the happy gods."

Scanning Notes

593 The υ in θυμός is long.

595 The α in θεά is long.

596 The first α in μειδήσασα is long.

ὡς ἴδον Ἥφαιστον διὰ δώματα ποιπνύοντα. 600
Ὣς τότε μὲν πρόπαν ἦμαρ ἐς ἠέλιον καταδύντα 601
δαίνυντ᾿, οὐδέ τι θυμὸς ἐδεύετο δαιτὸς ἐΐσης, 602
οὐ μὲν φόρμιγγος περικαλλέος, ἣν ἔχ᾿ Ἀπόλλων, 603
Μουσάων θ᾿, αἳ ἄειδον ἀμειβόμεναι ὀπὶ καλῇ. 604
Αὐτὰρ ἐπεὶ κατέδυ λαμπρὸν φάος ἠελίοιο, 605
οἱ μὲν κακκείοντες ἔβαν οἰκόνδε ἕκαστος, 606
ἧχι ἑκάστῳ δῶμα περικλυτὸς ἀμφιγυήεις 607

---

600 ὡς—as.

ποιπνύω—bustle, hurry, puff. ποιπνύοντα is onomatopoetic, its sound suggesting the puffing of Hephaestus as he moves about, serving the gods. The gods are laughing at the sight of Hephaestus bustling about serving the wine. The lame, unattractive god who is more at home in the forge is a comic contrast to those who usually serve the gods: Hebe, the beautiful goddess of youth, or Ganymede, a boy so beautiful that Zeus had him carried to Mt. Olympus and made the gods' cupbearer. Thus, the quarrel that threatened to break out among the gods is averted, quite unlike the quarrel with which book 1 opened, which will not be resolved for quite some time. Hephaestus, the peacemaker, succeeds among the gods as Nestor could not among men. And Zeus's authority is supreme, as Agamemnon's is not.

601 πρόπας, -πασα, -παν—the whole, all.

602 δαίνυντ᾿ = ἐδαίνυντο.

θυμός—"desire."

ἔϊσος, -η, -ον—fairly divided.

603 οὐ μέν = οὐ μήν—nor indeed.

φόρμιγξ, -ιγγος, ἡ—phorminx (a type of lyre).

περικαλλής, -ές—very beautiful; περικαλλέος—gen. sing. fem.

ἥν—relative pronoun, referring to the φόρμιγξ.

ἔχ᾿ = ἔχε = εἶχε—imperfect.

604 Μοῦσα, -ης, ἡ—Muse, one of the goddesses of literature, music, and dance. In the first line of the *Iliad*, Homer invoked one of these goddesses to help him tell this story.

ἄειδον = ἤειδον—imperfect.

ἀμειβόμεναι—responsively, alternately, in turn (literally, "answering"); present middle participle of ἀμείβω.

ὄψ, ὀπός, ἡ—voice.

οὐδέ τι θυμὸς ἐδεύετο δαιτὸς ἐΐσης, / οὐ μὲν φόρμιγγος περικαλλέος . . . / Μουσάων θ᾿ . . . (lines 602–4)—"and no desire went unfulfilled in regard to the fairly divided meal or, indeed, in regard to the very beautiful lyre . . . or the

Fig. 5. Apollo holding a lyre. Painting by the Providence Painter on an Attic red-figure amphora, ca. 480 B.C. (Courtesy of the Museum of Art, Rhode Island School of Design; gift of Mrs. Gustav Radeke.)

Muses." (In other words, they were well satisfied with their food, Apollo's lyre playing, and the singing of the Muses.)

605   λαμπρός, -ή, -όν—bright, shining.

φάος, -εος, τό—light.

606   κατακείω—go to rest; κακκείοντες = κατακείοντες—present active participle.

ἔβαν = ἔβησαν.

ἕκαστος, -η, -ον—each one; although singular, it describes οἱ: "each one of them."

607   ἧχι—where.

ἑκάστῳ—for each.

περικλυτός, -ή, -όν—famous, renowned.

ἀμφιγυήεις, -εσσα, -εν—lame in both legs (an epithet of Hephaestus).

Scanning Notes

600   The υ in ποιπνύοντα is long.

602   The υ in θυμός and the ι in ἐΐσης are long.

603   Although the α in Ἀπόλλων is long, the first syllable is scanned short. Why?

604   The α in Μουσάων and the α in καλῇ are long.

605   The υ in κατέδυ is long.

606   The word οἰκόνδε was originally spelled Ϝοικόνδε.

Ἥφαιστος ποίησεν ἰδυίῃσι πραπίδεσσι·   608
Ζεὺς δὲ πρὸς ὃν λέχος ἤϊ' Ὀλύμπιος ἀστεροπητής,   609
ἔνθα πάρος κοιμᾶθ' ὅτε μιν γλυκὺς ὕπνος ἱκάνοι·   610
ἔνθα καθεῦδ' ἀναβάς, παρὰ δὲ χρυσόθρονος Ἥρη.   611

608   **ἰδυίῃσι**—perfect active participle of οἶδα, dat. plur. fem.
      πραπίδες, -ων, αἱ—mind, understanding, skill.
      ἰδυίῃσι πραπίδεσσι—"with knowing mind,'" "with cunning skill."
609   **λέχος, -εος, τό**—bed.
      ἤϊ' = ἤϊε.
610   **ἔνθα**—where.
      πάρος—before, in the past.
      κοιμάω, (aor.) **ἐκοίμησα**—lull to sleep; *middle*—lie down to sleep, sleep;
      κοιμᾶθ' = ἐκοιμᾶτο—imperfect middle.
      ὅτε—whenever.
      ὕπνος, -ου, ὁ—sleep.
      ἱκάνοι—present optative, 3rd pers. sing.
611   **ἔνθα**—there.
      καθεύδω—go to bed, sleep; καθεῦδ' = ἐκάθευδε.
      ἀναβάς—"going up [onto his bed]."
      παρά—"beside him."
      χρυσόθρονος, -ον—golden-throned.

In the first book of the *Iliad,* Homer introduces the main characters and describes the quarrel that will have fatal results for so many Greeks and Trojans. Because of the opening seven lines, Achilles' actions and predictions, Athena's words, and Zeus's promise to Thetis, we think we know what to expect in the coming books: Achilles will refuse to fight for the Greeks, and as a result, many of them will die in battle. When they realize they cannot win without Achilles, the Greeks will offer him gifts and honors to return. To guide their expectations, ancient audiences had not only these indications but a general familiarity with the story. Homer does not, however, rush to present the expected events. By interrupting the traditional sequence of events with Agamemnon's call for a retreat in book 2, the duel between Menelaus and Paris in book 3, and a series of other episodes, he teases the audience with alternate ending possibilities and keeps them guessing as to when the expected outcomes will take place. In the remainder of the *Iliad,* Homer's artistry makes even a familiar story with a known end suspenseful and surprising.

    The *Iliad* is often described as a poem about war, but book 1, which depicts no battles at all, shows that it is also about how people deal with anger, pride, power, honor, responsibility, disappointment, and the knowledge of mortality. It is about consequences, how the decisions of one person can affect many others. Although set in ancient Greece, it has relevance for all times, places, and cultures. Dealing with power responsibly, being forced to give up something we want very much to keep, having to sacrifice for the common good, refusing to cooperate when our wishes are thwarted, taking a position on principle and sticking to it despite the consequences, contemplating the briefness of our lives—these are all part of being human. While Achilles is unique in knowing more specifically than most when he will die, we are all μινυνθάδιοι and must grapple with the questions of how to live honorably and what choices to make within the brief time allotted for any human life. In book 1 of the *Iliad*, Homer shows how Agamemnon and Achilles face and meet or fail to meet these challenges. The rest of the *Iliad* reveals the consequences of their choices.

Scanning Notes

609   You would expect δέ to be scanned long because it is followed by two consonants. However, if the first consonant is a mute or stop (π, β, φ, κ, γ, χ, τ, δ, or θ) and the second is either λ or ρ, the preceeding syllable can be scanned short, as it is here.

610   The α in ἱκάνοι is long.

611   The υ in χρυσόθρονος is long.

Appendix 1
Criticism

The *Iliad* has been analyzed, critiqued, and explained for a very long time, and the notes in this book include ideas suggested by many people. To give proper credit to them and to indicate books or articles for further investigation, the sources are listed here. They are arranged by the line number and the word or idea to which the note refers.

1   θεά   Elizabeth Minchin, "The Poet Appeals to His Muse: Homeric Invocations in the Context of Epic Performance," *Classical Journal* 91, no. 1 (October-November 1995): 26–27.

2   οὐλομένην   Clyde Pharr, *Homeric Greek: A Book for Beginners,* rev. John Wright (Norman: University of Oklahoma Press, 1985), 28.

3   Ἄϊδι   Simon Pulleyn, ed., *Homer: Iliad, Book One* (Oxford: Oxford University Press, 2000), 41–43; 119.

4–5   αὐτοὺς δὲ ἑλώρια τεῦχε κύνεσσιν / οἰωνοῖσί τε πᾶσι   James Redfield, "The Proem of the *Iliad:* Homer's Art," *Classical Philology* 74, no. 2 (April 1979): 103–5.

7   introductory lines (lines 1–7)   Richard Rutherford, *Homer,* Greece and Rome New Surveys in the Classics, no. 26. (Oxford: Oxford University Press, 1996): 30–31.
      Homer's originality   Joachim Latacz, *Homer: His Art and His World,* trans. James P. Holoka (Ann Arbor: University of Michigan Press, 1996), 75–79.

14   στέμματ'   Simon Pulleyn, ed., *Homer: Iliad, Book One* (Oxford: Oxford University Press, 2000), 125.

15   σκήπτρῳ   Mark W. Edwards, "Convention and Individuality in *Iliad* I," *Harvard Studies in Classical Philology* 84 (1980): 6.

17   ἐϋκνήμιδες   C. M. Bowra, "*ΕΥΚΝΗΜΙΔΕΣ ΑΧΑΙΟΙ,*" *Mnemosyne (Bibliotheca Classica Batava)* 14 (1961): 97–110.

19   εὖ δ᾽ οἴκαδ᾽ ἱκέσθαι   James V. Morrison, *Homeric Misdirection: False Predictions in the Iliad* (Ann Arbor: University of Michigan Press, 1992), 26–27.

21   end of Chryses' speech   Thomas D. Seymour, *The First Six Books of Homer's Iliad,* rev. ed. (Boston: Ginn, 1929), commentary on line 21; Simon Pulleyn, ed., *Homer: Iliad, Book One* (Oxford: Oxford University Press, 2000), 128.

26   κοίλῃσιν   Lionel Casson, *The Ancient Mariners: Seafarers and Sea Fighters of*

the *Mediterranean in Ancient Times,* 2d ed. (Princeton: Princeton University Press, 1991), 39.

30 ἡμετέρῳ ἐνὶ οἴκῳ, ἐν ῎Αργεϊ, τηλόθι πάτρης   Jasper Griffin, *Homer on Life and Death* (Oxford: Clarendon, 1980): 107; Johannes Th. Kakridis, "The First Scene with Chryses in the *Iliad,*" in *Homer Revisited* (Lund: New Society of Letters, 1971), 131.

32 characterization of Agamemnon   Mark W. Edwards, "Convention and Individuality in *Iliad* I," *Harvard Studies in Classical Philology* 84 (1980): 7–8; Oliver Taplin, "Agamemnon's Role in the *Iliad,*" in *Characterization and Individuality in Greek Literature,* ed. Christopher Pelling (Oxford: Clarendon, 1990): 79–80.

43 ἔκλυε   George Eckel Duckworth, *Foreshadowing and Suspense in the Epics of Homer, Apollonius, and Vergil* (New York: Haskell, 1966), 10.

45 φαρέτρην   W. B. Stanford, "Varieties of Sound-Effects in the Homeric Poems," *College Literature* 3, no. 3 (1976): 223.

47 νυκτὶ ἐοικώς   Mark W. Edwards, *Homer: Poet of the Iliad* (Baltimore: Johns Hopkins University Press, 1987), 177.

52 βάλλ᾽   Mark W. Edwards, "Convention and Individuality in *Iliad* I," *Harvard Studies in Classical Philology* 84 (1980): 11; J. R. Sitlington Sterrett, ed., *Homer's Iliad: First Three Books and Selections* (New York: American Book Company, 1907), N68.

αἰεί   Johannes Th. Kakridis, "The First Scene with Chryses in the *Iliad,*" in *Homer Revisited* (Lund: New Society of Letters, 1971), 129.

identification of the disease   Frederick Bernheim and Ann Adams Zener, "The Sminthian Apollo and the Epidemic among the Achaeans at Troy," *Transactions of the American Philological Association* 108 (1978): 11–14; Lionel Casson, *The Ancient Mariners: Seafarers and Sea Fighters of the Mediterranean in Ancient Times,* 2d ed. (Princeton: Princeton University Press, 1991), 37.

55 λευκώλενος   Allen Rogers Benner, *Selections from Homer's Iliad* (New York: Irvington, 1903), xxv; Simon Pulleyn, ed., *Homer: Iliad, Book One* (Oxford: Oxford University Press, 2000), 140–41.

84 use of epithets   André Michalopoulos, *Homer* (New York: Twayne, 1966), 69–70.

117 βούλομ᾽ and other first-person verbs of wanting   Simon Pulleyn, ed., *Homer: Iliad, Book One* (Oxford: Oxford University Press, 2000), 159.

120 loss of property   W. B. Stanford, "Homer," in *Ancient Writers: Greece and Rome,* vol. 1, ed. T. James Luce (New York: Scribner's, 1982), 4.

133 αὐτὸς . . . αὐτὰρ . . . αὔτως   A. Shewan, "Alliteration and Assonance in Homer," *Classical Philology* 20, no. 3 (July 1925): 206–7.

141 νῆα μέλαιναν   Lionel Casson, *The Ancient Mariners: Seafarers and Sea Fighters of the Mediterranean in Ancient Times,* 2d ed. (Princeton: Princeton University Press, 1991), 38.

157 ἠχήεσσα Clyde Pharr, *Homeric Greek: A Book for Beginners,* rev. John Wright (Norman: University of Oklahoma Press, 1985), 94.

159 κυνῶπα Margaret Graver, "Dog-Helen and Homeric Insult," *Classical Antiquity* 14, no. 1 (April 1995): 46–47, 49.

180 position of Μυρμιδόνεσσιν Clyde Pharr, *Homeric Greek: A Book for Beginners* (Norman: University of Oklahoma Press, 1959), 111.

183 ἐμῇ, ἐμοῖς G. S. Kirk, *The Iliad: A Commentary,* vol. 1, *Books 1–4* (Cambridge: Cambridge University Press, 1985), 70.

184 Agamemnon's implication G. S. Kirk, *The Iliad: A Commentary,* vol. 1, *Books 1–4* (Cambridge: Cambridge University Press, 1985), 70.

185 κλισίηνδε Mary O. Knox, "Huts and Farm Buildings in Homer," *Classical Quarterly* 21, no. 1 (May 1971): 27–31.

190 παρὰ μηροῦ Thomas Day Seymour, *Life in the Homeric Age* (1907; reprint, New York: Biblo and Tannen, 1963), 666.

191 τοὺς μὲν ἀναστήσειεν Edwin D. Floyd, "Homer's *Iliad,* Book I, Line 191," *Explicator* 35, no. 4 (summer 1995): 186–88.

   ἐναρίζοι Simon Pulleyn, ed., *Homer: Iliad, Book One* (Oxford: Oxford University Press, 2000), 175.

195 imperfect and aorist tenses Clyde Pharr, *Homeric Greek: A Book for Beginners,* rev. John Wright (Norman: University of Oklahoma Press, 1985), 105.

222 Athena's intervention J. T. Hooker, "The Visit of Athena to Achilles in *Iliad* I," *Emerita* 58 (1990): 28–30.

234 σκῆπτρον Frederick M. Combellack, "Speakers and Scepters in Homer," *Classical Journal* 43, no. 4 (January 1948): 209–17.

243 irony of Achilles' prediction Andrew Lang, *Homer and the Epic* (London and New York: Longmans, Green, & Co., 1893; reprint, New York: AMS, 1970), 84.

245 throwing the staff to the ground Jasper Griffin, *Homer on Life and Death* (Oxford: Clarendon, 1980): 11–12; Cathy L. Callaway, "The Oath in Epic Poetry" (Ph.D. diss., University of Washington, 1990), 74.

265 interpolation of the line J. R. Sitlington Sterrett, ed., *Homer's Iliad: First Three Books and Selections* (New York: American Book Company, 1907), N100; G. S. Kirk, *The Iliad: A Commentary,* vol. 1, *Books 1–4* (Cambridge: Cambridge University Press, 1985), 80.

271 κατ᾽ ἔμ᾽ αὐτόν Hans Van Wees, *Status Warriors: War, Violence, and Society in Homer and History* (Amsterdam: J. C. Gieben, 1992), 364.

284 quarrel between Agamemnon and Achilles Sarah B. Pomeroy, Stanley M. Burstein, Walter Donlan, and Jennifer Tolbert Roberts, *Ancient Greece: A Political, Social, and Cultural History* (New York: Oxford University Press, 1999), 55–61; A. W. H. Adkins, "Homeric Values and Homeric Society," *Journal of Hellenic Studies* 91 (1971): 1–14; Oliver Taplin, "Agamemnon's Role in the *Iliad,*" in *Characterization and Individuality in Greek Literature,* ed. Christopher Pelling (Oxford: Clarendon, 1990), 65; C. M. Bowra, *Tradition and Design in*

the Iliad (Oxford: Clarendon, 1930), 17–19, 194–95; James M. Redfield, "The Wrath of Achilles as Tragic Error," in *Essays on the Iliad: Selected Modern Criticism,* ed. John Wright (Bloomington: Indiana University Press, 1978), 86–87; Walter Donlan, "Homer's Agamemnon," *Classical World* 65, no. 4 (December 1971): 109–15; C. H. Whitman, *Homer and the Heroic Tradition* (Cambridge: Harvard University Press, 1958), 189; Charles Segal, "Nestor and the Honor of Achilles *(Iliad* 1.247–84)," *Studi Micenei ed Egeo-Anatolici* 13 (1971): 94, 96–97; Jonathan Shay, "Achilles: Paragon, Flawed Character, or Tragic Soldier Figure?" *Classical Bulletin* 71, no. 2 (1995): 117–24; Jasper Griffin, *Homer on Life and Death* (Oxford: Clarendon, 1980): 70–73.

287 ὅδ' ἀνήρ Clyde Pharr, *Homeric Greek: A Book for Beginners,* rev. John Wright (Norman: University of Oklahoma Press, 1985), 127; J. R. Sitlington Sterrett, ed., *Homer's Iliad: First Three Books and Selections* (New York: American Book Company, 1907), N102.

289 repetition of forms of πᾶς A. Shewan, "Alliteration and Assonance in Homer," *Classical Philology* 20, no. 3 (July 1925): 206–7; Walter Leaf, ed. *The Iliad, with Apparatus Criticus, Prolegomena, Notes, and Appendices,* vol. 1, *Books I–XII,* 2d ed. (Amsterdam: Adolf M. Hakkert, 1960): 25; Harmut Erbse, ed., *Scholia Graeca in Homeri Iliadem (Scholia Vetera),* vol. 1 (Berlin: Walter de Gruyter, 1969), 89.

290 Agamemnon's use of αἰχμητήν Clyde Pharr, *Homeric Greek: A Book for Beginners,* rev. John Wright (Norman: University of Oklahoma Press, 1985), 129.

303 irony of the Greeks fighting over a woman Douglas M. Knight "Dramatic and Descriptive Order in the *Iliad,*" *Yale Classical Studies* 14 (1955): 110.

316 ἀτρυγέτοιο D. M. Jones, "Etymological Notes," *Transactions of the Philological Society* (1953): 51; Simon Pulleyn, ed., *Homer: Iliad, Book One* (Oxford: Oxford University Press, 2000), 207–8.

341 λοιγόν Simon Pulleyn, ed., *Homer: Iliad, Book One* (Oxford: Oxford University Press, 2000), 211.

351 χεῖρας ὀρεγνύς Walter Burkert, *Greek Religion,* trans. John Raffan (Cambridge: Harvard University Press, 1985), 75; Simon Pulleyn, *Prayer in Greek Religion* (Oxford: Clarendon, 1997), 188–91.

352 μινυνθάδιον George Eckel Duckworth, *Foreshadowing and Suspense in the Epics of Homer, Apollonius, and Vergil* (New York: Haskell, 1966), 28–29; Moses Hadas, *A History of Greek Literature* (New York: Columbia University Press, 1950; paperback ed., 1965), 18; Richard Rutherford, *Homer,* Greece and Rome New Surveys in the Classics, no. 26 (Oxford: Oxford University Press, 1996), 40.

369 Χρυσηΐδα G. S. Kirk, *The Iliad: A Commentary,* vol. 1, *Books 1–4* (Cambridge: Cambridge University Press, 1985), 91; Allen Rogers Benner, *Selections from Homer's Iliad* (New York: Irvington, 1903), 232.

388 scansion of ἠπείλησεν J. R. Sitlington Sterrett, ed., *Homer's Iliad: First Three Books and Selections* (New York: American Book Company, 1907), N112.

404 dual names   G. S. Kirk, *The Iliad: A Commentary,* vol. 1, *Books 1–4* (Cambridge: Cambridge University Press, 1985), 94.

406 οὐδ᾽ ἔτ᾽ ἔδησαν as a pun   Clyde Pharr, *Homeric Greek: A Book for Beginners,* rev. John Wright (Norman: University of Oklahoma Press, 1985), 142.

story of the revolt   Bruce Karl Braswell, "Mythological Innovation in the *Iliad,*" *Classical Quarterly* 21, no. 1 (May 1971): 18–19.

429 ἐϋζώνοιο   Thomas Day Seymour, *Life in the Homeric Age* (1907; reprint, New York: Biblo and Tannen, 1963): 167; Allen Rogers Benner, *Selections from Homer's Iliad* (New York: Irvington, 1903), xxiv.

439 scansion   J. R. Sitlington Sterrett, ed., *Homer's Iliad: First Three Books and Selections* (New York: American Book Company, 1907), N118.

474 Chryses episode   Robert J. Rabel, "Chryses and the Opening of the *Iliad,*" *American Journal of Philology* 109 (1988): 473–81; Oliver Taplin, "Homer," in *The Oxford History of the Classical World,* ed. John Boardman, Jasper Griffin, and Oswyn Murray (Oxford: Oxford University Press, 1986), 54–55.

489 contrast between images of speed and Achilles' inactivity   Simon Pulleyn, ed., *Homer: Iliad, Book One* (Oxford: Oxford University Press, 2000), 16, 245–46.

497 μέγαν οὐρανὸν Οὔλυμπόν τε   G. S. Kirk, *The Iliad: A Commentary,* vol. 1, *Books 1–4* (Cambridge: Cambridge University Press, 1985), 106.

507 ἠτίμησεν   Simon Pulleyn, ed., *Homer: Iliad, Book One* (Oxford: Oxford University Press, 2000), 251.

512 ἀλλ᾽ ἀκέων δὴν ἧστο   Mark W. Edwards, "Convention and Individuality in *Iliad* I," *Harvard Studies in Classical Philology* 84 (1980): 25.

538 ἀργυρόπεζα   Simon Pulleyn, ed., *Homer: Iliad, Book One* (Oxford: Oxford University Press, 2000), 258.

543 Hera's words   Gertrud Lindberg, "Hera in Homer to Ancient and Modern Eyes," in *Greek and Latin Studies in Memory of Cajus Fabricius,* ed. Sven-Tage Teodorsson (Göteborg, Sweden: Acta Universitatis Gothoburgensis, 1990): 69.

567 characterization of Hera   Gertrud Lindberg, "Hera in Homer to Ancient and Modern Eyes," in *Greek and Latin Studies in Memory of Cajus Fabricius,* ed. Sven-Tage Teodorsson (Göteborg, Sweden: Acta Universitatis Gothoburgensis, 1990), 68–70.

568 ὣς ἔφατ᾽, ἔδεισεν δέ   Simon Pulleyn, ed., *Homer: Iliad, Book One* (Oxford: Oxford University Press, 2000), 246, 265.

600 ποιπνύοντα   Clyde Pharr, *Homeric Greek: A Book for Beginners,* rev. John Wright (Norman: University of Oklahoma Press, 1985), 167.

comparison of Hephaestus/Nestor and Zeus/Agamemnon   Richard Rutherford *Homer,* Greece and Rome New Surveys in the Classics, no. 26 (Oxford: Oxford University Press, 1996), 46.

611 expectations for the rest of the *Iliad*   James V. Morrison, *Homeric Misdirection: False Predictions in the Iliad* (Ann Arbor: University of Michigan Press, 1992), 35–49.

Appendix 2
Some Basic Homeric Forms and Grammar

This appendix does not contain every Homeric form or explain every aspect of Homeric grammar. It includes some of the major Homeric variations from Attic Greek, as well as some of the most frequently used forms and constructions found in book 1. For more complete coverage, consult a standard grammar, such as Herbert Weir Smyth's *Greek Grammar* (1920; revised by Gordon M. Messing, 1956. Cambridge: Harvard University Press, 1984) or D. B. Monro's *A Grammar of the Homeric Dialect* (Oxford: Clarendon, 1891; reprint, Philadelphia: W. H. Allen, 1992).

Nouns and Adjectives

First Declension Endings

	Fem.	Masc.
Sing.		
nom.	-η, -α, -ᾱ	-ης, -ᾱς, -α
gen.	-ης, -ᾱς	-ᾱο, -εω, -ω
dat.	-ῃ , -ᾳ	-ῃ, -ᾳ
acc.	-ην, -αν, -ᾱν	-ην, -ᾱν
voc.	-η, -α, -ᾱ	-η, -α, -ᾱ
Dual		
nom., acc., voc.	-ᾱ	-ᾱ
gen., dat.	-ῃιν	-ῃιν
Plur.		
nom., voc.	-αι	-αι
gen.	-ᾱων, -έων, -ῶν	-ᾱων, -έων, -ῶν
dat.	-ῃσι(ν), -ῃς, -αις	-ῃσι(ν), -ῃς
acc.	-ᾱς	-ᾱς

146

Second Declension Endings

	Masc./Fem.	Neut.
Sing.		
nom.	-ος, -ως, -ους	-ον
gen.	-οιο, -ου, -ω, -οο	-οιο, -ου, -ω, -οο
dat.	-ῳ	-ῳ
acc.	-ον, -ων	-ον
voc.	-ε, -ος	-ον
Dual		
nom., acc., voc.	-ω	-ω
gen., dat.	-οιϊν	-οιϊν
Plur.		
nom., voc.	-οι	-α
gen.	-ων	-ων
dat.	-οισι(ν), -οις	-οισι(ν), -οις
acc.	-ους, -ως	-α

Third Declension Endings

	Masc./Fem.	Neut.
Sing.		
nom.	-ς, —	—
gen.	-ος, -ους, -ως	-ος, -ους, -ως
dat.	-ι, -ῑ, -ῳ	-ι, -ῑ
acc.	-α, -ν, -η, -ω	—
voc.	-ς, —, stem	—
Dual		
nom., acc., voc.	-ε	-ε
gen., dat.	-οιϊν	-οιϊν
Plur.		
nom., voc.	-ες, -εις, -ους	-α, -η, -ω
gen.	-ων	-ων
dat.	-εσσι(ν), -σι(ν), -εσι(ν)	-εσσι(ν), -σι(ν), -εσι(ν)
acc.	-ς, -ας, -ῑς, -ῡς, -εις	-α, -η

Common Nouns with Irregular Forms

	ἡ νηῦς, "ship"	ὁ Ζεύς, "Zeus"
Sing.		
nom.	νηῦς	Ζεύς
gen.	νηός, νεός	Διός, Ζηνός
dat.	νηΐ	Διί, Ζηνί
acc.	νῆα	Δία, Ζῆνα, Ζῆν
voc.	νηῦ	Ζεῦ
Dual		
nom., acc., voc.	νῆε	—
gen., dat.	νηοῖιν	—
Plur.		
nom.	νῆες, νέες	—
gen.	νηῶν, νεῶν	—
dat.	νήεσσι(ν), νέεσσι(ν), νηυσί(ν)	—
acc.	νῆας, νέας	—
voc.	νῆες	—

Pronouns

Personal Pronouns

	I, we	you	he, she, it, they
Sing.			
nom., voc.	ἐγώ, ἐγών	σύ, τύνη	—
gen.	ἐμεῖο, ἐμέο, ἐμεῦ, μευ, ἐμέθεν	σεῖο, σέο, σεο, σεῦ, σευ, σέθεν, τεοῖο	εἷο, ἕο, ἕο, εὗ, εὐ, ἕθεν, ἕθεν
dat.	ἐμοί, μοι	σοί, τοι, τεΐν	ἑοῖ, οἷ, οἱ
acc.	ἐμέ, με	σέ, σε	ἑέ, ἕ, ἑ, μιν
Dual			
nom., acc., voc.	νῶϊ, νώ	σφῶϊ, σφώ	σφωε
gen., dat.	νῶϊν	σφῶϊν, σφῶν	σφωϊν

	I, we	you	he, she, it, they
Plur.			
nom., voc.	ἡμεῖς, ἄμμες	ὑμεῖς, ὕμμες	—
gen.	ἡμείων, ἡμέων	ὑμείων, ὑμέων	σφείων, σφέων, σφεων, σφῶν
dat.	ἡμῖν, ἄμμι(ν), ἥμιν, ἦμιν	ὑμῖν, ὕμμι(ν), ὕμιν	σφίσι(ν), σφισι(ν), σφι(ν)
acc.	ἡμέας, ἄμμε, ἥμεας, ἦμας	ὑμέας, ὕμμε	σφέας, σφεας, σφε, σφας

Other Pronouns

The following pronouns have the same forms in the Homeric dialect as in Attic Greek, with ending variations similar to those seen on nouns and adjectives.

relative pronoun:	ὅς, ἥ, ὅ
intensive pronoun:	αὐτός, -ή, -ό
demonstrative pronouns:	(ἐ)κεῖνος,-η,-ο
	ὅδε, ἥδε, τόδε
	οὗτος, αὕτη, τοῦτο

In most forms, the indefinite pronouns (τις, τι) and interrogative pronouns (τίς, τί) are the same in Homer as in Attic. The following are Homeric variations.

	Indefinite	Interrogative
gen. sing.	τεο, τευ	τέο, τεῦ
dat. sing.	τεῳ, τῳ	τέῳ, τῷ
gen. plur.	τεῶν	τέων
acc. plur. neut.	ἄσσα	—

The Definite Article

The definite article *(the)* in Attic Greek (ὁ, ἡ, τό) is common in Homer but is more frequently used there as a demonstrative pronoun *(this, that),* personal pronoun *(he, she, it),* or relative pronoun *(who, which)* than as an article.

	Masc.	Fem.	Neut.
Sing.			
nom., voc.	ὁ	ἡ	τό
gen.	τοῦ, τοῖο	τῆς	τοῦ, τοῖο
dat.	τῷ	τῇ	τῷ
acc.	τόν	τήν	τό
Dual			
nom., acc., voc.	τώ	τώ	τώ
gen., dat.	τοῖιν	τοῖιν	τοῖιν
Plur.			
nom., voc.	οἱ, τοί	αἱ, ταί	τά
gen.	τῶν	τάων, τῶν	τῶν
dat.	τοῖσι(ν), τοῖς	τῇσι(ν), τῇς	τοῖσι(ν), τοῖς
acc.	τούς	τάς	τά

Case Usages

Nominative

Nominative for vocative—The nominative case may be used for the vocative case.

δημοβόρος βασιλεύς, ἐπεὶ οὐτιδανοῖσιν ἀνάσσεις· (*Il.* 1.231)
[You] people-devouring king, since you rule worthless men.

Genitive

Genitive absolute—A participle agreeing with a noun (or a pronoun) in the genitive case that is not connected grammatically with the main construction of the sentence and that expresses the time, cause, condition, or circumstances under which an action takes place.

οὔ τις ἐμεῦ ζῶντος καὶ ἐπὶ χθονὶ δερκομένοιο / σοὶ κοίλης παρὰ νηυσὶ βαρείας χεῖρας ἐποίσει (*Il.* 1.88–89)
while I'm alive and breathing [literally, with me living and having sight on earth], no one beside the hollow ships will lay violent hands on you

Genitive of comparison—Used with comparative adjectives or adverbs to indicate the standard to which the comparison is made.

ἄμφω δὲ νεωτέρω ἐστὸν ἐμεῖο· (*Il.* 1.259)
You both are younger than I.

Genitive of separation—Indicates that from which something is separated.

ἀλλὰ σὺ τόν γ᾽ ἐλθοῦσα, θεά, ὑπελύσαο δεσμῶν, (*Il.* 1.401)
But you, goddess, came and released him from the bonds,

Genitive of source—Indicates source.

δεινὴ δὲ κλαγγὴ γένετ᾽ ἀργυρέοιο βιοῖο· (*Il.* 1.49)
And a terrible noise arose from the silver bow.

Partitive genitive—Can indicate the whole of which someone or something is a part.

τῶν δ᾽ ἄλλων οὔ τις ὁρᾶτο· (*Il.* 1.198)
Not anyone of the others saw.

The partitive genitive can also indicate the part touched, grabbed, and so on with verbs implying taking hold of in some fashion (this is sometimes called a quasi-partitive genitive).

στῆ δ᾽ ὄπιθεν, ξανθῆς δὲ κόμης ἕλε Πηλεΐωνα (*Il.* 1.197)
She stood behind [him] and grabbed the son of Peleus by his blond hair

Dative

Dative of advantage or disadvantage—Indicates for whose advantage or disadvantage something is done.

ἤδη νῦν Δαναοῖσιν ἀεικέα λοιγὸν ἄμυνον. (*Il.* 1.456)
Now at once ward off ruinous destruction from the Greeks [for the advantage of the Greeks].

καὶ δή μοι γέρας αὐτὸς ἀφαιρήσεσθαι ἀπειλεῖς, (*Il.* 1.161)
and you yourself threaten to take from me [to my disadvantage] the gift of honor,

Dative of cause—Indicates cause or reason.

ἧς ὑπεροπλίῃσι τάχ᾽ ἄν ποτε θυμὸν ὀλέσσῃ. (*Il.* 1.205)
Because of his arrogant behavior, he will one day soon lose his life.

Dative of interest—Indicates to or for whom something refers or is done. Can convey the idea of possession.

τίμησόν μοι υἱόν (*Il.* 1.505)
honor my son

Dative of manner—Indicates how or in what manner something is done.

τήν ῥα βίῃ ἀέκοντος ἀπηύρων (*Il.* 1.430)
whom they took away by force against his will

Dative of means—Indicates the means by which something is done.

νέοι δὲ παρ᾽ αὐτὸν ἔχον πεμπώβολα χερσίν. (*Il.* 1.463)
The young men beside him were holding the five-pronged forks with their hands.

Dative of place, or locative dative—Indicates location.

ἄμφω ὁμῶς θυμῷ φιλέουσά τε κηδομένη τε (*Il.* 1.196)
loving and caring for both of them equally in her heart

εὗρεν δ᾽ εὐρύοπα Κρονίδην ἄτερ ἥμενον ἄλλων / ἀκροτάτῃ κορυφῇ πολυδειράδος Οὐλύμποιο· (*Il.* 1.498–99)
She found the far-thundering son of Cronus sitting apart from the others, on the highest peak of many-ridged Olympus.

Dative of possession—Indicates possession when that which is possessed is the subject of the verb εἰμί or a similar verb.

τώ οἱ ἔσαν κήρυκε καὶ ὀτρηρὼ θεράποντε (*Il.* 1.321)
who were his heralds and busy attendants

Dative of time when—Indicates when something occurs.

τῇ δεκάτῃ δ᾽ ἀγορήνδε καλέσσατο λαὸν Ἀχιλλεύς· (*Il.* 1.54)
on the tenth [day], Achilles summoned the troops to an assembly.

Accusative

Accusative of extent of time—Indicates how long something lasted.

πᾶν δ᾽ ἦμαρ φερόμην, (*Il.* 1.592)
I fell all day,

Accusative of respect—Indicates in what respect the meaning of a verb or adjective is limited or applied; a very common construction.

πόδας ὠκὺς Ἀχιλλεύς (*Il.* 1.58)
swift-footed Achilles [Achilles, swift with respect to his feet]

ἀλλὰ φθινύθεσκε φίλον κῆρ (*Il.* 1.491)
but he kept pining away in his heart [with respect to his heart]

Verbs

Verb Forms

Augments—These are frequently left off for metrical reasons.

νοῦσον ἀνὰ στρατὸν ὦρσε κακήν, ὀλέκοντο δὲ λαοί, (*Il.* 1.10)
he let loose a deadly plague on the army, and the troops were dying,
[This line has one augmented and one unaugmented verb.]

Tmesis—In Homer's time, some prepositions and verbs were used to convey an idea that in later times would be expressed by a compound verb formed from their union. This occurred because most prepositions were originally adverbs, and Homer often used them in this way to modify a verb's meaning. In later Greek, the two parts evolved into a compound verb. The technical name for the separation is *tmesis* (from the verb τέμνω, "cut"). This is not really a very accurate name, since the preposition has not been "cut" from the verb. Rather, in Homeric Greek, they have not yet joined together.

Ἦμος δ᾽ ἠέλιος κατέδυ καὶ ἐπὶ κνέφας ἦλθε, (*Il.* 1.475)
When the sun set and darkness came on,

Second-person singular—In the second-person singular middle/passive endings -σαι and -σο, the sigma is often lost between vowels, but the vowel contractions that take place in Attic Greek do not occur. In other words, you will see -εαι or -ηαι instead of -ει or -η, -σαο instead of -σω.

ἀλλ᾽ ἴθι, μή μ᾽ ἐρέθιζε, σαώτερος ὥς κε <u>νέηαι</u>. (*Il.* 1.32)
But go, don't provoke me, so you may return safely.

ἀλλὰ σὺ τόν γ᾽ ἐλθοῦσα, θεά, <u>ὑπελύσαο</u> δεσμῶν, (*Il.* 1.401)
But you, goddess, came and released him from the bonds,

Third-person plural—The endings -αται and -ατο are sometimes used for the middle/passive endings -νται and -ντο.

ἄλλοι τε Τρῶες μέγα κεν <u>κεχαροίατο</u> θυμῷ, (*Il.* 1.256)
and the other Trojans would rejoice very much in their hearts,

Third-person plural—The ending -εν for the Attic -ησαν is frequently seen in the aorist passive third-person plural.

οἱ δ᾽ ἐπεὶ οὖν <u>ἤγερθεν</u> ὁμηγερέες τ᾽ ἐγένοντο, (*Il.* 1.57)
When they were assembled and gathered together,

Present middle imperative, second-person singular—This form with the ending -εο, rather than -ου, is found several times in book 1.

πολέμου δ᾽ <u>ἀποπαύεο</u> πάμπαν (*Il.* 1.422)
refrain completely from war

Present active infinitive—The following endings occur.

-μεναι	ἔμμεναι (= Attic εἶναι) (*Il.* 1.117)
-έμεναι	ἐριζέμεναι (= Attic ἐρίζειν) (*Il.* 1.277)
-έμεν	ἀγέμεν (= Attic ἄγειν) (*Il.* 1.443)
-ειν	ἄγειν (*Il.* 1.338)

The Verb "To Be"

	Sing.	Dual	Plur.
present indicative	εἰμί		εἰμέν
	ἐσσί, εἶς	ἐστόν	ἐστέ
	ἐστί	ἐστόν	εἰσί, ἔασι

	Sing.	Dual	Plur.
imperfect indicative	ἦα, ἔα, ἔον		ἦμεν
	ἦσθα, ἔησθα	ἦστον	ἦτε
	ἦεν, ἔην, ἤην, ἦν	ἤστην	ἦσαν, ἔσαν

infinitive   εἶναι, ἔμμεναι, ἔμμεν, ἔμεναι, ἔμεν

participle   ἐών, ἐοῦσα, ἐόν

The Verb "To Go"

	Sing.	Dual	Plur.
present indicative	εἶμι		ἴμεν
	εἶσθα	ἴτον	ἴτε
	εἶσι	ἴτον	ἴασι
imperfect indicative	ἤϊα, ἤϊον		ἤομεν
	ἤεισθα	ἴτον	ἦτε
	ἤϊε, ἦε, ἤει, ἴε	ἴτην	ἤϊσαν, ἦσαν, ἤϊον, ἴσαν

infinitive   ἴμεναι, ἴμεν, ἰέναι

participle   ἰών, ἰοῦσα, ἰόν

Verb Tenses

Future tense—It is not unusual for Homer to use κε(ν) with a future indicative verb to indicate some type of limitation or condition.

πάρ' ἔμοιγε καὶ ἄλλοι / οἵ κέ με τιμήσουσι, (*Il.* 1.174–75)
And [there are] others beside me, who in that case will honor me,

Gnomic aorist—An aorist used as the verb in a statement expressing a general truth or what always happens; translated with an English present tense.

ὅς κε θεοῖς ἐπιπείθηται, μάλα τ' ἔκλυον αὐτοῦ. (*Il.* 1.218)
The gods certainly hear the man who obeys them [literally, *[He] who obeys the gods, him they certainly hear*].

Aorist participle—A common form in Homer; can indicate the same time as the main verb rather than time before it.

μειδήσασα δὲ παιδὸς ἐδέξατο χειρὶ κύπελλον· (*Il.* 1.596)
and smiling, she took the cup from her son with her hand.

Perfect tense—Often indicates something true in the present and should be translated with an English present tense.

κλῦθί μευ, ἀργυρότοξ᾽, ὃς Χρύσην ἀμφιβέβηκας (*Il.* 1.37)
Hear me, lord of the silver bow, you who protect Chryse

Subjunctive

Subjunctive for future—The subjunctive is frequently used to express a future idea. It may be used with κε(ν) or ἄν.

οὐ γάρ πω τοίους ἴδον ἀνέρας οὐδὲ ἴδωμαι, (*Il.* 1.262)
I've not ever seen nor will I see such men,

ἐγὼ δέ κ᾽ ἄγω Βρισηΐδα καλλιπάρῃον (*Il.* 1.184)
but I shall take away the fair-cheeked Briseis

Short-vowel subjunctive—Long thematic vowels (the -η or -ω before verb endings) of the subjunctive are often shortened (to -ε or -ο), especially in plural or dual forms. This short-vowel subjunctive is most frequently seen in the endings -εται, -ομεν, and -ετε.

ἀλλ᾽ ἄγε δή τινα μάντιν ἐρείομεν ἢ ἱερῆα, (*Il.* 1.62)
But come, let us ask some seer or priest,

Hortatory subjunctive—A first-person subjunctive used to express exhortation or warning.

νῦν δ᾽ ἄγε νῆα μέλαιναν ἐρύσσομεν εἰς ἅλα δῖαν, (*Il.* 1.141)
now come, let us drag the dark ship into the glorious sea,

Deliberative subjunctive—A present or aorist subjunctive, usually but not always in the first person, used to pose a question about what may be proper or advantageous to do or say.

τίη τοι ταῦτα ἰδυίη πάντ᾽ ἀγορεύω; (*Il.* 1.365)
Why should I tell you all these things that you already know? [literally,
Why should I tell all (these things) to you knowing these things?]

Purpose clause—A dependent clause expressing purpose can be introduced by
ὡς, ὅπως, ἵνα, ὄφρα, or ἕως. μή is used for the negative. The verb is subjunctive after a primary tense (present, future, perfect, or future perfect), optative (sometimes subjunctive) after a secondary tense (imperfect, aorist, or
pluperfect). ἄν or κε(ν) may be used with the subjunctive.

ἦ ἵνα ὕβριν ἴδῃ ᾽Αγαμέμνονος ᾽Ατρεΐδαο; (*Il.* 1.203)
So that you may see the arrogance of Agamemnon, the son of Atreus?

Future-more-vivid condition—εἰ, αἴ, or ἤν (with or without κε(ν) or ἄν)
+ a subjunctive in the protasis and a subjunctive (or a future indicative or another form referring to the future) in the apodosis. Sometimes κε(ν) or ἄν is
used in the apodosis.

αὐτὰρ ᾽Αχαιοὶ / τριπλῇ τετραπλῇ τ᾽ ἀποτείσομεν, αἴ κέ ποθι Ζεὺς /
δῶσι πόλιν Τροίην εὐτείχεον ἐξαλαπάξαι. (*Il.* 1.127–29)
*But the Greeks will repay you threefold and fourfold, if ever Zeus
grants that we sack the well-walled city of Troy.*

ὁ δέ κεν κεχολώσεται ὅν κεν ἵκωμαι. (*Il.* 1.139)
And he to whom I [will] come will be angry. [This sentence contains a
future-more-vivid conditional relative clause, which operates on the
same principle as a future-more-vivid condition.]

Present general condition—An expression of a general truth or a customary
or repeated action: εἰ, αἴ, ἤν, ὁππότε, ὅτε, ἐπεί (with or without κε(ν) or ἄν)
+ a subjunctive in the protasis and a primary indicative verb (present, future,
gnomic aorist, perfect, or future perfect) in the apodosis.

ἀτὰρ ἤν ποτε δασμὸς ἵκηται, / σοὶ τὸ γέρας πολὺ μεῖζον,
(*Il.* 1.166–67)
*But if ever it comes time for a division [of the spoils], your gift of
honor [is] much greater,*

ὅς κε θεοῖς ἐπιπείθηται, μάλα τ᾽ ἔκλυον αὐτοῦ. (*Il.* 1.218)
The gods certainly hear the man who obeys them. [This sentence

contains a present general conditional relative clause, which operates on the same principle as a present general condition.]

αἴ κε(ν) + subjunctive—Expresses the idea "in the hope that" or "on the chance that."

αἴ κε πίθηαι (*Il*. 1.207)
in the hope that you might obey

ὄφρα + subjunctive (with or without κε(ν) or ἄν)—May express the idea "until," "until the time when."

τόφρα δ᾿ ἐπὶ Τρώεσσι τίθει κράτος, ὄφρ᾿ ἄν ᾿Αχαιοὶ / υἱὸν ἐμὸν τίσωσιν (*Il*. 1.509–10)
Bestow victory on the Trojans, until the time when the Greeks honor my son

The Optative

Future (possible) wishes—The optative without κε(ν) or ἄν to express a wish referring to the future.

τείσειαν Δαναοὶ ἐμὰ δάκρυα σοῖσι βέλεσσιν. (*Il*. 1.42)
May the Greeks pay for my tears with your arrows.

Potential optative—ἄν or κε(ν) + optative to express a future possibility or likelihood; sometimes occurs without ἄν or κε(ν).

κείνοισι δ᾿ ἂν οὔ τις / τῶν οἳ νῦν βροτοί εἰσιν ἐπιχθόνιοι μαχέοιτο· (*Il*. 1.271–72)
Not any of the men alive now could fight with those men.

Future-less-vivid condition—εἰ + optative in the protasis and an optative (or a subjunctive or an indicative) + κε(ν) or ἄν in the apodosis; sometimes occurs without ἄν or κε(ν).

ἦ κεν γηθήσαι Πρίαμος Πριάμοιό τε παῖδες / ἄλλοι τε Τρῶες μέγα κεν κεχαροίατο θυμῷ, / εἰ σφῶϊν τάδε πάντα πυθοίατο μαρναμένοιϊν, (*Il*. 1.255–57)
Indeed, Priam and the children of Priam would rejoice and the other Trojans would be very glad in their hearts, if they should learn all these things about the two of you fighting,

Participles

Participle rather than a relative clause—A participle will often be used where in English you might expect a relative clause.

θεοὶ . . . Ὀλύμπια δώματ᾽ ἔχοντες (*Il.* 1.18)
the gods who have [literally, *the gods having*] *Olympian homes*

Future participle of purpose—The future participle can be used to express purpose.

ἦλθον ἐγὼ παύσουσα τὸ σὸν μένος, (*Il.* 1.207)
I came to stop your rage,

Infinitives

Infinitive of purpose—An infinitive can be used to express purpose.

ἔξαγε κούρην / καί σφῶϊν δὸς ἄγειν· (*Il.* 1.337–38)
bring out the woman and give her to these two to take away.

Infinitive used as imperative—An infinitive can be used to express a command.

ἀλλὰ σὺ τόν γ᾽ ἐπέεσσι καθάπτεσθαι μαλακοῖσιν· (*Il.* 1.582)
But address him with gentle words.

Glossary

A, α
ἄαπτος, -ov—invincible
ἀγαθός, -ή, -όv—brave, valiant, noble
Ἀγαμέμνων, -ονος, ὁ—Agamemnon, king of Mycenae, son of Atreus
(Ἀτρεΐδης)
ἀγάννιφος, -ov—snowy, snowcapped, snow-covered
ἄγγελος, -ου, ὁ—messenger
ἄγε—come! (imperative of ἄγω, used as an interjection)
ἀγείρω, (aor.) ἤγειρα, (aor. pass.) ἠγέρθην—gather, assemble, collect
ἀγέραστος, -η, -ov—without a prize of honor
ἀγλαός, -ή, -όv—splendid, shining
ἀγνοιέω, (aor.) ἠγνοίησα—be unaware, fail to notice
ἀγοράομαι, (aor.) ἠγορησάμην—address (an assembly), talk
ἀγορεύω—speak, say, declare, speak of, tell of
ἀγορή, -ῆς, ἡ—assembly
ἀγορητής, -οῦ, ὁ—speaker, orator
ἄγω, ἄξω, ἤγαγον—bring, lead, carry off, take away
ἀδάκρυτος, -η, -ov—tearless
ἀείδω—sing about, sing
ἀεικής, -ές—disgraceful, grievous, ruinous
ἀέκων, -ουσα, -ον—unwilling
ἄζομαι—respect, stand in awe of
ἀθάνατος, -η, -ον—immortal
ἀθερίζω—disregard, treat with disrespect
Ἀθηναίη, -ης, ἡ = Ἀθήνη
Ἀθήνη, -ης, ἡ—Athena, goddess of the arts and war
αἰ, αἴ—if, if only, whether; (+ κε(ν) + subjunctive) in the hope that
Αἴας, -αντος, ὁ—Ajax, one of the leading Greek warriors
Αἰγαίων, -ωνος, ὁ—Aegaeon, the name used by humans for Briareus, one of
the Hecatoncheires (hundred-handed giants)
Αἰγεΐδης, -αο, ὁ—son of Aegeus (= Theseus)
αἰγίοχος, -η, -ον—aegis-holding, aegis-bearing (see note on line 202)
αἰγλήεις, -εσσα, -εν—bright, shining
αἰδέομαι, αἰδέσομαι, ἠδεσάμην—respect, have regard for

161

Ἀΐδης, -αο, ὁ—Hades, god of the underworld

αἴδομαι—respect, have regard for

αἰεί, αἰέν—always

αἴθε—introduces a wish

Αἰθιοπεύς, -ῆος, ὁ—Ethiopian

αἶθοψ, -οπος—bright, sparkling

αἷμα, -ατος, τό—blood

αἰνά—(adv.) calamitously, grievously, for misfortune, for sorrow

αἰνός, -ή, -όν—terrible, fear-inspiring

αἰνῶς—greatly, terribly

αἴξ, αἰγός, ὁ, ἡ—goat

αἱρέω, αἱρήσω, εἷλον or ἕλον—take, seize

αἶσα, -ης, ἡ—fate, life span, one's appointed lot

αἴτιος, -η, -ον—to blame, guilty, at fault

αἰχμητής, -ᾱο, ὁ—spearman, warrior

αἶψα—at once, immediately

ἀκέων, -ουσα, -ον—in silence, silent

ἀκούω, ἀκούσομαι, ἤκουσα—hear (+ gen.)

ἄκρος, -η, -ον—high

ἄλγος, -εος, τό—pain, hardship, trouble, suffering

ἀλεγίζω—care for, care about (+ gen.)

ἀλέξω—aid, defend

ἅλιος, -η, -ον—of the sea

ἀλλ᾽ = ἀλλά

ἀλλά—but

ἄλλῃ—elsewhere

ἄλλομαι, (aor.) ἄλμην—jump, leap

ἄλλος, -η, -ο—other, another

ἄλλοτε—on another occasion

ἄλοχος, -ου, ἡ—wife

ἅλς, ἁλός, ἡ—sea

ἅμα—(prep.) along with, together with, at the time of (+ dat.); (adv.) at the same time

ἀμβρόσιος, -η, -ον—ambrosial, immortal, sweet-smelling

ἀμείβω, ἀμείψω, ἤμειψα—exchange; *middle*—answer, reply

ἀμείνων, -ον—better, greater

ἀμύμων, -ον—excellent, blameless

ἀμύνω, (aor.) ἤμυνα—ward off, defend against, protect from, keep off

ἀμύσσω, ἀμύξω—tear, scratch

ἀμφηρεφής, -ές—closed, covered at both ends, closely covered

ἀμφί—(prep.) around (+ acc.); (adv.) on both sides, around

ἀμφιβαίνω, ἀμφιβήσω, ἀμφέβησα, ἀμφιβέβηκα—protect

ἀμφιγυήεις, -εσσα, -εν—lame in both legs

ἀμφικύπελλος, -ον—double, two-handled

ἄμφω—both (nom. and acc. dual)

ἄν—adds an idea of indefiniteness or indicates a condition (no exact English equivalent)

ἀνά—on, upon (+ dat.); upon, up through, throughout (+ acc.)

ἀναβαίνω, ἀναβήσω, ἀνέβησα or ἀνέβην—take on board, go up, ascend, embark, go on board

ἀνάγω—lead, bring; *middle*—put to sea, sail

ἀναδύομαι, ἀναδύσομαι, ἀνεδυσάμην or ἀνέδυν—rise up from out of, emerge from out of (+ gen. or acc.)

ἀναθηλέω, ἀναθηλήσω—bloom again

ἀναιδείη, -ης, ἡ—shamelessness

ἀναιδής, -ές—shameless

ἀναιρέω, ἀναιρήσω, ἀνεῖλον—take, seize, take up

ἀναΐσσω, ἀναΐξω, ἀνήϊξα—spring up, leap up

ἄναξ, ἄνακτος, ὁ—lord, king, protector

ἀναπετάννυμι, (aor.) ἀνεπέτασσα—spread out, unfold, unfurl

ἀνάποινον—(adv.) without a ransom

ἀνάσσω, ἀνάξω, ἤναξα—be lord or master of, rule over, be king over (+ gen. or dat.)

ἀναφαίνω—reveal, show

ἀνδάνω—be acceptable, please

ἀνδροφόνος, -ον—man-slaying

ἀνεκτός, -όν—endurable

ἄνεμος, -ου, ὁ—wind

ἀνέχω, ἀνέξω, ἀνέσχον—lift up, hold up, raise; *middle*—bear up, endure, hold up under

ἀνήρ, ἀνδρός, ὁ—man

ἀνθερεών, -ῶνος, ὁ—chin

ἄνθρωπος, -ου, ὁ—man, human being

ἀνίστημι, ἀναστήσω, ἀνέστησα or ἀνέστην—stand up, get up, rise, make to stand up

ἀνορούω, (aor.) ἀνόρουσα—spring up, jump up

ἀντάξιος, -η, -ον—equivalent in value, of equal value

ἄντην—openly

ἀντιάω, ἀντιάσω, ἠντίασα—partake of, accept (+ gen.); share (+ acc.)

ἀντιβίην—hostilely, antagonistically

ἀντίβιος, -η, -ον—hostile

ἀντίθεος, -η, -ον—godlike

ἀντίον—against (+ gen.)

ἀντίος, -η, -ον—meeting, to meet

ἀντιφέρομαι—set oneself against, oppose

ἀνώγω, ἀνώξω, ἤνωξα—order, command

ἀπαμείβομαι—answer, reply
ἀπαμύνω, (aor.) ἀπήμυνα—ward off (+ acc.) from (+ dat.)
ἀπάνευθε—(adv.) far away, away; (prep.) apart from, far from (+ gen.)
ἅπας, ἅπασα, ἅπαν—all
ἀπατηλός, -ή, -όν—deceitful
ἀπαυράω—take away, rob, deprive; ἀπούρας—aorist active participle
ἀπειλέω, ἀπειλήσω, ἠπείλησα—threaten (+ dat.)
ἀπείρων, -ονος—boundless
ἀπερείσιος, -ον—boundless, immeasurable, unlimited
ἀπήμων, -ον—unharmed, unhurt, safe
ἀπηνής, -ές—harsh, unfeeling
ἀπιθέω, (aor.) ἠπίθησα—disobey (+ dat.)
ἄπιος, -η, -ον—distant
ἀπό—from (+ gen.)
ἀποβαίνω, ἀποβήσω, ἀπέβησα—depart, go away
ἀποδέχομαι, (aor.) ἀπεδεξάμην—accept
ἀποδίδωμι, ἀποδώσω, ἀπέδωκα—give up, restore, give back
ἀποεῖπον (aor.)—refuse
ἄποινα, -ων, τά—ransom
ἀπόλλυμι, ἀπολέσσω, ἀπώλεσα—destroy; *middle*—be destroyed, perish
Ἀπόλλων, -ωνος, ὁ—Apollo, god of archery, music, and prophecy
ἀπολυμαίνομαι—purify or cleanse oneself of pollution (by washing)
ἀπολύω, ἀπολύσω, ἀπέλυσα—release
ἀπονοστέω, ἀπονοστήσω, ἀπενόστησα—return home, return
ἀπονόσφιν—apart from, keeping away from (+ gen.)
ἀποπαύω—hinder; *middle*—cease from, refrain from (+ gen.)
ἀποστείχω, (aor.) ἀπέστιχον—go away, go back
ἀποτίνω, ἀποτείσω, ἀπέτεισα—pay back, repay
ἀπριάτην—(adv.) without a price
ἅπτω, ἅψω, ἧψα—fasten; *middle*—take hold of, grasp, touch (+ gen.)
ἀπωθέω, ἀπώσω, ἀπέωσα—push away, push back, drive off
ἄρ, ἄρα, ῥα—then, in fact; frequently untranslatable
ἀράομαι, ἀρήσομαι, ἠρησάμην—pray
ἀραρίσκω, (aor.) ἦρσα—join, fit, suit
ἀργαλέος, -η, -ον—difficult, hard
Ἀργεῖοι, -ων, οἱ—Argives (a name Homer uses for the Greeks)
Ἄργος, -εος, τό—Argos, the area in the Peloponnese ruled by Agamemnon
ἀργός, -ή, -όν—swift
ἀργύρεος, -η, -ον—silver, made of silver
ἀργυρόπεζος, -α, -ον—silver-footed (see note on line 538)
ἀργυρότοξος, -ον—equipped with a silver bow, (god) of the silver bow
ἀρείων, -ον—better, superior

ἀρήγω, ἀρήξω, ἤρηξα—help, support (+ dat.)

ἀρήν, ἀρνός, ὁ, ἡ—lamb

ἀρητήρ, -ῆρος, ὁ—priest

ἀριστεύς, -ῆος, ὁ—best man, chief, leader

ἄριστος, -η, -ον—best, bravest, noblest

ἄρνυμαι—win, gain, achieve

ἀρχός, -οῦ, ὁ—leader, commander

ἄρχω, ἄρξω, ἦρξα—lead, begin

ἄσβεστος, -η, -ον—unquenchable, inextinguishable, ceaseless

ἆσσον—nearer

ἀστεροπητής, -ᾶο, ὁ—lightning hurler

ἀτάρ—but, however

ἀταρτηρός, -ή, -όν—harsh, abusive

ἀτελεύτητος, -ον—unaccomplished, unfulfilled

ἄτερ—apart from, away from (+ gen.)

ἄτη, -ης, ἡ—folly, moral blindness

ἀτιμάζω, ἀτιμάσω, ἠτίμασα—dishonor, treat with disrespect, insult

ἀτιμάω, ἀτιμήσω, ἠτίμησα—dishonor, treat with disrespect, insult

ἄτιμος, -ον—unhonored, slighted, dishonored

Ἀτρεΐδης, -αο, ὁ—son of Atreus (= Agamemnon or Menelaus)

Ἀτρεΐων, -ωνος, ὁ—son of Atreus (= Agamemnon or Menelaus)

ἀτρύγετος, -ον—barren, unfruitful (see note on line 316)

αὖ—again, this time

αὐδάω—speak

αὐδή, -ῆς, ἡ—speech, voice

αὐερύω, (aor.) αὐέρυσα—draw up, draw back, pull up

αὖθι—there

αὐτάρ—but, however, indeed (may mark a contrast with a preceding phrase
    containing μέν)

αὖτε—but, but now, again, on the other hand, now, hereafter (can express a
    feeling of irritation, vexation, or impatience)

ἀϋτή, -ῆς, ἡ—battle cry, war cry

αὐτῆμαρ—on the same day

αὐτίκα—immediately, at once

αὖτις—again, back again, later, by and by

αὐτός, -ή, -ό—self, same; him, her, it (3rd pers. pronoun in cases other than
    nominative)

αὐτοῦ—there

αὔτως—thus, so

ἀφαιρέω, ἀφαιρήσω, ἀφεῖλον—take away, take away from

ἄφαρ—at once, immediately

ἄφενος, -εος, τό—riches, wealth

ἀφίημι, ἀφήσω, ἀφῆκα—send away, dismiss, drive off
ἀφύσσω, ἀφύξω, ἤφυσα—accumulate, draw up (as water from a well), dip out
(as wine from a jar)
Ἀχαιίς, -ίδος—(fem. adj.) Achaean
Ἀχαιοί, -ῶν, οἱ—Achaeans (a name Homer uses for the Greeks)
Ἀχιλεύς, -ῆος, ὁ—Achilles, greatest Greek hero, son of Peleus and Thetis
Ἀχιλλεύς = Ἀχιλεύς
ἄχνυμαι—be distressed, grieve
ἄχος, -εος, τό—distress, pain, anguish
ἄψ—back, backward, back again

Β, β
βαθύς, -εῖα, -ύ—deep
βαίνω, βήσω, ἔβησα or ἔβην, βέβηκα—come, go, walk, set out
βάλλω, (aor.) ἔβαλον—throw, shoot
βαρύ—heavily, deeply
βαρύς, -εῖα, -ύ—heavy, violent
βασιλεύς, -ῆος, ὁ—king, chief
βέλος, -εος, τό—arrow, missile
βένθος, -εος, τό—depth
βῆ = ἔβη—see βαίνω
βηλός, -οῦ, ὁ—threshold
βίη, -ης, ἡ—strength, force, might
βιός, -οῦ, ὁ—bow
βουλεύω, βουλεύσω, ἐβούλευσα—plan
βουλή, -ῆς, ἡ—plan, counsel, advice, purpose
βουληφόρος, -ου, ὁ—leader, member of the βουλή (council of the most
important leaders)
βούλομαι, βουλήσομαι—wish, want, prefer
βοῦς, βοός, ὁ, ἡ—cow, bull, ox
βοῶπις, -ιδος—(fem. adj.) ox-eyed, large-eyed, calm-eyed, beautiful
(see note on line 551)
Βριάρεως, -ω, ὁ—Briareus, one of the Hecatoncheires (hundred-handed
giants)
Βρισεύς, -ῆος, ὁ—Briseus, father of Briseis
Βρισηΐς, -ΐδος, ἡ—Briseis, the woman allotted to Achilles as a prize
βροτός, -οῦ, ὁ—mortal, mortal man
βωμός, -οῦ, ὁ—altar
βωτιάνειρα—(fem. adj.) hero-nourishing

Γ, γ
γ' = γε
γαῖα, -ης, ἡ—earth, the ground, land

γαίω—rejoice, exult
γάρ—for, namely; often simply adds emphasis
γε—(enclitic) at least; indeed (often simply adds emphasis)
γείνομαι, (aor.) ἐγεινάμην—bear, give birth to
γέλως, γέλωτος, ὁ—laughter
γενεή, -ῆς, ἡ—generation
γεραιός, -ή, -όν—old
γέρας, -αος, τό—prize, gift of honor
γέρων, -οντος, ὁ—old man
γηθέω, (aor.) ἐγήθησα—rejoice, be glad
γῆρας, -αος, τό—old age
γίγνομαι, γενήσομαι, ἐγενόμην—become, be, occur, happen, arise, be born
    (γένετ᾽ = ἐγένετο)
γιγνώσκω, γνώσομαι, ἔγνων—know, learn, recognize
γλαυκῶπις, -ιδος—gleaming-eyed, bright-eyed (possibly "gray-eyed,"
    "green-eyed," or "owl-eyed")
γλυκύς, -εῖα, -ύ—sweet; γλυκίων, -ον—comparative
γλῶσσα, -ης, ἡ—tongue
γόνυ, γουνός, τό—knee
γουνάζομαι, γουνάσομαι—beg, entreat
γυνή, γυναικός, ἡ—woman

Δ, δ
δ᾽ = δέ
δαιμόνιος, -η, -ον—foolish, possessed, misguided
δαίμων, -ονος, ὁ, ἡ—god, goddess
δαίνυμι—give a feast; *middle*—eat, feast
δαίς, δαιτός, ἡ—feast, banquet, meal
δάκρυ, -υος, τό—tear
δακρύω, (aor.) ἐδάκρυσα—weep, cry; *aorist*—burst into tears
δαμάζω, δαμάω, ἐδάμασα—subdue, overcome, tame
Δαναοί, -ῶν, οἱ—Danaans (a name Homer uses for the Greeks)
δασμός, -οῦ, ὁ—division
δατέομαι, δάσ(σ)ομαι, ἐδασ(σ)άμην, δέδασμαι—divide up, allot
δέ—and, but, then, for, while, although
-δε—suffix indicating motion toward (ex.: Οὐλυμπόνδε—to Mt. Olympus)
δείδω, δείσομαι, ἔδεισα, δέδοικα—fear, be afraid
δειλός, -ή, -όν—cowardly
δεινός, -ή, -όν—terrible, awful, fearful, dreadful
δέκατος, -η, -ον—tenth
δέμας, -αος, τό—body, stature, build
δεξιτερός, -ή, -όν—right
δέος, δείους, τό—fear

δέπας, -αος, τό—cup
δέρκομαι—see, look
δέρω, (aor.) ἔδειρα—skin, flay
δεσμός, -οῦ, ὁ—restraint, bond, any means of binding
δεύομαι, δευήσομαι, ἐδεύησα—lack, be without, be stinted in the matter of
    (+ gen.)
δεῦρο—to this place, here
δεύτερον—a second time
δέχομαι, δέξομαι, ἐδεξάμην—accept, receive
δέω, δήσω, ἔδησα—tie up, bind
δή—indeed, now, really (adds emphasis; often untranslatable with a single
    English word)
δηθύνω—linger, delay, tarry
δηλέομαι, δηλήσομαι, ἐδηλησάμην—lay waste, destroy
δημοβόρος, -ον—devouring the people's goods, devouring the people's
    property (literally "people-devouring")
δήν—long, for a long time
διά—by means of, through (+ acc.)
Δία—acc. of Ζεύς
διάνδιχα—between two ways, between two courses
διαπέρθω, διαπέρσω, διέπραθον—sack, utterly destroy, devastate
διαπρήσσω—accomplish, traverse
διατμήγω, (aor.) διέτμαγον, (aor. pass.) διετμάγην—separate, part
δίδωμι, (δι)δώσω, ἔδωκα—give, grant
διείρομαι—ask about
διέπω—attend to, accomplish
Διί—dat. of Ζεύς
διίστημι, διαστήσω, διέστην—stand apart, separate
διίφιλος, -η, -ον—dear to Zeus
δικάζω—decide, give decision on
δικασπόλος, -ου, ὁ—judge
διογενής, -ές—descended from Zeus, divine
δῖος, -α, -ον—godlike, glorious, divine
Διός—gen. of Ζεύς
διοτρεφής, -ές—cherished by Zeus, Zeus-nurtured
δίπτυξ, -υχος—double-folded
δολομήτης, -ου, ὁ—deceiver, crafty-minded one
δόρυ, δουρός, τό—spear
Δρύας, -αντος, ὁ—Dryas, a Lapith leader
δύναμαι, δυνήσομαι—be able
δύω or δύο (indeclinable)—two
δυωδέκατος, -η, -ον—twelfth
δῶ, το (indeclinable)—house, home

δωδέκατος, -η, -ον—twelfth
δῶμα, -ατος, τό—home, house, palace (often plural with singular meaning)
δῶρον, -ου, τό—gift

E, ε
ἑ—him, her, it (acc. sing. of εἷο)
ἐάω—permit, allow, let, leave, let alone, let be
ἐγγυαλίζω, ἐγγυαλίξω, ἠγγυάλιξα—give, grant, bestow
ἐγώ, ἐμεῖο—I, me
ἔγωγε—I (emphatic); I, at any rate; I, at least
ἐγών = ἐγώ
ἐδητύς, -ύος, ἡ—food
ἕδος, -εος, τό—seat
ἐείκοσι(ν)—twenty
ἐέλδωρ, τό (indeclinable)—wish, desire
ἕζομαι, ἕσσομαι, εἷσα—sit down, take a seat; with ἀνά—put on board a ship
ἐθέλω, ἐθελήσω, ἠθέλησα—wish, want
ἕθεν = εἷο (gen.)—of him, her, it
ἔθεσαν = ἔθηκαν
ἔθηκαν—from τίθημι
ἔθηκε—from τίθημι
εἰ—if; εἴ τε . . . εἴ τε—whether . . . or
εἰ δ᾽ ἄγε—come! come on! come now!
εἴδομαι—seem
εἴλω, (aor.) ἔλσα—hem in, crowd together
εἰμί—be, exist
εἶμι—go, come
εἵνεκα—on account of, because of, for the sake of (+ gen.)
εἷο (gen.)—of him, her, it
εἷος—while
εἶπον (aor.)—say, tell, speak, name
εἴρομαι—ask, question
εἴρω, ἐρέω—tell, say, speak
εἰς—into, to (+ acc.)
εἷς, μία, ἕν—one
ἔϊσος, -η, -ον—well-balanced, trim (of ships); fairly divided (of a meal)
εἴσω—to (+ acc.)
εἴτε = εἴ τε—see εἰ
ἐκ—(prep.) out of, from (+ gen.); (adv.) out
ἑκάεργος, -ου, ὁ—far-worker, far-shooter
ἕκαστος, -η, -ον—each, each one, every
ἑκατηβελέτης, -αο—(adj.) far-shooting
ἑκατηβόλος, -ον—far-shooting

ἑκατόγχειρος, -ον—(adj.) hundred-handed; *as a noun*—the hundred-handed one, one of the Hecatoncheires (hundred-handed giants)

ἑκατόμβη, -ης, ἡ—hecatomb, sacrificial offering of a number of animals (originally one hundred cows); the animals for the sacrifice

ἕκατος, -ου, ὁ—the far-shooter (= Apollo)

ἐκβαίνω—disembark, go forth, step out; *with an object*—set ashore

ἐκβάλλω, (aor.) ἔκβαλον—throw out, hurl out, let go

ἐκ . . . ἐρέω—from ἐξερέω

ἐκηβόλος, -ον—(adj.) far-shooting, sharp-shooting; *as a noun*—the far-shooter (= Apollo)

ἔκπαγλος, -ον—terrible

ἐκπάγλως—terribly, exceedingly

ἐκπέρθω, ἐκπέρσω, ἐξέπερσα or ἐξέπραθον—sack, utterly destroy; plunder, carry off from (+ gen.)

ἐκτάμνω, (aor.) ἐξέταμον—cut out

Ἕκτωρ, -ορος, ὁ—Hector, son of King Priam of Troy and leader of the Trojan forces

ἐλαύνω—stir up, set in motion

ἔλαφος, -ου, ὁ, ἡ—deer

ἐλάω, ἐλάσω, ἤλασα—drive away, rustle

ἐλελίζω, (aor.) ἐλέλιξα—shake, make tremble

ἑλικῶπις, -ιδος (fem. adj.); ἑλίκωψ, -ωπος (masc. adj.)—quick-eyed, flashing-eyed; possibly "black-eyed" or "dark-eyed"

ἑλίσσω—curl, wind

ἕλκω—draw, drag

ἕλον—aorist of αἱρέω

ἑλώρια, τά—prey

ἐμέ—acc. sing. of ἐγώ

ἐμέθεν—gen. sing. of ἐγώ

ἐμεῖο—gen. sing. of ἐγώ

ἐμεῦ—gen. sing. of ἐγώ

ἐμός, -ή, -όν—my, mine

ἔμπης—nevertheless

ἐμπρήθω, ἐμπρήσω, ἐνέπρησα—blow, inflate

ἐμφύω, ἐμφύσω, ἐνέφυσα, ἐμπέφυκα—cling closely

ἐν—(prep.) in, on, among (+ dat.); (adv.) in, therein

ἐναντίον—opposite, facing (+ gen.)

ἐναρίζω—kill

ἐνδέξια—from left to right

ἔνδοθι—within

ἔνειμι—be in

ἕνεκα—because of, on account of (+ gen.)

ἔνθα—then, where, there

ἐνθάδε—here, to this place

ἐνί = ἐν

ἐννῆμαρ—for nine days

ἐνόρνυμι, ἐνόρσω, ἐνῶρσα—arouse, stir up; *middle*—arise, rise among

ἐντός—within, inside (+ gen.)

ἐξ = ἐκ

ἐξάγω—bring out, lead out

Ἐξάδιος, -ου, ὁ—Exadius, a Lapith leader

ἐξαιρέω, (aor.) ἔξελον—select, choose

ἐξαλαπάζω, ἐξαλαπάξω, ἐξηλάπαξα—sack, utterly destroy

ἐξαυδάω—speak out, tell

ἐξαῦτις—again

ἐξείης—one after another

ἐξερέω (fut.)—speak out, say, tell

ἐξίημι—remove, appease, satisfy

ἔοικα (perfect; translate as present)—be like, resemble (+ dat.); be fitting, be suitable

ἐός, ἐή, ἐόν—his, her, its, his own, her own, its own

ἐπαγείρω—bring together

ἐπαίτιος, -ον—to blame, blameworthy

ἐπαπειλέω, (aor.) ἐπηπείλησα—threaten against (+ dat.)

ἐπαρήγω, ἐπαρήξω, ἐπήρηξα—help (+ dat.)

ἐπάρχομαι—pour the first drops of wine

ἐπασσύτερος, -η, -ον—in quick succession, one right after the other

ἐπαυρίσκω, (aor.) ἐπαῦρον—enjoy, appreciate (+ gen.)

ἐπεί—when, since

ἔπει—dat. sing. of ἔπος

ἔπειμι, ἐπείσομαι—come upon

ἔπειτα—then, after that, next

ἐπέοικε (impersonal)—it is proper, it is right, it is seemly (+ acc. and infinitive)

ἐπερέφω, ἐπερέψω—roof over, build

ἐπέρχομαι, (aor.) ἐπῆλθον—come near, approach, come on

ἐπευφημέω, ἐπευφημήσω, ἐπευφήμησα—approve, shout assent, speak favorably, agree

ἐπί—on, upon, at, by, beside (+ gen. or dat.); to, upon (+ acc.)

ἐπιγνάμπτω, (aor.) ἐπέγναμψα—restrain, repress

ἐπιείκελος, -ον—like (+ dat.)

ἐπιεικής, -ές—suitable, proper

ἐπιέλπομαι—hope, expect

ἐπιέννυμι—clothe in

ἐπικραιαίνω, (aor.) ἐπεκρήηνα—grant, fulfill, accomplish

ἐπιλείβω—pour over

ἐπιμέμφομαι—blame, find fault with (+ gen.)
ἐπινεύω, ἐπινεύσω, ἐπένευσα—nod, nod in agreement
ἐπιπείθομαι—obey (+ dat.)
ἐπιπλέω—sail over
ἐπιρρώομαι, (aor.) ἐπερρωσάμην—ripple down, flow down, roll down
ἐπισσεύομαι—hurry, urge on, be eager
ἐπιστέφω, (aor.) ἐπεστεψάμην—fill to the brim
ἐπιτέλλω, (aor.) ἐπέτειλα—lay (a command) on, impose, inflict; order, command
ἐπιτηδές—as are needed, in sufficient number
ἐπιτίθημι—put into, bestow upon
ἐπιφέρω, ἐποίσω, ἐπήνεικα—bear upon, bring against, lay on, lay upon
ἐπιχθόνιος, -ον—upon the earth, earthly
ἐποίχομαι, ἐποιχήσομαι—go against, attack; (with ἱστόν) work at, apply oneself to, ply
ἕπομαι, ἕψομαι, ἑσπόμην—follow, go along with, accompany (+ dat.)
ἐπόμνυμι, ἐπομοῦμαι—swear
ἔπος, -εος, τό—word, speech, matter
ἔργον, -ου, τό—work, deed, thing
ἔρδω, ἔρξω, ἔρξα—do, make, sacrifice
ἐρεθίζω, ἐρεθίσω, ἠρέθισα—provoke, irritate, anger
ἐρέθω—provoke, tease, torment
ἐρέτης, -αο, ὁ—rower, oarsman
ἐρετμόν, -οῦ, τό—oar
ἐρέω—ask
ἐρητύω, (aor.) ἠρήτυσα—hold back, restrain
ἐριβῶλαξ, -ακος—with large clods, fertile
ἐριδαίνω—quarrel
ἐρίζω, ἐρίσω, ἤρισα—quarrel
ἔρις, -ιδος, ἡ—quarrel, strife, contention, rivalry
ἕρκος, -εος, τό—defense against, barrier, hedge (+ gen.)
ἕρμα, -ατος, τό—prop, beam, support (used to keep ships upright when they were on shore)
ἔρος, -ου, ὁ—desire
ἐρύομαι, (aor.) εἰρυσσάμην, (perf.) εἴρυμαι—preserve, protect, defend, obey, respect
ἐρύω, ἐρύω, εἴρυσ(σ)α—drag, draw (a sword), draw off, pull off
ἔρχομαι, ἐλεύσομαι, ἦλθον or ἤλυθον, εἰλήλουθα or ἐλήλυθα—come, go
ἐρωέω, ἐρωήσω—flow, rush forth
ἐς—(prep.) into, to (+ acc.); (adv.) into [something], in
ἐσθλός, -ή, -όν—good, excellent, fine
ἐσσί = εἶς (2nd pers. sing. of εἰμί)
ἑταῖρος, -ου, ὁ—companion, friend
ἕταρος, -ου, ὁ—companion, friend

ἑτέρωθεν—from the other side, on the other side
ἐτήτυμον—truly, actually
ἔτι—still, yet, again
ἔτλην (aor.)—dare, venture
ἑτοιμάζω, (aor.) ἡτοίμασα—prepare, make ready
ἐύ, εὖ—well, successfully, properly, justly
ἐΰδμητος, -ον—well-built
ἐΰζωνος, -ον—beautifully belted, well-belted (see note on line 429)
εὔκηλος, -ον—quiet, undisturbed, calm
ἐϋκνήμις, -ιδος—well-greaved
εὐνή, -ῆς, ἡ—anchor stone (a stone, attached to a rope and thrown off the
    front of a ship to hold it in place)
εὑρίσκω, (aor.) εὗρον—find
εὐρύ—(adv.) widely
Εὐρυβάτης, -αο, ὁ—Eurybates, one of Agamemnon's heralds
εὐρύοπα (nom. and acc.)—far-thundering
εὐρύς, -εῖα, -ύ—wide, broad
ἐύς, (gen.) ἐῆος—good, noble
εὖτε—when
εὐτείχεος, -ον—well-walled, well-fortified
ἐϋφρονέων, -ουσα, -ον—prudently, sensibly; well-meaning, with good intent
εὔχομαι, εὔξομαι, ηὐξάμην—pray, boast, claim
εὐχωλή, -ῆς, ἡ—vow
ἔφατο—from φημί; imperfect middle with active meaning
ἐφετμή, -ῆς, ἡ—request, command
ἐφίημι, ἐφήσω, ἐφῆκα—let go at, shoot, send upon, inflict, cause, drive to,
    incite, lay on
ἐχεπευκής, -ές—sharp
ἔχθιστος, -η, -ον—most hated, most odious, most hostile
ἐχθοδοπέω, (aor.) ἠχθοδόπησα—quarrel with (+ dat.)
ἔχω, ἕξω, ἔσχον or ἔσχεθον—have, hold

Z, ζ
ζάθεος, -η, -ον—very sacred, holy
Ζεύς, Διός, ὁ—Zeus, king of the gods and husband of Hera
ζώω—live

Η, η
ἤ, ἠέ, ἦε—or, than, whether; ἤ . . . ἤ—either . . . or, whether . . . or
ἦ—indicates a question
ἦ—surely, truly, indeed
ἦ—he spoke, she spoke (imperfect, 3rd pers. sing., of ἠμί)
ἠγάθεος, -η, -ον—very sacred, very holy

ἡγέομαι, ἡγήσομαι, ἡγησάμην—lead (+ dat.)
ἠδέ—and, also; ἠμὲν . . . ἠδέ—just as . . . so
ἤδη—already, at once, now
ἤδη—pluperfect of οἶδα, 3rd pers. sing.
ἦδος, -εος, τό—enjoyment, pleasure
ἡδυεπής, -ές—sweet-speaking
ἦε, ἠέ—or
ἠέλιος, -ου, ὁ—sun (= Attic ἥλιος)
ἠέριος, -η, -ον—early in the morning
Ἠετίων, -ωνος, ὁ—Eetion, king of Thebe
ἦκα—aorist of ἵημι
ἦλος, -ου, ὁ—nail, ornamental stud
ἦμαι—sit
ἦμαρ, ἤματος, τό—day
ἡμεῖς, ἡμέων—we, us
ἠμέν—truly, surely, just as; ἠμὲν . . . ἠδέ—just as . . . so
ἡμέτερος, -η, -ον—our
ἠμί, (imperf.) ἦν—speak, say
ἡμῖν—dat. of ἡμεῖς
ἦμος—when
ἤν—if
ἦος—while
ἤπειρος, -ου, ἡ—land
ἦρα (acc. sing.)—what is pleasing or agreeable, kindness
Ἥρη, -ης, ἡ—Hera, wife of Zeus and queen of the gods
ἠριγένειος, -α, -ον—early born
ἥρως, ἥρωος, ὁ—hero, warrior
ἤτοι—in truth, to be sure; when followed by a δέ clause, may simply stress
     the contrast
ἦτορ, -ορος, τό—heart
ἠΰκομος, -ον—with beautiful hair, having beautiful hair, beautiful-haired
ἠΰτε—like, as
Ἥφαιστος, -ου, ὁ—Hephaestus, lame son of Zeus and Hera; god of fire and
     all arts that use fire, especially metalworking
ἠχήεις, -εσσα, -εν—roaring, echoing
ἦχι—where
ἠώς, ἠοῦς, ἡ—dawn, morning
Ἠώς, Ἠοῦς, ἡ—Eos, goddess of dawn

Θ, θ
θ' = τε
θάλασσα, -ης, ἡ—sea
θαμβέω, θαμβήσω, ἐθάμβησα—wonder, be astonished, be amazed

θαμέες, θαμειαί, θαμέα—frequent, thick, numerous
θάνατος, -ου, ὁ—death
θαρσέω, (aor.) ἐθάρσησα—take courage, be bold
θεά, -ᾶς, ἡ—goddess
θείνω—beat, strike, hit
θέμις, θέμιστος, ἡ—law, right
-θεν—suffix indicating place from (ex.: οὐρανόθεν—from heaven)
θεοείκελος, -ον—godlike
θεοπροπέω—prophesy, predict
θεοπροπίη, -ης, ἡ—oracle, prophecy
θεοπρόπιον, -ου, τό—oracle, prophecy
θεός, -οῦ, ὁ, ἡ—god, goddess
θεράπων, -οντος, ὁ—attendant, companion
θεσπέσιος, -η, -ον—divine
Θεστορίδης, -αο, ὁ—son of Thestor (= Calchas)
Θέτις, -ιδος, ἡ—Thetis, sea goddess and mother of Achilles
θέω, θεύσομαι—run
Θήβη, -ης, ἡ—Thebe, a city near Troy
Θησεύς, -ῆος, ὁ—Theseus, a great Athenian hero
θίς, θινός, ἡ—beach, shore
θνήσκω, θανέομαι, ἔθανον, τέθνηκα—die, be killed
θνητός, -ή, -όν—mortal
θοός, -ή, -όν—swift
θρόνος, -ου, ὁ—chair, seat
θυγάτηρ, -τρός, ἡ—daughter
θυμός, -οῦ, ὁ—heart, soul, life, breath, mind, feelings, desire
θύω—rage
θωρήσσω, (aor.) ἐθώρηξα, (aor. pass.) ἐθωρήχθην—arm; *middle and passive*—arm oneself, put on a breastplate

I, ι
ἰάχω—roar
ἴδμεν—1st pers. plur. of οἶδα
Ἰδομενεύς, -ῆος, ὁ—Idomeneus, king of Crete
ἱερεύς, -ῆος, ὁ—priest
ἱερόν, -οῦ, τό—sacrifice
ἱερός, -ή, -όν—sacred, holy
ἵημι, ἥσω, ἧκα—send
ἱκάνω—come to
ἵκμενος, -η, -ον—favorable
ἱκνέομαι, ἵξομαι, ἱκόμην—arrive at, reach, come to
ἵκω—reach, come to
ἵλαος, -η, -ον—propitious, kind

ἱλάσκομαι, ἱλάσσομαι, ἱλασ(σ)άμην—appease, propitiate
Ἴλιος, -ου, ἡ—Ilium, Troy
ἵνα—so that, in order that
ἰός, -οῦ, ὁ—arrow
ἵππος, -ου, ὁ—horse
ἵπτομαι, ἵψομαι, ἱψάμην—afflict, punish
ἶσον—equally, as an equal, on equal terms
ἶσος, -η, -ον—equal
ἵστημι, στήσω, ἔστησα or ἔστην—stand, set up
ἱστίον, -ου, τό—sail; ἱστία—plural used for singular
ἱστοδόκη, -ης, ἡ—mast receiver, mast hold (a forked piece of wood in the
    stern [rear] of the ship, in which the mast would lie when it was lowered)
ἱστός, -οῦ, ὁ—loom, mast
ἴσχω—hold back, restrain
ἴφθιμος, -ον—strong, mighty, stalwart
ἶφι—with might, with power, by force

Κ, κ
καθάπτομαι—address, approach
καθέζομαι—sit down
καθεύδω—go to bed, sleep
κάθημαι—sit, sit down
καί—and, also, even, too
Καινεύς, -ῆος, ὁ—Caeneus, a Lapith leader
καίω, καύσω, ἔκηα—burn
κακός, -ή, -όν—bad, evil, destructive, disastrous
κακῶς—badly, harshly, wickedly
καλέω, (aor.) ἐκάλεσ(σ)α—call; *middle*—summon
καλλιπάρῃος, -ον—fair-cheeked, with beautiful cheeks
καλόν—well, sweetly
καλός, -ή, -όν—good, noble, brave, lovely, beautiful, pleasant
Κάλχας, -αντος, ὁ—Calchas, a Greek seer
κάμνω, καμέομαι, ἔκαμον—grow tired
καπνός, -οῦ, ὁ—smoke
κάρη, κρατός, τό—head
κάρηνον, -ου, τό—peak, summit
καρπαλίμως—quickly, at once
καρπός, -οῦ, ὁ—crop
καρτερός, -ή, -όν—powerful, strong, mighty
κάρτιστος, -η, -ον—strongest, mightiest, best
κατά—(prep.) down from (+ gen.), down through, down by, down along
    (+ acc.); (adv.) down
καταδέω, (aor.) κατέδησα—tie up, tie fast

καταδύω, (aor.) κατέδυν—go down, set

κατακαίω, κατακαύσω, κατέκηα, (aor. pass.) κατεκάην—burn, consume by fire

κατακαλύπτω, κατακαλύψω—cover up

κατακείω—go to rest

κατανεύω, κατανεύσω, κατένευσα—nod assent, nod in agreement

καταπέσσω, (aor.) κατέπεψα—digest, repress, swallow

καταπίπτω, (aor.) κάππεσον—fall down

καταρέζω, (aor.) κατέρεξα—stroke, caress, pat

κε, κεν—(enclitic) adds the idea of indefiniteness or indicates a condition (no exact English equivalent)

κεῖμαι, κείσομαι—lie, be placed

κεῖνος, -η, -ο = ἐκεῖνος, -η, -ο—that, that one, (plur.) those

κελαινεφής, -ές—of the dark clouds

κελαινός, -ή, -όν—dark

κέλευθος, -ου, ἡ—path, way, course, route, journey, voyage; plur.—κέλευθα, -ων, τά

κέλομαι, κελήσομαι—urge, exhort, tell, command, order, request

κεν = κε

κερδαλεόφρων, -ον—crafty, sly

κερτόμιος, -ον—cutting, sharp, bitter, reproachful

κεύθω—hide, conceal

κεφαλή, -ῆς, ἡ—head

κεχολωμένος—perfect passive participle of χολόω

κῆδος, -εος, τό—suffering, trouble, pain, sorrow

κήδω, κηδήσω, ἐκήδησα—trouble, distress; middle and passive—be concerned about, care for (+ gen.)

κῆλον, -ου, τό—arrow

κήρ, κηρός, ἡ—death, destruction

κῆρ, κῆρος, τό—heart

κῆρυξ, -υκος, ὁ—herald

Κίλλα, -ης, ἡ—Cilla, a town near Troy

κινέω, κινήσω, ἐκίνησα, (aor. pass.) ἐκινήθην—move; middle and passive—go, come, move

κιχάνω, κιχήσομαι, ἐκιχησάμην—come upon, find, overtake

κίω—come, go

κλαγγή, -ῆς, ἡ—scream, shriek, noise

κλάζω, κλάγξω, ἔκλαγξα—rattle, clang

κλαίω—weep, cry

κλέπτω—hide, steal, deceive

κλισίη, -ης, ἡ—hut, shelter (see note on line 185)

Κλυταιμνήστρη, -ης, ἡ—Clytemnestra, wife of Agamemnon

κλυτοτέχνης, -ου, ὁ—renowned artisan

κλύω, (aor.) ἔκλυον—hear (+ gen.)
κνέφας, -αος, τό—darkness, night
κνίση, -ης, ἡ—odor of roast meat, steam or smell of burnt offerings, fat
κοῖλος, -η, -ον—hollow
κοιμάω, (aor.) ἐκοίμησα—lull to sleep; *middle*—lie down to sleep, sleep
κολεόν, -οῦ, τό—sheath or scabbard (of a sword)
κολῳός, -οῦ, ὁ—quarrel, disturbance
κόμη, -ης, ἡ—hair
κομίζω, κομιῶ, ἐκόμισα—care for, attend to; *middle*—rescue, come to the
    relief of
κορυφή, -ῆς, ἡ—peak, summit
κορωνίς, -ίδος—curved
κοσμήτωρ, -ορος, ὁ—commander
κοτέω—be angry
κότος, -ου, ὁ—grudge, resentment, rancor, wrath
κουλεόν, -οῦ, τό—sheath or scabbard (of a sword)
κούρη, -ης, ἡ—girl, young woman, daughter
κουρίδιος, -η, -ον—wedded, legally married
κοῦρος, -ου, ὁ—young man
κραδίη, -ης, ἡ—heart
κραίνω—accomplish, perform, bring to pass, fulfill; κρήηνον—aorist
    imperative
κρατερός, -ή, -όν—harsh, stern, powerful
κρατέω—have power, rule over (+ gen.)
κράτος, -εος, τό—might, power, victory
κρείσσων, -ον—stronger, of superior strength, more powerful, better
κρείων, -ουσα, -ον—ruling
κρήγυος, -ον—good, useful, helpful
κρητήρ, -ῆρος, ὁ—mixing bowl, krater
κρίνω, κρινέω, ἔκρινα—pick, choose, select
Κρονίδης, -αο, ὁ—son of Cronus (= Zeus)
Κρονίων, -ωνος, ὁ—son of Cronus (= Zeus)
κρυπτάδιος, -η, -ον—secret
κτείνω—kill, slay
κυάνεος, -η, -ον—dark
κυδιάνειρα—(fem. adj.) bringing honor to men, glory-bringing, making men
    illustrious
κύδιστος, -η, -ον—most glorious
κῦδος, -εος, τό—glory
κῦμα, -ατος, τό—wave, waves
κυνώπης—dog-faced; κυνῶπα—vocative
κύπελλον, -ου, τό—cup

κύων, κυνός, ὁ—dog
κώπη, -ης, ἡ—handle, hilt (of a sword)

Λ, λ
λαμβάνω, λήψομαι, ἔλαβον—seize, take hold of
λαμπετάω—shine, flash, gleam, blaze
λαμπρός, -ή, -όν—bright, shining
λαός, -οῦ, ὁ—(in sing. and plur.) army, troops, people
λάσιος, -η, -ον—hairy, shaggy
λείπω, λείψω, ἔλιπον, λέλοιπα—leave
λευκός, -ή, -όν—white
λευκώλενος, -ον—white-armed (see note on line 55)
λεύσσω—see
λέχος, -εος, τό—bed
λήγω, λήξω—leave off, cease, stop (+ gen.)
λήθω—escape the notice of, escape the observation of; *middle*—forget
    (+ gen.)
Λῆμνος, -ου, ἡ—Lemnos, an island in the Aegean Sea
Λητώ, -οῦς, ἡ—Leto, mother of Apollo and Artemis
λιάζομαι, (aor. pass.) ἐλιάσθην—withdraw
λιγύς, -εῖα, -ύ—clear-voiced
λίην—very, greatly, exceedingly; καὶ λίην—assuredly, most certainly, truly
λιμήν, λιμένος, ὁ—harbor
λίσσομαι, (aor.) ἐλισάμην—beg, beseech
λοίγιος, -η, -ον—dreadful, horrible
λοιγός, -οῦ, ὁ—destruction, ruin, death
λοιμός, -οῦ, ὁ—plague
λόχος, -ου, ὁ—ambush
λῦμα, -ατος, τό—dirt, defilement, filth, what is washed off
λύω, λύσω, ἔλυσα—loosen, free, set free, release, dismiss, cause to disperse;
    middle—ransom
λωβάομαι, (aor.) ἐλωβησάμην—maltreat, outrage, wrong
λωΐων, -ον—better, preferable

M, μ
μά—by (+ acc.) (used in an oath, followed by the accusative of the god or
    object invoked)
μάκαρ, -αρος—blessed, happy
μακρός, -ή, -όν—long, high, tall
μάλα—very, by all means, certainly
μαλακός, -ή, -όν—soft, gentle
μάλιστα—especially

μᾶλλον—more

μαντεύομαι, μαντεύσομαι, ἐμαντευσάμην—predict, prophesy

μάντις, -ιος, ὁ—seer, prophet

μαντοσύνη, -ης, ἡ—gift of prophecy

μάρναμαι—fight

μάρτυρος, -ου, ὁ—witness

μάχη, -ης, ἡ—battle, fight

μάχομαι or μαχέομαι, μαχήσομαι or μαχέσομαι, ἐμαχεσ(σ)άμην—fight, fight with, battle (can take a dative object)

μέγα—greatly, exceedingly, very

μεγάθυμος, -ον—great-hearted, high-spirited

μεγάλα—loudly

μέγαρον, -ου, τό—great hall, dining hall; *plur.*—house, palace

μέγας, μεγάλη, μέγα—large, great

μέγιστος, -η, -ον—greatest (superlative of μέγας)

μεθίημι, μεθήσω, μεθέηκα—let go, let fly, send, shoot, give up, dismiss

μεθομιλέω—associate with (+ dat.)

μειδάω, (aor.) ἐμείδησα—smile, laugh

μείζων, -ον—greater, larger (comparative of μέγας)

μείρομαι, (perf.) ἔμμορα—share, receive (+ gen.)

μέλας, μέλαινα, μέλαν—dark, black

μέλι, -ιτος, τό—honey

μέλλει (impersonal)—it is likely

μέλπω—sing the praises of

μέλω, μελήσω—be a concern

μέμονα (perfect; translate as present)—desire, be eager

μέν—in truth, indeed, certainly, to be sure (may call attention to or mark a contrast with a following statement, often one that contains δέ; frequently, there is no English equivalent)

Μενέλαος, -ου, ὁ—Menelaus, king of Sparta, brother of Agamemnon and husband of Helen

Μενοιτιάδης, -αο, ὁ—son of Menoetius (= Patroclus)

μένος, -εος, τό—fury, rage

μένω, μενέω, ἔμεινα—remain, stay

μερμηρίζω, (aor.) ἐμερμήριξα—ponder, think over, consider

μέροψ, -οπος—a word of unknown meaning; possibly "endowed with speech"

μέσος, -η, -ον—middle of

μετά—with (+ gen.); among, amid, in (+ dat.); to, toward, into the midst of, to join (+ acc.)

μεταλλάω—seek after, inquire about, question

μεταξύ—between

μετατρέπομαι—consider (+ gen.); turn around, turn toward

μετάφημι, μεταφήσω, μετέφησα—address, speak to
μεταφράζομαι—consider later, consider by and by
μετέειπον (aor.)—speak
μετόπισθε(ν)—afterward, behind
μή—not, lest
μηδέ—and not
μήν—indeed
μῆνις, -ιος, ἡ—anger, wrath
μηνίω, μηνίσω, ἐμήνισα—be angry, rage
μῆρα, -ων, τά—thigh pieces
μηρίον, -ου, τό—thigh piece, thighbone
μηρός, -οῦ, ὁ—thigh
μήτε—and not; μήτε . . . μήτε—neither . . . nor
μήτηρ, -τρός, ἡ—mother
μητίετα, -αο, ὁ—counselor, wise one
μιμνήσκω, μνήσω, ἔμνησα—remind
μιν—him, her, it (acc. sing. of εἷο)
μίνυνθα—short, for a short time
μινυνθάδιος, -η, -ον—short-lived
μιστύλλω—cut into small pieces, cut up
μογέω, (aor.) ἐμόγησα—suffer, struggle
μοῖρα, -ης, ἡ—share, portion, lot, fate; κατὰ μοῖραν—properly, rightly
μολπή, -ῆς, ἡ—song, singing
Μοῦσα, -ης, ἡ—Muse (the Muses are the goddesses of literature, music, and dance)
μυθέομαι, μυθήσομαι, ἐμυθησάμην—speak, tell
μῦθος, -ου, ὁ—word, command, speech, counsel, advice, thought
μυρίος, -η, -ον—countless
Μυρμιδών, -όνος, ὁ—Myrmidon, a follower of Achilles (see note on line 180)

N, ν
ναί—yes, in truth, indeed
ναίω—dwell, inhabit, be situated
νεικέω—quarrel with, rebuke, taunt
νέκταρ, -αρος, τό—nectar (the drink of the gods)
νέκυς, νέκυος, ὁ—corpse, dead body
νέομαι—go, return
νέον—just now
νέος, -η, -ον—young
Νέστωρ, -ορος, ὁ—Nestor, king of Pylos, the oldest of the Greek leaders
νεφεληγερέτα, -αο, ὁ—cloud-gatherer
νημερτές—truly
νηός, -οῦ, ὁ—temple

νηῦς, νηός, ἡ—ship
νικάω—prevail, be victorious
νοέω, νοήσω, ἐνόησα—think, consider, take thought of, direct one's mind,
    perceive, observe
νόος, -ου, ὁ—mind, understanding
νόσφι—apart from, away from (+ gen.)
νοῦσος, -ου, ἡ—sickness, plague, disease
νυ—(enclitic) indeed
νῦν—now
νύξ, νυκτός, ἡ—night
νωμάω, (aor.) ἐνώμησα—distribute

Ξ, ξ
ξανθός, -ή, -όν—blond, reddish yellow
ξίφος, -εος, τό—sword
ξυνδέω, (aor.) ξυνέδησα—tie up, bind
ξυνήϊος, -η, -ον—common; ξυνήϊα—common property
ξυνίημι, ξυνήσω, ξυνέηκα—bring together; hear, take heed of (+ gen. or acc.)

Ο, ο
ὁ, ἡ, τό—the, he, she, it, this, that, who, which
ὀβελός, -οῦ, ὁ—spit
ὅδε, ἥδε, τόδε—this
ὁδός, -οῦ, ἡ—road, journey, expedition
Ὀδυσ(σ)εύς, -ῆος, ὁ—Odysseus, king of Ithaca, Greek leader renowned for
    his craftiness
ὄζος, -ου, ὁ—branch, twig, shoot
ὄθομαι—care about, trouble oneself (+ gen.)
οἱ—him, her, it (dat. of εἷο)
οἶδα (perfect; translate as present)—know, know how
ὀϊζυρός, -ή, -όν—miserable, unhappy
οἴκαδε—home(ward), to home
οἴκοι—at home
οἰκόνδε—home(ward), to home
οἶκος, -ου, ὁ—house, home
οἰνοβαρής, -ές—wine guzzler, drunk
οἶνος, -ου, ὁ—wine
οἰνοχοέω—pour, pour wine
ὀΐομαι—think, imagine, suspect
οἶος, -η, -ον—alone
οἷος, -η, -ον—such as
ὀϊστός, -οῦ, ὁ—arrow
οἴχομαι—come, go

οἴω or ὀΐω or ὀΐομαι, οἰήσομαι, ὠισάμην—think, suppose, believe, intend, imagine, suspect
οἰωνοπόλος, -ου, ὁ—seer, augur, soothsayer, interpreter of birds
οἰωνός, -οῦ, ὁ—bird of prey
ὀλέκω—destroy, kill; middle—perish, die
ὀλίγος, -η, -ον—little, small, few
ὄλλυμι, ὀλέσ(σ)ω, ὤλεσ(σ)α—lose, destroy, kill, ruin
ὀλοιός, -ή, -όν—destructive, deadly
Ὀλύμπιος, -η, -ον—Olympian, on Mt. Olympus; ὁ Ὀλύμπιος—Zeus; Ὀλύμπιοι—Olympians, gods
Ὄλυμπος, -ου, ὁ—Mt. Olympus, the home of the gods
ὁμηγερής, -ές—collected, gathered together, assembled together
ὁμιλέω, (aor.) ὡμίλησα—associate with (+ dat.)
ὀμίχλη, -ης, ἡ—mist
ὄμμα, -ατος, τό—eye
ὄμνυμι, ὀμοῦμαι, ὤμοσσα—swear, take an oath
ὁμοῖος, -η, -ον—equal, similar
ὁμοιόω—compare, liken
ὁμοῦ—together, at the same time
ὁμῶς—together, alike, equally
ὄναρ, τό (indeclinable)—dream
ὀνείδειος, -ον—reproachful, injurious, abusive
ὀνειδίζω, (aor.) ὠνείδισα—reproach
ὄνειδος, -εος, τό—words of abuse, insult, reproach
ὀνειροπόλος, -ου, ὁ—interpreter of dreams
ὀνίνημι, ὀνήσω, ὤνησα—help, benefit, be of service to, delight
ὀνομάζω, ὀνομάσω, ὠνόμασα—call by name
ὀξύς, -εῖα, -ύ—sharp
ὄπιθεν—behind
ὀπίσσω—backward
ὁππότε—whenever, when
ὀπτάω, (aor.) ὤπτησα—cook, roast
ὅπως, ὅππως—how, so that, that
ὁράω, ὄψομαι, εἶδον or ἴδον—see
ὀρέγνυμι—stretch out, hold out
ὀρεσκῷος, -ον—having mountain lairs
ὅρκος, -ου, ὁ—oath
ὁρμαίνω, (aor.) ὥρμηνα—debate, turn over (in the mind), ponder
ὅρμος, -ου, ὁ—anchoring place, landing place
ὄρνυμι, ὄρσω, ὦρσα—stir up, start, let loose
ὄρος, -εος, τό—mountain
ὅς, ἥ, ὅ—who, which
ὅς, ἥ, ὅν—his own, her own, its own

ὅσοι, -αι, -α—as many as, all that
ὄσσε (nom./acc. dual neut.)—eyes
ὄσσομαι—look
ὄσσον—how much, by how much
ὅς τις, ἥ τις, ὅ τι—whoever, whatever; ὅ τι—(adv.) why
ὅτε—when, since, whenever, seeing that
ὅτι, ὅττι—that, because, since, seeing that, in that, why
ὀτρηρός, -ή, -όν—ready, busy
οὐ, οὐκ, οὐχ—not, no; οὔ τι—not at all
οὐδέ—and not, not even; οὐδέ τι—not at all, none whatever
οὐδείς, οὐδεμία, οὐδέν—no one, nobody, nothing
οὐδέν—not at all
οὐλόμενος, -η, -ον—destructive, ruinous
οὐλοχύται, -ῶν, αἱ—barley sprinkled at a sacrifice (barley was sprinkled on
    sacrificial victims before a sacrifice)
Οὔλυμπος, -ου, ὁ—Mt. Olympus, the home of the gods; Οὔλυμπόνδε—to
    Mt. Olympus
οὖν—then, therefore, in fact, now
οὔνεκα—because
Οὐρανίων, -ωνος—heaven-dwelling
οὐρανός, -οῦ, ὁ—the heavens, the sky; οὐρανόθεν—from the sky
οὐρεύς, -ῆος, ὁ—mule
οὖρος, -ου, ὁ—wind, breeze
οὖρος, -εος, τό—mountain
οὔτε—and not, nor; οὔτε . . . οὔτε—neither . . . nor
οὔ τι—(adv.) not at all
οὐτιδανός, -ή, -όν—good-for-nothing, worthless
οὗτος, αὕτη, τοῦτο—this
οὕτω(ς)—thus, in this way, so
ὀφείλω, (aor.) ὤφελον—ought, would that (+ infinitive)
ὀφέλλω—ought
ὀφέλλω—increase, glorify
ὀφθαλμός, -οῦ, ὁ—eye
ὄφρα—until, in order that
ὀφρύς, -ύος, ἡ—brow, eyebrow
ὄχα—by far
ὀχθέω, (aor.) ὤχθησα—be vexed with, be displeased with, be distressed, be
    troubled, be worried
ὄψ, ὀπός, ἡ—voice

Π, π
παιήων, παιήονος, ὁ—song of praise, paean
παῖς, παιδός, ὁ, ἡ—child, son, daughter

παλάμη, -ης, ἡ—palm, hand
παλίλλογος, -ον—gathered together again, collected again
παλιμπλάζομαι—be driven back; παλιμπλαγχθέντας—aorist passive
    participle, acc. plur. masc.
πάλιν—back
παλινάγρετος, -ον—revokable, able to be taken back
Παλλάς, -άδος, ἡ—Pallas, a name given to Athena (see note on line 200)
πάμπαν—wholly, entirely, completely
πανημέριος, -η, -ον—all day long, all the rest of the day
πάντῃ—in all directions, everywhere
παρά—from (+ gen.); beside, by (+ dat.); along, to (+ acc.)
παράφημι—urge, advise (+ dat. and infinitive)
παρέζομαι—sit by, sit near
πάρειμι, παρέσσομαι—be present, be at hand
παρεῖπον (aor.)—persuade, beguile, win over
παρέρχομαι, παρελεύσομαι—go by, pass by, outwit
πάρημαι—sit beside (+ dat.)
πάροιθε—in front of (+ gen.)
πάρος—before, at other times, in the past
πᾶς, πᾶσα, πᾶν—all
πατέομαι, (aor.) ἐπασάμην—taste, eat
πατήρ, -τρός, ὁ—father
πάτρη, -ης, ἡ—native land
Πάτροκλος, -ου, ὁ—Patroclus, Achilles' best friend
παύω, παύσω, ἔπαυσα—stop, restrain; middle—cease from (+ gen.)
πείθω, πείσω, ἔπεισα or ἔπιθον or πέπιθον, πέποιθα—persuade; middle—
    obey (+ dat.); perfect—trust, rely on
πειράω, πειρήσω, ἐπειρησάμην—try
Πειρίθοος, -ου, ὁ—Pirithous, king of the Lapiths (a people of northern
    Thessaly) and friend of the Athenian hero Theseus
πείρω, (aor.) ἔπειρα, (perf. mid./pass.) πέπαρμαι—pierce
πελάζω, (aor.) ἐπέλασα—bring into (+ dat.)
πέλομαι—be, become, come to be
πέμπω, πέμψω, ἔπεμψα—send, send or convey home
πεμπώβολον, -ου, τό—five-pronged fork
πένθος, -εος, τό—grief, sadness
πένομαι—work at, labor at
περ—(enclitic) even, although, very, at least, even though, at any rate (often
    adds emphasis, usually to the preceding word)
περί—above, beyond (+ gen.); around (+ dat. or acc.)
περίειμι—be superior to, excel (+ gen.)
περιέχομαι—protect (+ gen.); περίσχεο—aorist imperative
περικαλλής, -ές—very beautiful

περικλυτός, -ή, -όν—famous, renowned
περιλέπω, περιλέψω—strip off all around from (+ two accusatives)
περιφραδέως—very carefully, with great care
πεύθομαι, (aor.) ἐπυθόμην—learn, hear (+ gen. of the person or thing heard or learned about)
Πηλεΐδης, -εω, ὁ—son of Peleus (= Achilles)
Πηλεῖων, -ωνος, ὁ—son of Peleus (= Achilles)
Πηλεύς, -ῆος, ὁ—Peleus, father of Achilles
Πηληϊάδης, -εω, ὁ—son of Peleus (= Achilles)
πίμπλημι, πλήσω, ἔπλησα—fill
πίπτω, (aor.) ἔπεσον—fall, perish, die
πίων, πίειρα, πῖον—fat
πλάζω, πλάγξομαι, ἔπλαγξα—drive back
πλείων, -ον—more, greater, the greater part (comparative of πολύς)
πλέων, -ον—more (comparative of πολύς)
πλοῦτος, -ου, ὁ—wealth
ποδάρκης, -ες—swift-footed
ποθέω, ποθήσω, ἐπόθεσα—long for
ποθή, -ῆς, ἡ—longing for, yearning for (+ gen.)
ποθι—(enclitic) ever
ποιέω, ποιήσω, ἐποίησα—do, make
ποιμήν, -ένος, ὁ—shepherd, guardian
ποῖος, -η, -ον—what sort of? what kind of?
ποιπνύω—bustle, hurry, puff
πολεμίζω—fight
πόλεμος, -ου, ὁ—war, battle
πολιός, -ή, -όν—gray
πόλις, -ιος, ἡ—city
πολλά—earnestly, fervently
πολλάκι—many times, often
πολλόν—by far, much
πολλός, -ή, -όν = πολύς, πολλή, πολύ—many, much
πολύ—much, by far
πολυάϊξ, -ϊκος—rushing, impetuous
πολυβενθής, -ές—very deep
πολυδειράς, -άδος—many-ridged, with many peaks
πολύμητις, -ιος—crafty, shrewd
πολύς, πολλή, πολύ = πολλός, -ή, -όν—many, much
πολύστονος, -ον—causing many groans, grievous
Πολύφημος, -ου, ὁ—Polyphemus, a Lapith leader
πολύφλοισβος, -ον—loud roaring, ever roaring
πόνος, -ου, ὁ—work, toil
ποντοπόρος, -ον—seagoing

πόντος, -ου, ὁ—sea, the open sea, the deep sea

πόποι—alas! for shame!

πόρον (aor.)—give, bestow, grant

πορφύρεος, -η, -ον—dark, purple

Ποσειδάων, -ωνος, ὁ—Poseidon, god of the sea, brother of Zeus

πόσις, -ιος, ἡ—drink

ποτε—(enclitic) ever, at some time, at any time, once, someday

ποτί—on, upon, at (+ dat.); to (+ acc.)

πότνια—(fem. adj.) revered, honored

ποτόν, -οῦ, τό—drink

που—(enclitic) anywhere, doubtless

πούς, ποδός, ὁ—foot

πραπίδες, -ων, αἱ—mind, understanding skill

πρήσσω, πρήξω, ἔπρηξα—do, act, accomplish

Πρίαμος, -ου, ὁ—Priam, king of Troy

πρίν—(adv.) sooner, before that; (conj.) until, before (+ infinitive)

πρό—(adv.) before, forth; (prep.) in front of, before (+ gen.)

προβάλλω, προβαλέω, προέβαλον—scatter, sprinkle, throw

προβέβουλα (perfect; translate as present)—prefer to (+ gen.)

προερέσσω, (aor.) προήρεσ(σ)α—row forward

προερύω, (aor.) προέρυσσα—drag forward, launch

προθέω—rush forward

προϊάπτω, προϊάψω, προΐαψα—send, hurl

προΐημι, προήσω, προέηκα—send forth, let go, give up

πρόπας, -πασα, -παν—the whole, all

προπέμπω—send, dispatch

πρός—from, before, in the sight of (+ gen.); on, at, by (+ dat.); to, toward, against (+ acc.)

προσαυδάω, προσαυδήσω, προσηύδησα—speak to, address

προσέειπον (aor.)—address, speak to

πρόσθεν—before, formerly

πρόσσω—forward

πρόσφημι, προσφήσω, προσέφησα—speak to, address; προσέφη—imperfect

προσφωνέω—speak to, address

πρότερος, -η, -ον—sooner

πρότονος, -ου, ὁ—forestay (one of the ropes that hold the mast of a ship in place)

πρόφρων, -ονος—(adjective often used as adverb) zealous(ly), earnest(ly), cheerful(ly), eager(ly)

πρύμνη, -ης, ἡ—stern (rear part of a ship)

πρυμνήσιον, -ου, τό—stern cable (rope for fastening the stern, or rear, of the ship to the shore)

πρώτιστα—(adv.) first of all

πρῶτον, πρῶτα, τὸ πρῶτον, τὰ πρῶτα—(adv.) first
πρῶτος, -η, -ον—first
πτερόεις, -εσσα, -εν—winged
πτόλεμος, -ου, ὁ = πόλεμος
πτολίεθρον, -ου, τό—city
Πύλιοι, -ων, οἱ—Pylians, inhabitants of Pylos
Πύλος, -ου, ἡ—Pylos, the kingdom of Nestor, located on the southwest coast
   of the Peloponnese
πῦρ, πυρός, τό—fire, flame
πυρή, -ῆς, ἡ—funeral pyre
πω—(enclitic) yet, ever
πωλέομαι—go
πῶς—how?
πως—(enclitic) in some way, somehow, perhaps

P, ρ
ῥ᾿ = ἄρα—then, in fact
ῥα = ἄρα—then, in fact
ῥέζω, ῥέξω, ἔρεξα—perform, make, do
ῥέω—flow, run, pour
ῥηγμίς, -ῖνος, ἡ—breakers, the edge of the seashore
ῥίγιον—(neut. comp. adj.) more horrible, more terrible, worse
ῥίπτω, ῥίψω, ἔρριψα—hurl, throw, fling
ῥοδοδάκτυλος, -ον—rosy-fingered

Σ, σ
σαόω, σαώσω, ἐσάωσα—protect, rescue, preserve, save
σαώτερος, -η, -ον—safer
σέθεν—gen. sing. of σύ
σημαίνω—command, give orders to (+ dat.)
Σίντιες, -ων, οἱ—Sintians, inhabitants of Lemnos
σκαιός, -ή, -όν—left
σκηπτοῦχος, -ον—scepter-holding, scepter-bearing
σκῆπτρον, -ου, τό—staff
σκίδναμαι—scatter, disperse
σκιόεις, -εσσα, -εν—shady
Σμινθεύς, -ῆος, ὁ—Smintheus, a name given to Apollo (see note on line 39)
σόος, -η, -ον—safe
σός, σή, σόν—your, yours
σπλάγχνα, -ων, τά—entrails (heart, liver, spleen, etc.)
στεῖρα, -ης, ἡ—stem (the curved front part of a ship's keel that cuts through
   the water)
στέλλω, στελέω, ἔστειλα—take in, lower, roll up, furl

στέμμα, -ατος, τό—band of fabric, ribbon (see note on line 14)
στενάχω—groan
στῆθος, -εος, τό—breast, chest; "heart," i.e., the seat of emotion and feeling
   (always plural; translate as singular)
στρατός, -οῦ, ὁ—army, camp
στυγέω—be afraid, fear
στυφελίζω, (aor.) ἐστυφέλιξα—hurl, thrust
σύ, σεῖο—you
σύμπας, σύμπασα, σύμπαν—all
συμφράζομαι, συμφράσσομαι, συνεφρασάμην—make plans with, form
   plans with
σύν—with (+ dat.)
συνταράσσω, συνταράξω—disturb, spoil
συντίθημι, συνθήσω, συνέθηκα—take heed, hear
σφάζω, (aor.) ἔσφαξα—cut the throat
σφείων—them (gen. plur. of εἷο)
σφιν—them (dat. plur. of εἷο)
σφός, σφή, σφόν—their own
σφωΐτερος, -η, -ον—of you two, of you both
σχίζη, -ης, ἡ—firewood, a piece of split wood

T, τ
Ταλθύβιος, -ου, ὁ—Talthybius, one of Agamemnon's heralds
τἆλλα = τὰ ἄλλα—the other (things)
τανύω, τανύσω, ἐτάνυσσα—stretch, extend
ταρβέω, (aor.) ἐτάρβησα—fear, be afraid
ταῦρος, -ου, ὁ—bull
τάχα—quickly, soon
τε—(enclitic postpositive; often not translated when it indicates a general,
   common, or proverbial statement) and; τε . . . καί or τε . . . τε—both . . .
   and
τέκμωρ, τό (indeclinable)—sign, pledge
τέκνον, -ου, τό—child
τέκος, -εος, τό—child, offspring
τέλειος, -η, -ον—perfect, without spot or blemish
τελείω, τελέω or τελέσσω, ἐτέλεσσα, τετέλεκα, τετέλεσμαι, ἐτελέσθην—
   accomplish, bring to completion, bring to pass
τελήεις, -εσσα, -εν—perfect, unblemished
Τένεδος, -ου, ἡ—Tenedos, a small island near Troy
τεός, -ή, -όν—your, yours
τερπικέραυνος, -ον—delighting in the thunderbolt; possibly "thunderbolt-
   hurling," "thunderbolt-wielding"
τέρπω—delight, please

τέταγον (aor.)—seize, grasp

τέτληκα (perfect; translate as present)—dare, venture, have the courage, bring oneself to, be willing to, endure

τετραπλῆ—four times, quadruply

τεύχω, τεύξω, ἔτευξα or τέτυκον—make, cause to be or become, cause to happen, prepare

τηλόθεν—far, from far away

τηλόθι—far from (+ gen.)

τί—why?

τίη—why?

τίθημι, θήσω, ἔθηκα—put, place, cause, make

τίκτω, τέξω, ἔτεκον—give birth to, bear

τιμάω, τιμήσω, ἐτίμησα—honor

τιμή, -ῆς, ἡ—honor, retribution, satisfaction, compensation

τίνω, τείσω, ἔτεισα—pay, atone for

τίπτε—why?

τις, τι—(enclitic) some(one), some(thing), any(one), any(thing); οὔ τι—not at all

τίς, τί—who? what?

τίω, τίσω, ἔτισα—honor, esteem

τοι—(enclitic) certainly, you may be sure

τοι—(enclitic) dat. sing. of σύ (= σοί)

τοιγάρ—therefore, accordingly

τοῖος, -η, -ον—such

τομή, -ῆς, ἡ—stump, the end left after cutting

τόξον, -ου, τό—bow

τόσσον—so, so very

τόσσος, -η, -ον—so many, so much, so great, so large

τότε—then

τοὔνεκα—for this reason, therefore, because of this (= τοῦ ἕνεκα)

τόφρα—for so long a time

τρέφω, (aor.) ἔτραφον, (aor. pass.) ἐτράφην—bring up, nurture, breed; τράφεν = ἐτράφησαν (aorist passive, 3rd pers. plur.)

τριπλῆ—three times, triply

τρίς—three times, thrice

τρίτατος, -η, -ον—third

Τροίη, -ης, ἡ—Troy

Τρῶες, -ων, οἱ—Trojans

τυτθόν—a little

τῷ—so, therefore, thus

Υ, υ

ὕβρις, -ιος, ἡ—arrogance, insolence

ὑγρός, -ή, -όν—wet, liquid, watery

υἱός, -οῦ, ὁ—son
ὑμεῖς or ὕμμες, ὑμέων—you (plur.)
ὑμῖν—dat. of ὑμεῖς
ὑπείκω, ὑπείξω—yield, submit
ὑπέρ—on behalf of, for, over (+ gen.)
ὑπεροπλίαι, -ῶν, αἱ—arrogance, arrogant behavior, presumption
ὑπίσχομαι, ὑποσχήσομαι, ὑπεσχόμην—promise
ὕπνος, -ου, ὁ—sleep
ὑπό—(prep.) by, under, at the hands of (+ gen.); under (+ dat.); (adv.)
    beneath, under
ὑποβλήδην—interrupting
ὑποδείδω, ὑποδείσομαι, ὑπέδεισα—fear, be afraid of, dread, tremble before
ὑπόδρα—darkly, grimly, sternly
ὑπολύω, ὑπολύσω, ὑπέλυσα—set free, release from
ὕστατος, -η, -ον—last
ὕστερον—later, afterward
ὑφίημι, ὑφήσω, ὑφῆκα—let down, lower
ὑψιβρεμέτης, -ου—high-thundering
ὑψοῦ—(adv.) high

Φ, φ
φαίνω, φανέω, ἔφηνα, (aor. pass.) ἐφάνην—show, reveal, shine; *middle and passive*—appear, be visible
φάος, -εος, τό—light
φαρέτρη, -ης, ἡ—quiver
φάσγανον, -ου, τό—sword
φάτο = ἔφατο (imperfect middle with active meaning of φημί)
φέρτατος, -η, -ον—best, strongest, most powerful
φέρτερος, -η, -ον—better, more powerful
φέρω, οἴσω, ἤνεικα—carry, bring
φεύγω, φεύξομαι, ἔφυγον—flee, escape
φημί, φήσω, ἔφησα—speak, say, declare, assert; (ἔ)φατο—imperfect middle
    with active meaning, 3rd pers. sing.; ἔφη—imperfect, 3rd pers. sing.
φήρ, φηρός, ὁ, ἡ—wild animal, beast
Φθίη, -ης, ἡ—Phthia, region in Thessaly that was Achilles' home; also the
    name of the chief city there
φθινύθω—pine away, waste away
φθίνω, φθίσω, ἔφθισα, ἔφθιμαι—die, perish
φιλέω, φιλήσω, ἐφίλησα—love, hold dear
φιλοκτεανώτατος, -η, -ον—most greedy (for other men's possessions)
φίλος, -η, -ον—dear, beloved, pleasing; one's own
φλοιός, -οῦ, ὁ—bark
Φοῖβος, -ου, ὁ—Phoebus, a name given to Apollo, possibly meaning "bright"
    or "shining"

φορέω—carry

φόρμιγξ, -ιγγος, ἡ—phorminx (a type of lyre)

φράζω, φράσω, ἔφρασα—point out, show; *middle*—consider

φρήν, φρενός, ἡ—mind, thoughts, heart (often used in plural); *literally,* midriff, diaphragm (see note on line 55)

φρονέω, φρονήσω, ἐφρόνησα—think, think about, consider, intend

φυή, -ῆς, ἡ—form, physique, appearance, figure

φύλλον, -ου, τό—leaf

φύω, φύσω—produce, put forth, grow

φωνέω, φωνήσω, ἐφώνησα—raise the voice, speak

X, χ

χαίρω, χαιρήσω, κεχαρόμην—be glad, be happy, rejoice; χαίρετε—welcome! hail!

χαίτη, -ης, ἡ—hair, locks

χαλεπός, -ή, -όν—difficult

χαλκοβατής, -ές—with a bronze floor, bronze-floored

χαλκός, -οῦ, ὁ—bronze; a bronze knife, ax, or spear

χαλκοχίτων, -ωνος—bronze-clad (see note on line 371)

χαρίεις, -εσσα, -εν—pleasing, lovely, fine

χείρ, χειρός, ἡ—hand

χερείων, -ον—worse, inferior, less worthy

χέρης, -ες—low, humble, poor, inferior

χερνίπτομαι, (aor.) ἐχερνιψάμην—wash one's hands

χερσί—dat. plur. of χείρ

χέω—pour, shed; δάκρυ χέων—weeping, crying

χθιζός, -ή, -όν—yesterday's

χθών, χθονός, ἡ—earth, land

χόλος, -ου, ὁ—anger, wrath, rage

χολόω, χολώσω, ἐχόλωσα, κεχόλωμαι, ἐχολώθην—anger, enrage; *middle*—be angry

χραισμέω, χραισμήσω, ἔχραισμον—help, avail, benefit, keep off, help against (+ dat.)

χρειώ, -όος, ἡ—need

χρή (impersonal)—there is need, (one) ought

χρύσειος, -η, -ον—made of gold, golden

χρύσεος, -η, -ον—made of gold, golden, decorated with gold

Χρύση, -ης, ἡ—Chryse, a town near Troy

Χρυσηΐς, -ΐδος, ἡ—Chryseis, daughter of Chryses

Χρύσης, -αο, ὁ—Chryses, priest of Apollo, father of Chryseis

χρυσόθρονος, -ον—golden-throned

χώομαι, χώσομαι, ἐχωσάμην—be angry

Ψ, ψ

ψάμαθος, -ου, ἡ—sand

ψυχή, -ῆς, ἡ—soul, life, spirit

Ω, ω

ὦ, ὤ—oh! ὤ μοι—oh! alas!

ὧδε—thus, in this way, in the following way, so

ὠθέω, (aor.) ἔωσα—push, thrust

ὦκα—quickly

Ὠκεανός, -οῦ, ὁ—Oceanus, the river that was believed to circle the flat disc of the earth

ὠκύμορος, -ον—fated to die early, short-lived

ὠκύπορος, -ον—swift, swift-sailing

ὠκύς, -εῖα, -ύ—swift, fast, quick

ὠμοθετέω, (aor.) ὠμοθέτησα—place pieces of raw meat on

ὦμος, -ου, ὁ—shoulder

ὦρσα—aorist of ὄρνυμι

ὡς, ὥς, ὣς—so, thus, in this way, how, that, as